Choo is a woman of God who epitomizes what it means to put first things first. The Lord Jesus Christ is truly the cornerstone of her life. The level of intimacy that Choo has encountered with the Lord rests on the precipice between heaven and earth. This book compels the reader to take a journey beyond the Pearly Gates. The throne room of God will no longer be an ambiguous undefined location, but rather a very inviting and viable encounter with our Lord Jesus Christ. This book is a must-read for those who have ever doubted the authenticity of what awaits us beyond the veil.

—BILL WOLFSON
SENIOR PASTOR, CHURCH FOR ALL NATIONS
PARKLAND, WASHINGTON

Choo Thomas, whom I know to be a godly woman, gave me a condensed manuscript of *Heaven Is So Real!,* which I read several times. I am convinced she has had an authentic supernatural experience with our Lord Jesus Christ in the spiritual realm. Taken into heaven, she witnessed both current and future events that faithful Christians as well as unfaithful believers and nonbelievers will face when they leave this earth. As a result of these things, I believe a fresh anointing of the Holy Spirit has come upon Choo. In *Heaven Is So Real!,* she stresses the importance of absolute obedience to our Lord's direction if we are to please Him and be used by Him. This work is both a vivid description of what Choo saw in heaven and a graphic illustration of how we all should live while still on the earth.

—WALKER V. FREDERICK
CHURCH FOR ALL NATIONS
VOLUNTEER CHAPLAIN, PIERCE COUNTY JAIL
WASHINGTON

A wise man once said: "There is nothing more powerful than an idea whose time has come." More powerful than the right time for a good idea, however, is the appointed time for the Son of God to return. For He warns that when He comes back, His people must be prepared for Him. "You must be ready, for the Son of Man is coming at an hour when you do not expect Him," Jesus said in Matthew 24:44. For the last seven years, the Lord Jesus has given Choo Thomas visions with heavenly visitations so He could use her to help prepare His people for His coming in the season just ahead. This book can help you make yourself ready so that you needn't fear His return. May we greet Him with joyful expectation!

—ROSEMARY LAMBERT
PASTOR OF PRAYER AND INTERCESSION
PUGET SOUND CHRISTIAN CENTER
TACOMA, WASHINGTON

We have been close friends of Choo Thomas for years. Choo is a genuine Christian and her book is a result of her actual experiences. Jesus is using Choo to reach many people. Jesus is coming soon for His people.

—GEORGE AND LORRAINE FERRA

I have known Choo Thomas for almost two years now. I have watched her great love for the Lord and her obedience and dedication to Him. We have talked about the love God has for each of us and the way He wants us to grow in Him. Choo is the kind of witness for God that makes you want to know God more and more. I know that in talking to her, I want to be good enough to join her in this glorious kingdom she has told me so much about. Thank you Choo.

—BETTY GEIER
YOUR SISTER IN CHRIST

Choo has been part of Church For All Nations for several years, along with her husband Roger. I know Choo as a committed Christian, a woman of Godly character, fully committed to her husband and faithful in attendance in the Sunday morning worship services. She has a desire to see others know the Lord Jesus Christ as their Savior and Lord.

—PASTOR RAYMOND WUERCH
ASSOCIATE PASTOR, CHURCH FOR ALL NATIONS
SENIORS AND PASTORAL CARE MINISTRIES

HEAVEN

IS SO

REAL!

Charisma
HOUSE
A STRANG COMPANY

Choo Thomas

Most STRANG COMMUNICATIONS/CHARISMA HOUSE/CHRISTIAN LIFE/ EXCEL BOOKS/SILOAM/FRONTLINE/REALMS products are available at special quantity discounts for bulk purchase for sales promotions, premiums, fund-raising, and educational needs. For details, write Strang Communications/ Charisma House/Christian Life/Excel Books/Siloam/FrontLine/Realms, 600 Rinehart Road, Lake Mary, Florida 32746, or telephone (407) 333-0600.

HEAVEN IS SO REAL! by Choo Thomas
Published by Charisma House
A Strang Company
600 Rinehart Road
Lake Mary, Florida 32746
www.charismahouse.com

Unless otherwise noted, all Scripture quotations are from the New King James Version of the Bible. Copyright © 1979, 1980, 1982 by Thomas Nelson Inc., publishers. Used by permission.

Scripture quotations marked kjv are from the King James Version of the Bible.

Library of Congress Control Number: 2003104166
ISBN-13: 978-1-59185-789-1

08 09 10 11 — 11 10 9 8 7
Printed in the United States of America

Dedication

I would like to dedicate this book to our Lord Jesus, who chose me to do His End-Time work. He took care of everything this book required, from the beginning to the end of the publishing process. He spent thousands of hours with me over a seven-year period to prepare me for publishing this book and to train me for my ministry.

Awesome God, I praise You, Lord. I thank you so much, Holy Spirit, for helping me write *Heaven Is So Real!* Without Your help, I could not have done anything. I give You all the credit.

To the Father, the Son, and the Holy Spirit I give all the glory for this book. I pray that whoever reads it will glorify You, Lord. I love You and praise You, Lord.

Acknowledgments

I want to thank Lloyd Hildebrand for the great service he has rendered to me in both believing in this book and helping me to write it.

After the Lord showed me the divine revelations I have chronicled in *Heaven Is So Real!*, I had such a burden to communicate my experiences to others. But I felt very insecure with my own ability to do that. In addition to having a lack of confidence in myself, I questioned where I would find someone to help me write my book, and I questioned whether or not anyone would believe me when they heard my revelations of heaven—even though the Lord had told me that He would take care of every detail related to this book.

That's when the Lord brought Lloyd to me. Lloyd asked me to send him the manuscript, and upon reading my first draft he decided to help me write this book. He told me he believed everything in my manuscript and that he thought it would be a very exciting book to write. In particular, he said he thought the segment about the rapture would be the most exciting.

Lloyd is an excellent writer who is filled with the Holy Spirit. Thank you, Lloyd, and God bless you.

I want to say a special thanks to my husband, Roger. Because English is my second language and because Roger is used to my writing, he helped me with spelling and grammar throughout the book so that Lloyd could better understand what I was trying to say.

I sincerely appreciate all the work he did. And I especially appreciate his support of everything related to this book—whatever needed to be done—as well his support in every area of my ministry. He was also patient with me and did not complain during my seven years of preparation for ministry.

Thank you, honey. God's favor is on you.

Contents

To download the DVD version of *Heaven Is So Real!*
visit Choo Thomas's Web site at
www.choothomas.com.

Testimonials

I simply had to write to tell you how much I loved *Heaven Is So Real!*...At one point, I had to stop reading to put my head down and weep, not over your stunning account of the sights of heaven, but over the beautiful intimacy between you and the Lord Jesus....In 1991, after my children were all in school, I felt the Lord sending me back to college to complete my degree and begin a career as an English professor. While I am certain the Lord sent me back to school, I have long lamented the time that my studies and my career have demanded, and my relationship with the Lord has suffered from neglect because of this....Your story reminded me of times when I would be overwhelmed with the sense of His anointing and His presence, even while vacuuming my house....I consider my classroom my mission field, and I talk to my students about the Lord all the time....Yet, I cannot go on like this, just talking about Him rather than to Him, and your book has been a huge wakeup call to get me to stop and put Him first and foremost.... I am desperate to find Him again and find my way back to the warm and tender intimacy I used to experience with Jesus.

IN HIM,
P.

***

I would like to share with you that I was lost in faith in darkness and decided to pick up your book one day at the Christian bookstore here in San Diego. I could not put it down and I have shared the book with so many of my friends. It is such an inspirational book. I am so glad that I ran across your book. I so much understand what heaven is all about. I thank you and through the grace of God sharing this lovely, beautiful, and unbelievable book has opened my heart and faith even stronger....I am the only one in the family who was lost and have found my way back home to Lord.

MAKE IT A BEAUTIFUL AND BLESSED DAY,
C.

I had lived as a carnal Christian for many years and had been entangled in some terrible sins. I finally cried out to God, and over the past two years, He has graciously set me free. God has been showing me the emptiness of a life that does not have Him as its focus and then He led me to read your book. I believe every word you wrote. What I have read has certainly adjusted my theology in a radical way. Thanks to your obedience, I now have a clear understanding of what God desires and requires of us who believe. God's timely warning through *Heaven Is So Real!* has literally snatched me from the jaws of hell.

WITH MY SINCEREST THANKS AND DEEPEST APPRECIATION,

P.

***

I am in 7th grade and I just finished your book. At first I did it because my mom said that she would give me 50 bucks if I read it but now I don't need the 50 bucks anymore because I have Christ!! I'm a Christian and I have been a Christian for my whole life and I have never read a better Christian book in my life. You're so lucky that you got to go to heaven and meet God. You must be a awesome Christian. Well, sorry that I took up your time I was soooo blessed by this book that I just had to e-mail you. Well, it getting late, I have to go. BYE!!!

D.

***

I truly thank God for inspiring you to do His work. The book has really helped me re-examine my spiritual walk with the Lord just as it was purposed. I wasn't even halfway through the book before I began to repent of some things. Just the first few chapters changed me and now I'm putting God first and learning how to depend on Him day by day. Instead of trattling the fence I jumped over the fence and made up in my mind that I going to give God my all and all. I'd like to thank you for being obedient to the Lord because the book has helped me to be more obedient to the Word of God. You are blessed to have walked with the Lord in Heaven and I believe it's as beautiful as you say.

BE BLESSED,

T.

Testimonials

***

First, I would like to start off by saying I really enjoyed reading your book. I felt so much happiness because of all the wonderful things that our Lord Jesus Christ has in store for us in heaven. While reading your book, I felt uplifted and hungered for more of Christ. I had such a passion and peace that I shared your experiences with a girl on my bus. I told her about the reality of heaven and hell, and what awaits us in both places. She immediately felt a hunger to become a Christian, and that night her and her younger brother accepted Christ into their lives.

LOVE,

E.

***

It is not by chance that I got the book. It was the Lord who has chosen me to read it. After starting to listen to the CD, I began to discern God's voice for the first time. I have always wondered at Spirit-filled people who claim to have heard God speaking to them but I myself never knew the privilege.

After sharing with a friend about how God has answered all my daughter's prayers, I came home and felt so blessed. I began to thank the Lord for being so good to my daughter. Before I could finish my sentence I heard distinctly a voice that sounded exactly like my own voice saying, "She's my daughter too." I knew definitely it was not my subconscious or whatever they call it. I was so overjoyed. Now I know how God speaks to me. God has spoken to me several times after that...

I'm a changed person now. I pray more often and Jesus is always on my mind. I love Him more and more each day as I study His Word. I cry each time I'm reminded of what He did for us at Calvary. He has suffered enough for me. I will not let Him suffer more because of my sins. I want to be more like Him. With your description of Heaven I want to be ready for Him. I have never been afraid to die but after reading God's book I'm so eager to see Him and I hope to be in the category of "the pure in heart."... Thank you so much!

ANONYMOUS

I struggled a lot whether or not I should read the book. I was going to just check what kind of book it was and browsed through your book, the astonishing book.

But, oh my goodness! The whole book was sent to earth for me.

While turning the first few pages, I couldn't help shedding uncontrollable tears because the Holy Spirit was touching me. I fell on my knees and couldn't hold back my tears.

Is there another way to be moved to tears in this world?

Your witness and each word by the Lord were the vision, the voice, the look, and the being itself that made me endure until this day.

The spirit of the Lord touches us all through one thing. Within this truth I confessed continuously saying "Amen, amen. Father, I trust every single bit of this book."

The time while I was reading the book was so precious and the words the Lord was saying to me so bewitchingly beautiful that I could not get distracted by seconds. I was all focused on the Lord.

I was given a strong determined will to be resolute.

I was given a mission at church that I have to deal with.

I was given the hope to offer my three sons and my husband the Lord.

And I also told the Lord that I won't be displeased by the things I am not able to enjoy in this world.

Also, I was confirmed again that our pursuit and prayer should aim at only one thing that are the kingdom of the Lord and the crying out prayer for the children who are loved by the Lord yet who do not know Jesus.

IN LOVE,
S.

***

I have finished your book or better yet Jesus' book *Heaven Is So Real!*, and I want to thank you for being obedient and writing it. I could feel the Holy Spirit in each page. This book made some really important things crystal clear for me, especially that I have to guard my heart and repent daily to keep it pure. There are a lot of other parts of the book that are vital information for my walk with our Father and His wonderful, holy, Son Jesus, my Savior. Thank you, Choo. You will be in my prayers.

YOUR SISTER IN CHRIST JESUS,

J.

***

My English is not that good so I don't know how to express my feeling.

I'm sure that you wouldn't mind my broken English.

I started reading this book yesterday and I read half of the book.

I'm truly touched by Our Lord's endless love and patient. As I turned one page after page I feel more of His grace and love. I could feel the presence of God (I work in a small company, whenever I have some time, I read the book) and sometimes make me shake a bit, make me cry, smile, laugh sometimes I really want to stand up and dance like you did in the pond in heaven. If I wasn't in the office I would have done that.

Thank you so much to share that precious experience with million people. Thank you so much for showing me God's love and grace and urgency.

I don't have anything to offer Him but I want to give Him whole my heart and the best thing. I'm sure He knows me better than I do. I want to do something for Him.

TOUCHED BY GOD'S GRACE.

Y.

***

From the moment I began the book, I could not put it down. When I ordered it for myself, I also ordered two more copies for two close intercessor friends. Then, after reading only a couple of chapters, I went online and ordered 12 more copies to give out as Christmas presents!! I gave a copy on Sunday to my pastor's wife with a note attached to it saying "PREPARE FOR BLAST-OFF!!!!!!!" I guaranteed her that she has not ever read anything so powerful.

I want you to know that I know by the Spirit of God that you have an extraordinary relationship with our Lord and that you have had extraordinary experiences visiting heaven. You have inspired me. I have lived a very consecrated life and do very much relate to you when you say that you are not interested in conversations that don't revolve around our Lord Jesus. But...even though I have lived a very consecrated life, I want you to be encouraged that your book has shaken the core of me to rise up to a new level of consecration. I pray that I, too, will be given the grace to live such a disciplined, obedient life as you, Choo.

WITH LOVE,
C.

***

I usually don't open the many e-mail advertisements for books, CDs, and conferences, HOWEVER, the advertisement for your book was different. I was drawn to it like a magnet and after reading the write-up, I just had to get it. I received it in the mail on November 29 and began reading it that very day. I finished reading it on December 7 and, of course, I am greatly moved to the core of my being. How awesome and how very sobering!!! Next to the Bible, this is one of the most life-changing books I have read. While I have been seeking the Lord for more of Him and to walk in Kingdom realms with Him, my fervour and determination to walk in obedience and purity has greatly intensified. Thank you very much for your abandonment to God and His purposes for your life and the great cost you have paid (and are still paying) in order for His people to hear the heart cry of our Heavenly Bridegroom.

I feel a strong sense of responsibility to get this book into the hands of whoever the Lord leads me to give it to. I've already bought three for other people (including my pastors). My one friend, to whom I gave the book yesterday, has reported to me this evening that she too is stirred deeply in her heart to follow the Lord with new resolve and consecration. My husband has accepted Christ as His Savior, but has grown at a slow pace and is still struggling with the flesh, the world and the devil. After a very serious and tearful exhortation from me, he is now reading it and I pray the Lord will awaken in him the same urgency to walk closely with the Lord as He did in me.

YOUR SISTER IN CHRIST,
J.

Testimonials

***

I do not know how to express my sincere gratitude and thanks for this wonderful book, *Heaven Is So Real!* You really wakes me up from my slumberland which I never aware that it is so near to the opening pit of hell! You make me repent and ask for forgiveness each time when I read Jesus' warning and reminder to all the unfaithful and disobedient Christians. Thank you, Sis. Choo! I really envy you with your amazing relationship with our dear Lord Jesus Christ. You really deserve such special love, attention and rewards from our dear Lord because you are the most obedient, pure hearted and loving person that I've ever known. God truly blesses you abundantly, sister.

WITH BIG HUGS AND KISSES,

S.

***

This book itself emphasizes to me repeatedly of how great is God's grace and mercy to us man. Jesus loves me and you so much that He's willing to shed His blood on the cross despite the terrible suffering and public humiliation so that we can be reconciled to God. Now He is again, I believed, reaching out to us through this book. He is reminding the Christians of His love for them by the wonderful things He has prepared for them in the eternal kingdom. Do you know that it's all completed and done?! As I flipped the pages I could feel His urgency, His eagerness to come to bring us back. I guess the only thing that's delaying Him is us. Should He come now, a great multitude will not be able to enter into the eternal kingdom to be with Him!…

I'm really thankful for the bold step Choo took to write and publish this book. It's her sheer leap of faith that is not only going to help many come to know Christ but revive many more Christians around the world. For Choo, I would sum her in two words, OBEDIENT and PURE in heart, though that wouldn't even do enough justice.

BY E.

***

Choo Thomas presents a basic message in her book beyond the amazing things she sees with Jesus: Follow God with all your heart and obey Him and His commandments. God's place is prepared for us, but WE have to be ready for it. Our time is short.

We must be obedient servants to our Lord in this life and with a much greater promise of an amazing life to come that makes me long for heaven even more.

D.

***

I don't believe I've ever read a more important Christian book, other than the Bible. The Lord Jesus is coming soon, as evidenced by the preparations He's made in Heaven, and what He has revealed to the writer.

By the love and grace of God, the Lord Jesus is giving all people (Christian and un-believers) a forewarning to be prepared, along with a wonderful description of what eternal life will be like with Him in Heaven.

I pray that those who read the book will share in the urgency to be "born again" by repenting of their sins and receiving Jesus Christ as their Lord and Savior, just like the Bible says in Romans 10:9–10, so that they too shall be saved. The free gift of salvation and a relationship with Jesus is available to everyone that simply asks.

S.

***

Heaven Is So Real! has opened the eyes of my heart and mind to see much more clearly and to realize deeply about heaven which has already been prepared and is waiting for all of us.

My experience while I was reading and at the same time translating this book was really amazing. During translating this book which took about 3 months, I woke up nearly at 5:00 every morning and immediately sat down in front of my son's computer for 2 hours as I had to be ready for work. Then, if there were no prayer meetings or any other church activities in the evening, I continued translating this book till 10.00 at night.

How beautiful and such a blessing for me to read, describe and know more deeply of His words through the journeys with Him. Like Sister Choo Thomas, I cried many times, rejoicing and praising the Lord as if He spoke to me personally, many times His words hit me and caused me to cry tears of marvel for He knows 100% who I am inside out.

If this book has encouraged and motivated me to serve the Lord in sharing the gospel of salvation to the lost especially our

Testimonials

loved ones, friends and neighbors, I believe the same impact will happen in the lives of other concerned Christians.

Let all of us always be reminded that Jesus is coming soon and _Heaven Is So Real!_ for His obedient children.

IN HIS LOVE,
O.

***

Sister, I just want to thank you so much for your response to the Lord, though you honestly shared the process of your hesitations about why the Lord would bless you in such a way. I just loved the book so very very much and will go through it again for there are so many powerful things to be learned from it. Especially in the last four years the Lord has been working also in my life in preparing me for specific ministry in these last days. As you were describing the things about heaven I just found myself going along with you and letting your eyes catch things that I missed but just enjoying in some way all over again, the things the Lord showed me for what I had to learn....

The Lord told you that the book would affect many peoples' lives and I can witness that as I see the hunger of people to get the book. I guess the one part is that the Lord has changed me so much that He can now be just what He wants to be through me. These past few weeks I have watched the Lord amaze us as He walked among us and manifested His power in so many ways. I have never seen anything like it before in my ministry and I am excited to say the least. Many prophetic words have been spoke about our ministry and I am now seeing the fulfillment of it.

So I just want to say thank you so much for allowing the Lord to select you and prepare you for His ministry. I understand why He says you are special, because you respond just the way He wants. The other day, as the morning began the Lord said to me, "Remember to walk in My presence; ignore the things of the flesh and walk in the secret place." Oh, what a safe place to be; hidden with Him so that absolutely nothing causes us to deviate from the exactness of His leading.

THANKFULLY AND PRAYERFULLY YOURS,
J.

xvii

***

As a pastor, prison chaplain, and Pentecostal, I approached this work with a mixture of skepticism and anticipation. I looked for signs of true inspiration, and yet was alert for manipulation and opinion-masked-as-revelation. I read in this "double-minded" manner for fifty pages or so, and then tumbled upon a section that came through to me with such Holy Ghost anointing that I cast aside my doubts and prayed, "Lord, speak to me through this last day revelation!"

The passage contained a vision of the pit of hell. Many have claimed such visions, but never have I read such a frank, heart-rending description. Thomas tells of seeing her own beloved mother in that pit! I was dumbfounded, and humbled. I saw the broken heart of God, and was awakened to the urgency of the time in which we live.

The honesty and pain of this glimpse into Hades so gripped me that I shared it this past Sunday three times. First, with my adult Sunday school class, then with a group of male prisoners, and finally with a group of female inmates. In each case, as I read of this mother in hell, there were gasps. Usually, when ministers read from the pulpit, we limit ourselves to a short paragraph. I read nearly two pages of her book, and was met with silence and amazement. Each time I read, I felt such an anointing.

I dare not rate this book on its style, plot, or any other such "objective" standards. This book claims to be an account of visions from God. I believe it is and encourage believers see what God says about heaven, hell, the importance of our witness, and of holy living in these last days.

Thank you, Choo Thomas, for your sacrificial and humble obedience to an extraordinarily difficult calling!

T.

***

I am a American soldier currently fighting in the war in Iraq. Two years ago I did not know Jesus and I was stationed in Korea where I met my wife...who was a Christian.

Even though I went to church with my wife because I love her so much I still really didn't understand, I guess I didn't have the will to learn. My wife then suddenly became to be extremely religious she began speaking in tongues and going to church almost 7 days a week. I then became a little more religious myself understanding listening wanting to learn.

I then was deployed to Iraq and without my wife was kind of lost, until one day she's going crazy over your book heaven is so real, she begged me to read. So finally I read it and have more faith and more belief than I can handle! I wanting to read the Bible just stop and talk to God whenever I have questions about anything I love it, I love u, I love Jesus! Me and my wife both want to thank u for sacrifices enable to teach us of the days to come and Jesus loves more than we will ever know.

GOD BLESS!!!!

YOUR BROTHER B.

***

I just wanted you to know how great your book has been for me and countless others.

It started with a phone call from my husband, who is stationed in Iraq. Although we are both "Christians," I don't think we both really ever knew what our purpose on this earth was for. So my husband called me and wanted me to read this book, *Heaven Is So Real!*

To be honest, I had no interest in reading it at all but since my husband wanted me to I thought I would just to appease him! To make a long story short I ordered the book, from a local bookstore, left in at the store for a week before I went and bought it! Then I started reading it a week ago. I'm only beginning chapter 12 today but the message was loud and clear. God wants me to love His people and share the gospel of our Lord Jesus Christ! I never thought I would be one of those sold out for Jesus types!

I don't know yet all about what you have seen in heaven but I know that God has called you to ministry so that He can minister to others like me. It is a contagious! I have been sharing this book with everyone I know!...

MAY THE WHOLE WORLD HEAR!

M.

***

As lots of people say that we are living in the last days, I have had a strong passion to know more about our Lord Jesus and

His coming. In *Heaven Is So Real!*, the author, Choo Thomas, wrote about her experience and conversation with Lord Jesus. When I heard about this book, I ordered it immediately from online and read it. The book was much more than I ever expected. Jesus was talking to me through the book. And the Holy Spirit was coming onto me with shaking my body when I was reading His Word. I tell you humbly that this book is next to the Holy Bible to know our Lord Jesus and His coming. The LORD Savior loves us so much. He wants all people to be obedient and pure-hearted as water. He wants all nations to be prepared for His coming and to be saved. The book is powerful enough to prepare for His coming and to make strait the way for the Lord.

YOUR BROTHER IN CHRIST,
J.

***

While reading your testimony I could see and understand why Jesus in the beginning took you very slowly through your experience at first. Building your faith each time He would visit you and showing you that you have nothing to fear. I could sense you warming up and asking Jesus more and more questions as you begin to grow and gain confidence in the Lord Jesus. It was wonderful to walk with you, in my mind's eye, as Jesus revealed some of the hidden mysteries of the Kingdom to you. The best part is that He is coming soon to rapture His church and we shall forever be with the Lord.

Heaven Is So Real! is a book that glorifies Jesus and denounces sin and disobedience to God. It is a balanced account that shows the amazing goodness of the Lord toward the faithful but also shows the consequences for living in sin and rebellion against God which is eternal hell fire (the pit). This book is chuck full of subtle clues that only Jesus would know and could reveal. This is the work of the Lord. Glory to God!.

IN HIS SERVICE,
PASTOR D.

***

I wish that you could see how many lives you have changed through *Heaven Is So Real!* So many people around me have bought several copies to give to their friends and family members and they constantly tell me that their lives and relationship with God has changed by reading *Heaven Is So Real! Heaven Is So Real!* really clarified many things to a lot of people and our desires to enter Heaven has been re-strengthened. Isn't this so amazing how Jesus is changing our lives!...

Heaven Is So Real! was advertised on Full Gospel Church's website, on newspapers, journals, and on posters. Before it even hit the bookshelves, I was very fortunate to receive a copy in English from the person who translated the book, but others had to stand in long lines to buy a copy. The first day the book was out, thousands of copies were immediately sold out. Constantly, a sign saying "Sold Out" would be hanging outside the bookstores people had to wait for the next day to buy a book! So many books have been sold due to that many people felt that this was too great of a book to just keep it to themselves. People are buying several copies to give to their unsaved friends and family members. Even my Sunday school students have read it and burning desires to go to Heaven has taken place in their hearts. *Heaven Is So Real!* is not only sold at the bookstores in churches but also in the largest bookstores in Korea. As of today, it is the number one best seller in the Christian section! Glory to God!

LOVE,
S.

***

I thank and praise God for your obedience and His persistent love! *Heaven Is So Real!* completely changed my life. I now have real hope of Heaven and even more real closeness to my beloved Jesus.

God has so set me free and blessed me indescribably through your book—or rather, His book.

I can't tell you how much I cried and laughed and yearned for Jesus throughout the read. I felt as if I was there with you and Jesus walking along the beach, visiting Heaven and its glorious splendor.

I think about Jesus at every waking moment and can't—and certainly don't want to—get Him out of my mind. He so preoccupies all my thoughts. He is SO good.

I am so eager each day to get on my knees and seek His face, His will, His Word. I love to be in His presence.

Since I've read the book, the Scriptures—most especially the four Gospels—come alive!

Reading *Heaven Is So Real!* I was astounded and mesmerized by each word Jesus spoke. I had to read and re-read every precious word He spoke. He forgave my sins, healed my heart, and revived my backslidden, dying soul.

GOD BLESS YOU!

S.

***

My wife is also a Korean American and she heard about your book from Pastor Cho in Korea. She bought a copy and read it, and WOW, it was awesome! It changed her Christian life forever! She couldn't wait to tell me about it. I was very interested, so I ordered a copy and read it. Unbelievable! It really changes lives! The Lord is speaking directly to us through your book!

Thank you, Choo, you truly are the Lord's "Special Daughter." Thank you for your dedicated prayer life, and for listening and obeying our Lord and Savior so that we can all enjoy this glimpse into our future.

This book is a "Serious Wake Up Call" for all Christians in this world. It woke me up that's for sure, and my prayer now is that it will "wake up" everyone that reads it. I bought 10 copies already for some of my friends and I plan on buying more. The Lord truly is coming soon, and we need to be ready! Thank you, Choo, for obeying Jesus, but most importantly.

THANK YOU LORD!!!!!

J.

***

Thank you for the book *Heaven Is So Real!* I don't quite know what to say. This book has shaken my world to the core. I have cried, (I didn't think I would), felt fear, sensed doubt that I have missed the mark in what I thought of as "loving the Lord," felt so unworthy of His consideration and done some serious soul searching. In other words this book has had a life changing effect on me. I am in the process of re-evaluating my life, daily choices, and most of all my commitment to God. I don't want to be cut off from God or miss out on heaven. All of my life is under the magnifying glass right now.

LOVE,

A.

***

I do most of my serious reading just before retiring. I had just started reading the book *Heaven Is So Real!*, and read the first few chapters. After going to sleep, I had a strange occurrence early in that morning of February 2nd. Sometime after 1:00 a.m. when I went to the bathroom, I dreamed that I could see a bright light although it was not brilliant. I stirred and quickly went back to sleep. Just before 1:58 a.m. I saw a light that was terribly bright, like looking into the sun without sunglasses. I awoke shaking! Was this the power of suggestion from the book, or was it a happening like what happened to Choo Thomas many times? Perhaps I will find out. I have never seen a bright light in my dreams before. I have accepted it as a sign that the book is important, very important.

G. AND A.

Foreword

Heaven! Just the mention of the word stirs something deep within the hearts and minds of people. We sing songs about it, hear sermons about it, and have loved ones there. One day we expect to go there ourselves. But how real is heaven?

Heaven is real to the author because of her encounters with Jesus Christ. This book reveals the personal story of Sister Choo Thomas who traveled to heaven with Jesus several times, and He took her sightseeing in heaven. You will read about her strong faith in heaven, the kingdom of God, which will make believers realize the importance of personally meeting God and receiving answers from Him through prayer. With such experiences of faith, people will come to realize the importance of a life of faith.

I have read this book in English three times, and I have received a lot of insight about heaven and have been blessed. In fact, I was so deeply impressed and inspired by it that I had it translated into Korean for Korean people to read and be blessed. Among religious books, it has become the number one best seller in Korea.

Please do not consider this a theological thesis or a book on doctrine. Just read it and enjoy it as the author's personal experience and testimony about what she has seen and heard in heaven.

Whether you are a Christian or not, *Heaven Is So Real!* is a very moving and inspiring story which you should read with an open heart. It will help you understand more fully the great blessings that God has prepared for His children in eternal heaven.

–DR. DAVID YONGGI CHO
SENIOR PASTOR
YOIDO FULL GOSPEL CHURCH
SEOUL, KOREA

Preface

I N THIS BOOK I will be sharing with you the experiences I have had in
heaven with Jesus. From the outset, I want you to understand the circumstances surrounding each of these visits to heaven.

A passage from the first letter by the apostle Paul to the Christians in
ancient Corinth will help make this clear. It says:

> Behold, I tell you a mystery: We shall not all sleep, but we shall all
> be changed—in a moment, in the twinkling of an eye, at the last
> trumpet. For the trumpet will sound, and the dead will be raised
> incorruptible, and we shall be changed.
>
> For this corruptible must put on incorruption, and this mortal
> must put on immortality. So when this corruptible has put on
> incorruption, and this mortal has put on immortality...then shall
> be brought to pass the saying that is written: "Death is swallowed
> up in victory."
>
> —1 CORINTHIANS 15:51–54

This pericope of Scripture refers to the End Times, when those who
know the Lord will go to be with Him forever. When this happens, we will
have to exchange our mortal bodies for incorruptible, heavenly bodies.

Preface

Every time I have gone to heaven with Jesus this exchange actually has occurred. God would give me a new body—a body in which I looked remarkably like I did when I was a teenager. Sometimes this transformation would take place at a beach on earth that He escorted me to. Other times I would be clothed in my incorruptible body in my bedroom at home.

People often ask me, "Were your experiences in heaven like visions or dreams, or did you actually go there?" My only response to these questions is that I know I've seen heaven, and I know that *heaven is so real.* Whether we place my experiences in the category of supernatural dreams, visions or actual experiences, I will leave to the theologians. All I can say is that they were very real to me.

Each time the Lord has visited me, I have been lying on my bed under the total control of the anointing of the Holy Spirit. Just before He visits each time, my earthly body quivers and quakes for at least twenty minutes. I do not understand everything about this, but I know that He is releasing His power into my being. Sometimes these preparatory periods last for a half-hour or more.

Please don't ask me why this is necessary, because only He knows the reason for each experience. He has simply told me, over and over again, that He is getting me ready for the ministry He has called me to.

Usually when this occurs, my body shakes and my stomach tightens. Deep groans emerge from my spirit, and I perspire profusely. I believe the groans are those described by the apostle Paul: "Likewise the Spirit also helps in our weaknesses. For we do not know what we should pray for as we ought, but the Spirit Himself makes intercession for us with groanings which cannot be uttered" (Rom. 8:26).

I believe the perspiring comes from the heavy anointing of the Lord. The Bible often describes the presence of the Lord in terms of fire, heat and glory, and now I know what these images mean. I personally have experienced the intense heat of His presence.

Usually these manifestations are followed quickly and suddenly by a tremendous surge within and a pulling, jerking sensation without. Then I see my transformed body with the Lord on the earthly beach. After He takes me to heaven, we always return to the same beach we started from.

Whenever and whatever has happened, which I admit I do not fully understand, my earthly body has remained in bed during each of my visits to heaven. During these experiences I am both a participant and an observer.

I have been able to see everything—all of what has happened to me—with the eyes of my earthly body. I have been able to observe all that has happened as I have gone with Jesus to the beach, as my body has been transformed and as He has escorted me to heaven.

My earthly body often reacts to my experiences in heaven as I am having them. It participates in the dancing, rejoicing, praising, laughing, crying and other manifestations occurring in my transformed body. ·

When my transformed body is happy, my physical body reacts with happiness. When my heavenly body is sad, my physical body reacts with tears. When my transformed body sings, I sing; when it dances, I move my hands; when it laughs, I laugh. When I, as a young woman within my transformed body, am talking with the Lord, my earthly body responds with words from my heart; and my mouth and head move accordingly.

I watch my transformed body as I walk with the Lord in heaven. When I sings songs of joy and praise, I can see the happiness reflected on my face. My voice, quite miraculously, emanates from my earthly body.

When I, in my transformed body, ascend to and descend from heaven, my real body feels as if it is being lifted up and gently lowered. These sensations last for only a second. Sometimes, when my physical body feels as if it is being lifted from my bed, I have screamed in fright.

Even though I can see the features of my own transformed face quite vividly, I cannot see the Lord's face. However, I can see His hair, hands and clothing, and I can tell that He has a very large frame. His wavy hair is parted in the middle, is curled in at the bottom, comes down to His neck and is as white as silk. The skin on His hands is olive-colored, and His fingers are long and slender.

I can see the Lord's mouth moving when He speaks to me. His stature and build make Him appear as if He is a young man, perhaps between the ages of thirty and forty. His height, it seems, is approximately six feet.

Although I can't make out His distinct facial features, I can tell when He is angry, happy, sad or concerned. I know Him to be very gentle and loving, and He enjoys playful moments. Remember, however, I am seeing the Lord's spirit body (just like I am able to see my spirit body).

Preface

Since May 27, 1996, the Lord has taken me to the earthly beach early every Monday morning in fulfillment of a promise He made to me. We often have walked along together in the sand. Sometimes He has lifted me in His arms and spun me around like a child. During such playful moments, the Lord and I have greatly enjoyed each other's presence, and we both have laughed with genuine joy.

The Lord has a very human personality, even though He is the Son of God. I love Him more than my life. He is a person of very few words. When He speaks, He always does so purposefully. He shares only those things He thinks are significant for us to know.

When He disappears after the exhilarating visits to heaven, my transformed body disappears as well, and my physical body is free to move in accord with its own needs and desires. At this point my body feels relaxed and restful.

After these marvelous experiences, I can get out of bed—immediately, if I choose to—but usually I lie there and reflect on the wonderful experiences I've just seen and lived. Then I write these experiences in my journal.

I am amazed that the Lord called me to write this book. I am a Korean-American whose use of the English language is somewhat limited. Nonetheless, the Lord chose me to do His work. He told me to tell everything I experienced and heard, and that is the purpose of this book.

How thankful I am that I have been privileged to have this foretaste of glory so I can share it with you. God wants me to let you know that He already has prepared a place for you in heaven if you only will believe in His Son and receive Him as your personal Lord and Savior.

I want only to do the will of the Lord. My prayer for you as you read this book is the same as the apostle Paul's prayer for his beloved Ephesian brothers and sisters, recorded in his letter to them:

> That the God of our Lord Jesus Christ, the Father of glory, may give to you the spirit of wisdom and revelation in the knowledge of Him, the eyes of your understanding being enlightened; that you may know what is the hope of His calling, what are the riches of the glory of His inheritance in the saints, and what is the exceeding greatness of His power toward us who believe, according to the working of His mighty power which He worked in Christ when He raised Him from the dead and seated Him at His right hand in the heavenly places, far above all principality and power and might and

dominion, and every name that is named, not only in this age but also in that which is to come.

—EPHESIANS 1:17–21

I ask only that you receive this book in the same way it was written—with total openness to the Lord and His will. Evaluate my experiences in the light of the Word of God. I believe you will find that the things I share about heaven and my experiences with the Lord are thoroughly biblical.

—CHOO THOMAS
TACOMA, WASHINGTON
FEBRUARY, 1997

Introduction

In My Father's house are many mansions;
if it were not so, I would have told you.
I go to prepare a place for you.

—JOHN 14:2 (EMPHASIS ADDED)

THROUGH A PROPHETIC utterance given by a pastor named Larry Randolph, God spoke directly to me on December 3, 1995. Pastor Randolph prophesied:

> I saw the blessing of the Lord in the realm of prophetic ministry and the Lord opening your spirit in a great way to prophetic ministry, dreams and words of knowledge...I saw the Lord speaking to you in the night seasons, between 11 P.M. and 3 A.M....[He will] begin to awaken you and visit you, give you dreams, visions and insight...God told me that you're one of the daughters that He's put His Spirit upon to prophesy.

Pastor Randolph spoke these words over me during a special Sunday service at Puget Sound Christian Center in Tacoma, Washington. As he did, the familiar anointing of the Holy Spirit welled up deep in my spirit, and my body began to shiver and quake under the power of God.

I began to weep tears of joy and gratitude as I realized that God had chosen me to be one of His servants in these last days. The Lord flooded me with His loving warmth, and the heat of His presence made the experience seem as if I were resting on a feather bed on a summer day.

I was reminded of the words of the prophet Joel:

> And it shall come to pass afterward that I will pour out My Spirit on
> all flesh; your sons and your daughters shall prophesy, your old men
> shall dream dreams, your young men shall see visions; And also on
> My menservants and on My maidservants I will pour out My Spirit in
> those days. And I will show wonders in the heavens and in the earth.
> —JOEL 2:28–30

Could it be, I wondered, that these prophetic words were being fulfilled here and now? Was I to be one of the Lord's special maidservants
who would see wonders in heaven and earth?

What an honor to be selected as a vessel of the Lord's love, grace and
power in these last days. Certainly this prophetic calling of God was not
something I would have chosen for myself, because I am ordinarily a
very shy person. I soon learned that all the shyness and bashfulness van-
ishes when I am experiencing the anointing of the Holy Spirit.

I recalled another scripture:

> You did not choose Me, but I chose you and appointed you that
> you should go and bear fruit, and that your fruit should remain,
> that whatever you ask the Father in My name He may give you.
> —JOHN 15:16

Clearly, God was choosing me to go forth in His name in order to
bear lasting fruit—fruit that would remain. He was showing me the
power of prayer and the importance of getting close to Him.

> Abide in Me, and I in you. As the branch cannot bear fruit of itself,
> unless it abides in the vine, neither can you, unless you abide in Me.
> I am the vine, you are the branches. He who abides in Me, and I in
> him, bears much fruit; for without Me you can do nothing.
> —JOHN 15:4–5

The overwhelming excitement and burning anointing of the Holy Spirit
continued to intensify as the pastor went on with his prophetic utterance. I
literally felt as if I were on fire for God. Pastor Randolph continued:

> There's been a misunderstanding at times in the way you respond to
> God or the way you connect with God. The Lord says He's going to
> remove the misunderstanding…they won't say, "She's an enigma."
> They'll say, "She's just different."…It's a godly difference…God

has given you a uniqueness. He's going to minister to you in a unique way. He's going to speak to you things that only friends would tell friends. He's going to give you secrets in the night seasons.

To be a close, personal friend of God's, as Abraham was, has been my heart's desire since I became a Christian. I treasure moments alone with the Lord. I know His voice, and when my heart is quiet before Him, He is able to speak to me: "My sheep hear My voice, and I know them, and they follow Me" (John 10:27).

Through this compelling message from God, I knew the Father was answering the cry of my heart—to get to know Him better by building an intimate personal relationship with Jesus. My heart was soaring like an eagle while I listened to Him speaking to me through Pastor Randolph:

> It's not showing off what God gives you; it's keeping secrets. God's going to tell you things about people that you'll never tell people. You'll pray for and intercede [for them], and hold them up in prayer because you're going to be a friend of God—and that's a true prophet. It's just a friend of God. A friend of God.
>
> He's going to tell you secrets about other people's lives and about things He's doing in the earth. So, get ready in 1996 for a fresh anointing of the prophetic to come upon your life. And in the new year, as you wait before the Lord, God's going to put a fresh Spirit upon you, an anointing of prophecy is going to come upon you.

I knew the words were beautiful and deeply meaningful even though I did not understand all they implied. I felt as if I were clay in the hands of the divine Potter, and He was shaping me, molding me and forming me in preparation for a special ministry that would begin in the very near future. As I spun on the Potter's wheel, under a mighty anointing of the Spirit of God, I sensed that major changes were already taking place deep in my spirit.

A tinge of fear was soon extinguished by the oil of the Spirit that seemed to drip over every part of my being. My mind tried to find its way into the old channel of questioning, because I felt so unworthy to receive such a wonderful personal message and calling.

How can God use me? I thought. *I am a Korean-American, and my use of the English language is not as proficient as it should be. Why would God pick me to be His friend? Why me?*

It was all so surprising, but even though I was a young Christian I had already learned the truth of Jesus' words, "Without Me you can do nothing" (John 15:5). I decided right then and there to accept the Lord's message by faith, and in my heart I prayed: *Father, thank You for giving me this word. I will always say yes to You.*

This was my commitment even though I did not fully understand everything the Lord was saying. One thing I did realize, however, was that He would have to prepare me for the ministry He was leading me into.

I remembered the words of one of my favorite verses: "Trust in the LORD with all your heart, and lean not on your own understanding; in all your ways acknowledge Him, and He shall direct your paths" (Prov. 3:5–6).

Little did I realize where those paths would lead me, but I was firm in my resolve to trust the Lord without leaning on my own understanding. After all, isn't this the essence of the spiritual life? We're spiritual beings on a human journey. Our true essence is our spirits. Heaven is our true home, and as I've discovered, *heaven is so real.*

Since the moment God called me to a prophetic ministry I have learned that many believers don't truly believe. Some are not sure that heaven even exists. Others don't seem to care. Too many go through life as if this world is all there is.

God has shown me an entirely different picture. He has taken me to heaven seventeen different times, and He wants me to let everyone know that *heaven is so real!* When we truly understand this, it changes everything about us—our motives, attitudes, values, relationships, dreams, plans and perspective. My prayer for you is, you will catch more than a glimpse of heaven as you read and that you will be changed—as I was—and experience the security of knowing Jesus has already prepared a place for you and your loved ones.

—CHOO THOMAS
TACOMA, WASHINGTON
FEBRUARY, 1997

PART ONE

Visitations and Visions

Chapter 1

On Heaven's Road

*I press toward the goal
for the prize of the upward call of
God in Christ Jesus.*

—Philippians 3:14

My NAME IS Choo Nam Thomas, and I am Korean-American. I am the only daughter of my parents, who are deceased, and I have two brothers: one younger and one older. I am married and have two children, a son and a daughter, both of whom are married. I also have two grandsons and two granddaughters.

In Korea, my family was not religious in any way. I never heard about Jesus until I went to church. I had only heard about church and God.

I became a Christian in February 1992. I literally fell in love with Jesus after I attended church a couple of times. When I found out what He did for me, I made up my mind that I wanted to give all of my being to Him for the rest of my life.

God responded by answering my prayers, and this enabled my faith to grow stronger day by day. I began to lose my old desires each day, very quickly. I could think only about Jesus every waking moment. I was so much in fear of God that I couldn't knowingly do anything against His will. I wanted only to please Him, and I wanted to know everything about Him so I could tell others.

A VISION AND THE FIRE OF GOD

I RECEIVED THE fire of the Holy Spirit while I was praying at home in January 1994. About a month later, I saw the Lord's presence while I was worshiping at the Neighborhood Assembly of God in Tacoma, Washington. He was sitting by the pulpit. His legs were crossed, and I could see Him as clearly as a real person, except I couldn't see His face.

As I perceived Him, He had silky white hair and was wearing a pure white robe. His person was visible to me for almost five minutes. After seeing Him my body was on fire with unspeakable joy, and I became wholeheartedly committed to Jesus. Soon after this life-changing experience, my family and I began attending Puget Sound Christian Center in Tacoma, Washington.

I had another profound spiritual experience on Easter Sunday 1995. While attending services with my family at Puget Sound Christian Center, my body began to shake violently, and we had to stay for second service. I was experiencing the same phenomenon known among Quakers, Shakers and early Pentecostals.

Since then, my body never stops shaking in church or during my prayer time at home. Two weeks after this Easter Sunday experience, I received the gift of tongues while at home and began to sing in the Spirit. While watching a Benny Hinn crusade on television, I stood up and lifted my hands in prayer. Then I fell on the floor for almost three hours. The anointing of God's Holy Spirit was so strong that I couldn't get up, and all I could do was sing and talk in tongues and laugh.

During every worship service after that, I could see the presence of the Lord Jesus in church. The visions I continue to receive of Him are not quite as vivid as the first one, but they are just as real.

A WILLING VESSEL

I BELIEVE THESE exciting and unusual experiences are preparation for the work God has called me to. I have a strong desire to receive healing and soul-winning gifts, but I don't know how to serve Him, except by telling everyone who Jesus is.

At first, some family members and friends rejected my message and disliked me for always talking about Jesus. Now, however, things are different. No matter who I am with, I only want to talk about the Lord, and

He has given me the privilege of leading many people to Him, including my relatives and friends. All of my loved ones are saved now.

Jesus is always in my thoughts and on my tongue. When difficult times come, I think about what Jesus did for us. When I remember all that He has done, I realize nothing is too hard for me. When someone hurts me, I simply meditate on all Jesus did for me at Calvary, and peace comes instantly.

Preceding the Lord's first visit with me, I had some very special dreams about clouds. These dreams reminded me of something my father had once shared with me.

He told me that my mother had had a very special dream about clouds. He often mentioned that my mother also had had a special dream about me before she became pregnant with me. He said she never forgot that dream about a clear day that suddenly became very cloudy. The clouds came toward the front of the house. One of them came into the room where she was sleeping and filled the room with a white glow.

My mother had been sick most of her life, and she died when she was only forty. She never shared these dreams and visions with me, but my father told me many times about them, especially about the clouds. I never thought seriously about them until I had my own experience with dreams and visions.

My father's interpretation of the dream about the clouds was that I could have become very successful if I had been a boy, because in those days many Oriental men believed that only boys could attain success in life. I believe, however, that the dream was a sign from the Lord. As you read this book, you will see that clouds have played an important part in the preparatory work the Lord had done and continues to do in my life.

Since meeting Jesus, I have had a strong desire to pray for others. I have become a true prayer warrior. Intercessory prayer has become a way of life for me. I regularly attended a Bible study at a Korean-American church for about a year before my husband, Roger, was saved.

I didn't do any full-time church work or know many of God's words, but He chose me for His special work anyway. According to my Lord Jesus, He wanted me to first get to know Him and to learn to obey Him and focus only on Him. By showing me heaven and all the other visions I have been privileged to experience, He began to prepare me for the ministry He has called me to. Now I'm learning about Him through prayer and the study of His Word.

REVELATION OF HEAVEN

THE REMAINING CHAPTERS of this book, as you will soon discover, record some remarkable journeys that God has taken me on since I turned my life over to Him. He has asked me to record these experiences in this book so that others will see and understand. Why He chose me for this important work remains a mystery to me, but I do understand that He wants me to warn people in the world and in the church that we don't have much time left in which to complete the work He has called us to do.

The Father in heaven wants everyone to know how much He loves them and desires to bless them, if they will trust Him and obey His Word. He has shown me that many believers are, in reality, functional atheists—they don't really believe there is a heaven. I can say with all the certainty that it is possible for us—on this side of eternity—to know that *heaven is so real*. Furthermore, I now know that our God is able, as His Word says, to do "exceedingly abundantly above all that we ask or think, according to the power that works in us" (Eph. 3:20).

The purpose of this book is to give Him glory: "To Him be glory in the church by Christ Jesus throughout all ages, world without end. Amen" (Eph. 3:21).

Please read these pages with an open mind and heart, and let the Lord speak to you. He has a wonderful plan and purpose for your life. He has prepared a home for you in heaven. Like me, you can discover the thrill of knowing that you are bound for the Promised Land.

Chapter 2

All Power in Heaven and on Earth

*Then Jesus came and spoke to them
saying, "All authority has been given
to Me in heaven and on earth."*

—MATTHEW 28:18

THE YEAR 1996, AS pastor Larry Randolph had prophesied, became the most wonderful, exciting, meaningful and empowering year of my life. It all began on New Year's Eve 1995. The anointing of the Lord was so very real to me throughout the entire evening. In fact, His presence was literally so hot that I could hardly breathe.

I had experienced the presence and power of the Holy Spirit before, but this night was so different. It was a time of intense love and excitement, and I sensed that something uniquely wonderful yet mysterious was about to happen to me.

What I was experiencing defied reason and logic, but the presence of the Lord was so real that I felt like I could have reached out and held His hand tangibly. It was a spiritual reality, but it far exceeded anything I had ever experienced in the natural realm.

There was an expectancy in my heart. Somehow I realized that all I needed to do was to continue waiting in the presence of the Lord, and He would speak to me and show me wonderful things. Throughout that long, yet pleasant night, I held onto a verse from Jeremiah that contains a promise from our Father: "Call to Me, and I will answer you, and show you great and mighty things, which you do not know" (Jer. 33:3).

While I waited with eager anticipation, I could hear the firecrackers and other loud noises of revelers ringing in the new year. As 1995 turned to 1996, I continued waiting, and throughout the wee hours of the morning until daybreak I waited. Nothing happened, but I was determined to hear from God.

January 1, 1996, was a cold, damp day in the Northwest, but there was a precious warmth in my heart that no winter wind could chill. The Word of God spoke to my heart, "Wait on the LORD; be of good courage, and He shall strengthen your heart; wait, I say, on the LORD!" (Ps. 27:14).

Waiting—one of the hardest things in the world to do, and yet it is the key to so much empowerment in the spiritual life. The Lord wants us to wait in His presence, because it is in this way that we develop the patience we need to grow and to serve.

Even though I had not slept at all the previous night, on New Year's Day I felt rested, happy and alive while my family and I celebrated the holiday. From 9 P.M. until 11 P.M. of New Year's Day the heat of the Lord's presence reminded me to keep the night watch once again. I slept briefly, then awoke refreshed, yearning to hear the Lord's voice speaking to me.

This almost sleepless schedule continued throughout the first half of January. Still I had not heard the Lord. By faith, however, I sensed that He was preparing me for a personal encounter with Him.

TREMBLING IN THE NIGHT

ON JANUARY 19 I awoke at 3 A.M. My body was shaking. This had never happened in my sleep. Since Easter Sunday 1995, however, my body had been shaking during worship services at church and in moments of personal prayer.

There's something about the night—a time of quietness and few distractions—that affords a special opportunity for the Lord to draw close to His people. This was certainly the case with me.

Sometimes the anointing of God was so heavy on me that I felt as if I would faint. At other times it would leave me feeling dizzy and weak. Often I would lay in bed completely immobilized by the overpowering presence of God. It is all too wonderful to fully describe, but I will endeavor to show you what it was like.

The Bible is replete with examples of people quaking and shaking in the presence of the Lord. Sometimes this manifestation is accompanied by fear, but most of the time it is preparatory; God is about to do a great work through a yielded vessel. Certainly the latter was true with the prophet Jeremiah, who heard God's voice pleading with him: "'Do you not fear Me?' says the LORD. 'Will you not tremble at My presence?'" (Jer. 5:22).

The one who would become known as the "weeping prophet" answered God's plea: "My heart within me is broken because of the prophets; all my bones shake. I am like a drunken man, and like a man whom wine has overcome, because of the LORD, and because of His holy words" (Jer. 23:9).

The Word of God shows us that trembling and shaking are appropriate physical responses to the presence of the Lord. Other examples are found in Daniel 10:7; Psalm 99:1, 114:7; Habakkuk 3:16; and Matthew 28:4, as well as in Acts 4:31, one of my favorites: "And when they had prayed, the place where they were assembled together was shaken; and they were all filled with the Holy Spirit."

"I WANT TO TALK TO YOU"

ON THE NIGHT of January 19, the Lord's presence was so intense in my bedroom that I shook, perspired and felt very weak for more than an hour. Then I heard something. Was it the voice of my Lord and Master?

I turned my head on the pillow to look in the direction of the sound, and there, all aglow, was a figure dressed in white garments. The radiance that emanated from this unknown visitor was so brilliant that I could not see His face, but in my heart of hearts I knew that I had been blessed with a special visitation from the Lord.

How could this be happening to me? I wondered, as I began to tremble even more violently and weep tears of love and joy. It was the Lord—the Lord of heaven and earth—and He had willingly chosen to visit me in this special way. I felt so humbled by His presence. I could not stop crying.

"My daughter, Choo Nam, I am your Lord, and I want to talk to you. You have been My special daughter for a long time."

The impact of His voice, His words, His message hit me with a supernatural force that left me reeling. My body shook harder, and I felt my spirit rising within. The gift of tongues began to flow, followed by a clear interpretation.

I moved as close to the edge of my bed as possible so that I wouldn't waken my husband, Roger, asleep next to me. For a moment I wondered how he could possibly sleep with such brightness in the room and the incessant shaking that seemed powerful enough to make the bed collapse. But this was a special moment for me to receive from the Lord, so Roger continued to sleep.

The Lord spoke once more in His calmly reassuring yet very firm voice: *"Daughter, you are such an obedient child, and I want to give you special gifts. These gifts are going to serve Me greatly. I want you to be happy about these gifts."*

I knew at that moment God was choosing me to do an important work for Him and that this must become my single-minded purpose. I knew I had nothing to give Him except my heart and my life, and I was willing to do whatever He wanted, to go wherever He wanted. It was a night of commitment, challenge and purpose. My wonderful Lord was beginning to reveal His will to me.

I have known since then that when my body begins to shake from the inside out, God soon will be speaking to me. I also knew then that His words would be life and victory.

My body stopped trembling, and I fell into one of the most peaceful, restful sleeps I could remember having in years. Throughout the next day I felt so anointed and happy because I had met the Master face-to-face. That morning I asked Roger if he had felt or heard anything during the night.

He shook his head. "I guess I'm just a deep sleeper," he said.

God had chosen me for a specific work. It was too wonderful to imagine, and yet it was exciting beyond words. I opened my Bible to the book of John and read these stirring words that coincided with Pastor Randolph's prophecy: "You did not choose Me, but I chose you and appointed you that you should go and bear fruit, and that your fruit should remain, that whatever you ask the Father in My name He may give you" (John 15:16).

The Lord had chosen me to go and bear lasting fruit. This is what I wanted more than anything in the world. His Word, His presence, His anointing confirmed His calling in my life. I committed my heart to obeying the Lord from that moment on, no matter what the consequences.

Then my eyes fell to the preceding verses: "You are My friends if you do whatever I command you. No longer do I call you servants, for a servant does not know what his master is doing; but I have called you friends, for all things that I heard from My Father I have made known to you" (John 15:14–15).

God was confirming His *rhema* word to me—from Pastor Randolph— through His *logos*, the Bible. The pastor's words came back to me: "God's going to tell you things about people that you'll never tell people. You'll pray for and intercede, and hold them up in prayer because you're going to be a friend of God—and that's a true prophet; it's just a friend of God. A friend of God. He's going to tell you secrets about other people's lives and about things He's doing in the earth. So, get ready in 1996 for a fresh anointing of the prophetic to come upon your life."

Now it was happening, and I could hardly wait to discover what God would tell me next.

A PROPHECY FULFILLED

ON JANUARY 20 I awoke between 3 A.M. and 4 A.M. The anointing of the Lord's presence awakened me and was accompanied again by intense heat. I was half asleep, but suddenly the Lord's voice woke me completely, saying: *"Daughter, I am going to visit you many times before this work is done. Therefore, I want you to rest during daytime hours. I have many special plans for you. I will use you in a great way, but it will take awhile to get you ready for the work I've called you to do. You must write down what you hear during each of My visits."*

The whole experience stunned me, and I was amazed to think that He would visit me again and again. Surely one visit with the Lord should be enough. Yet He said He would be returning to me personally so that He could get me ready for the work He has for me to do.

Just as suddenly as He came into my bedroom, He departed. I could neither hear nor see Him. The shaking dissipated. His reassuring words, and His wonderful visit, left me feeling very happy, peaceful and certainly curious.

It was as if I had climbed a high mountain in my native land of Korea from which I could see clearly for miles and miles and as if I were breathing the rich, clean air of the mountain heights. My mind was focused, my heart was joyful, and I felt healthy and happy. I determined

9

to obey the voice of the Lord by taking one step at a time, because I knew He would lead me each step of the way.

HOUR OF EMPOWERMENT

IT HAPPENED AGAIN the next morning. Between 2 A.M. and 3 A.M. I awoke suddenly. My body was shaking uncontrollably, and I was perspiring heavily. The anointing of the Lord's presence was upon me.

The Lord said, *"You are My precious daughter. I will be with you always, wherever you are. I love you just as you are."*

As I lay there, soaking in His every word, I was overcome by awe and adoration. He went on: *"I am giving you the power that you will need for the work I've called you to do. I am preparing you to serve Me. Your body shakes as the power flows into you. I am giving you all the spiritual gifts. I am releasing your spirit so you will be completely free to serve Me."*

A few days before this I had had a dream during which I had climbed a mountain. When I reached the summit I was able to touch the clouds. The Lord reminded me of that dream and explained its spiritual significance to me.

"You will go to that height as you minister in My name," He said.

For the first time during one of His personal visits to me I raised a question.

"Lord," I said, "what do You want me to do? I don't really know anything about ministering."

"I will guide You and show You what I want You to do."

"What about my husband?" I asked.

"Don't worry about him. I will bless him and minister to him also."

Once again His words were wonderfully reassuring, liberating and empowering. Truly I felt the power of His words unleashing power in my spirit. When He stopped talking to me that morning, the shaking stopped as well.

ON FIRE FOR GOD

THESE WONDERFULLY NEW experiences were quickening my body with joy. My heart was soaring, and my mind was filled with childlike curiosity. Where I once had felt insecure, I felt completely free. I realized my new future would be entirely different because all my hopes and dreams truly depended on the Lord. I was truly alive, and it was a vibrant life beyond all my expectations.

On January 25 the Lord talked with me from 3 A.M. until 4 A.M. This time, I had awakened before He arrived on the scene, and while I lay silently in my bed, I anticipated another meeting with my Lord and Savior. The familiar shaking began precisely at 3:00. By now I had learned that this meant my Savior would soon be with me. I had learned to sense His presence, and when I turned in the direction where He usually stood, I saw Him.

His radiance, His strong voice, His loving presence always transport me into a different world. I'm sure it's the realm of eternity where time and space hold little significance, and physical and material things do not matter. It is a realm of the spirit—so bright and peaceful—a place where life takes on new meaning and purpose. It is a little bit of heaven on earth.

The shaking continued for twenty minutes. I began to view it as being like a spiritual transfusion. The power of the Holy Spirit was coursing through every nerve, sinew, muscle and organ of my body. It was setting me on fire with the power of God.

This must have been what the disciples experienced on the Day of Pentecost when the Lord baptized them with the Holy Spirit and fire. "And suddenly there came a sound from heaven, as of a rushing mighty wind, and it filled the whole house where they were sitting" (Acts 2:2). When the power of God falls, strangely wonderful things begin to happen in our lives.

That night Jesus spoke to me in His inimitable way, *"I am your Lord, My daughter. I want you to hear and remember everything I tell you. When you write it down, use My exact words. You are sleepy, but do not miss any of the words I tell you. I will be visiting you many times in the future because I have important work for you to do. You are the child I am going to use to do this work for Me, so be prepared."*

ANSWERED PRAYERS

A FEW DAYS later, on January 28, I awoke, shaking again. It was between 2:00 and 3:00 in the morning. I felt so overcome by the presence of the Lord that I was weak. My body was so hot that I was perspiring. It seemed as if I was dreaming, but I soon realized that this was no dream.

11

"I am your Lord, My daughter," Jesus said. Then I glanced toward the window, in the direction of His majestic voice, and I saw His radiant figure standing there.

"I know You have been so hungry to serve Me, but You did not know how to serve Me yet. I know you do not want to be embarrassed when you come before Me. I know all your thoughts, and I love your thoughts."

This message from my Savior spoke volumes to my heart. I now knew what once I had only believed—that Jesus hears and answers prayer. I had prayed that God would help me serve Him so I will not be embarrassed when I stand before Him. I had told Him, so many times, how much I wanted to serve Him, and I always told Him that I didn't know how.

It is for this reason that I always read the Bible both in English and Korean—to gain the deepest possible understanding of the Word of God so I can share it with others. Serving the Lord was my deepest desire after I learned what the Lord had done for me.

"Daughter, your prayers have been answered, and you will serve Me greatly. You will have much work to do for Me. What you will do for Me will please you. You are My faithful daughter, and that is why I am giving this important work for you to do."

The shaking subsided, and the Lord departed from my room. My mind was drawn to His Word: "Now this is the confidence that we have in Him, that if we ask anything according to His will, He hears us. And if we know that He hears us, whatever we ask, we know that we have the petitions that we have asked of Him" (1 John 5:14–15).

I now know the truth of this wonderful prayer promise. It is an infallible promise of the Word of God that He does, in fact, hear us when we pray according to His will, and His will is revealed in the Bible.

It is His will for us to bear lasting fruit in His name. It is His will for us to minister to others. It is His will for us to believe when we pray. It is His will for us to spend time in His presence, to wait upon Him.

Therefore, when I pray according to these aspects of His will, as they are revealed in His Word, I know that He hears me. This is a very firm realization to me now.

The visitations from the Lord have given me the growing confidence that comes from spending time with God. He was there; He is always there. I know He will never leave me or forsake me. He is my friend, my constant companion, my Lord and Master. He is my loving Savior.

I now know, beyond all doubt, that God loves me and hears and answers prayer. He knows my thoughts and feelings, and He cares.

MANY CHURCHES TO VISIT

THE NEXT DAY, January 29, provided me with an inkling of God's plans and purposes for the ministry He was preparing me for. He came to me early in the morning, just before daybreak, and said, *"Daughter, I want you to look at something."*

In the spirit He transported me to an unknown church—a very large church filled with dark-skinned men. There were no women present in this particular assembly. Jesus explained, *"You will visit many churches as you do My work."*

Never had I experienced anything like this. It was as if I were able to fly with the Lord to a different time and place. It was an incredible sensation. He told me more.

"My daughter, I have many surprises for you," He said, *"so expect to receive them all. I will be with you everywhere. You will never have to worry about anything while you are on this earth. I want you to be happy every day of your life."*

Then He disappeared. After this visit, I knew that each visit thereafter would provide me with new clues about my future. When the Lord told me that I would never have to worry again, I rejoiced because I had been prone to worry and insecurity since my early childhood. He was healing me on the inside while He was preparing me for ministry.

The sweetness of His presence can only be described as total peace. It enabled me to live and walk in the truth of His Word: "Peace I leave with you, My peace I give to you; not as the world gives do I give to you. Let not your heart be troubled, neither let it be afraid" (John 14:27).

Chapter 3

All Things Are Possible

But Jesus looked at them and said to them,
"With men this is impossible, but with God
all things are possible."

—MATTHEW 19:26 (EMPHASIS ADDED)

O N FEBRUARY 1 the Lord visited with me as soon as I went to bed, around 11 P.M. Because of the trembling of my body that always accompanied the Lord's visits, Roger was now sleeping in the guest bedroom. It was a good thing he had made this change, because on this particular evening the shaking was more intense than ever before, and it was accompanied by other manifestations of the Lord's presence as well.

Immediately the Lord spoke to me, *"My precious daughter, I must show you My presence and talk with you before this work begins."*

His radiant presence had always been stunningly brilliant, but this time He was dressed in white and shining like the sun. His form was beautiful to behold, and so very compelling.

I responded this time by speaking in tongues and singing in the spirit. As I sang, my hands lifted in front of me and they began to move in rhythm with the singing. It was as if I were dancing, but I remained in bed.

I lost control of the movement of my hands and watched them sway back and forth as if they were being moved by a silent wind. It was the wind of the Spirit of God that was moving them, and, upon realizing this, I was overcome with joy and began to laugh. Though I could not see the Lord's face, I heard Him laughing as well.

This phenomenon is known as "holy laughter" in some circles. I can say without any reservation that I know it is a manifestation of the Lord's presence.

The Bible tells us:

> Make a joyful shout to the LORD, all you lands! Serve the LORD with gladness; come before His presence with singing. Know that the LORD, He is God; it is He who has made us, and not we ourselves; we are His people and the sheep of His pasture. Enter into His gates with thanksgiving, and into His courts with praise. Be thankful to Him, and bless His name. For the LORD is good; His mercy is everlasting, and His truth endures to all generations.
> —PSALM 100:1–5

We should not be surprised by joy and laughter when it occurs during times of worship and adoration in the presence of the Lord. It is thoroughly biblical, and we will spend all eternity in His presence, singing, worshiping, laughing, celebrating and experiencing His pleasures. In fact, this is what He wants for us because we are His children. The name of Isaac—the miracle child of Abraham—literally means "he laughs," and God wants us to enjoy His presence through the gift of laughter.

Although many of the psalms are songs of sadness, there are some that reflect the joy and laughter that are the true inheritance of God's people. For example, we read in Psalm 126: "When the LORD brought back the captivity of Zion, we were like those who dream. Then our mouth was filled with laughter, and our tongue with singing. Then they said among the nations, 'The Lord has done great things for us, whereof we are glad" (vv. 1–3).

When people raise questions about the shaking, singing in the Spirit and holy laughter, I point them to these passages. Solomon, the writer of Ecclesiastes, tells us that there is "a time to weep, and a time to laugh" (Eccles. 3:4). It's a shame that so many people believe Christianity needs to be stiff and formal, when it is clear that the Lord wants us to experience a full measure of joy. Nehemiah proclaimed, "The joy of the LORD is your strength" (Neh. 8:10), and the Book of Proverbs declares, "A merry heart does good, like medicine" (17:22). Now I know the true meaning of these healing words.

I was really encouraged by the laughter of my Lord as He visited with me that night. He seemed so pleased with me. As I sang in the spirit, even my own voice took on a different quality. It was my voice—I knew that—but it sounded so different, so beautiful, clear and resonant.

Around midnight the Lord said, *"I love you, My daughter, and I will continue to visit you."* As He departed I felt lighter and freer than I had ever felt before, and I was thrilled with the prospect that He would soon revisit me.

EXPECT MANY SURPRISES

THE NEXT DAY, February 2, began with a very special visitation from the Lord. He began to share many things with me, as He had promised, *"I am releasing all the power you will need to do the work I've chosen you to do."* As I did the night before, I was trembling and singing in the Spirit.

The Lord continued His personal message to me: *"Daughter, the way I am going to use you will be so different. Many of My children will be surprised. I have gifts for all My children, but I will give each one different gifts. Daughter, I want you to be pleased with what you are going to receive."*

It was an exhilarating promise. The Lord assured me that He was preparing me for a special ministry. I wanted only to please Him.

From 2:20 A.M. to 4:18 A.M. the next day He returned to my room to tell me more about the power of prayer. He stood before me in glowing garments of white.

"My daughter, do not be afraid to pray for others, because you are receiving the gift of healing and all the other spiritual gifts," He said. *"I know that you always want to pray for others and to make them happy. That is why I am giving you these spiritual gifts."*

At first His words were difficult for me to hear. I felt very unworthy to receive so much from my Lord and Master.

He went on: *"You have a special heart, and that is why I answer your prayers. I notice that your heart is pure, and you are an obedient daughter. I trust you with many things. This is why I have chosen you to do this important work. Your faith makes Me very happy, and so does your will power. Your heart is strong and independent, and I am very pleased."*

Obeying the Lord has been so important to me as a Christian. My main goal has always been to please Him. It was so wonderful to hear Him tell me I was pleasing to Him and that He had purified my heart and had seen my obedience. His message to me that night made me even more determined to follow Him in all my ways.

"This is why your faith has grown so strong and you gave up the worldly things for Me," Jesus continued. *"If you were not what you are, I could not use you for the work I have prepared. What I am going to do with you will surprise you, My daughter. I am your Lord. Remember, nothing is impossible for Me on earth or in heaven. I will release My power to you so I can use you."*

The way the Lord addressed me as "My daughter" over and over again always caused me to shed tears of love. He was so different from my earthly father. The Lord was tender, respectful, encouraging and sensitive in all His dealings with me. I knew that He knew my needs before I expressed them to Him. I knew that He was my safe place—my "Rock of refuge"—and that compared with Him, any other "refuge" was sinking sand.

He then explained the shaking in my body. *"Your body shakes for a long time because you need power for this work. I want you to expect many surprises."*

More surprises? I wondered, with joy. I felt like I had already experienced enough to last a lifetime. His visits, my time in prayer and the Word, the precious moments of worship at my church—all of these were having deeply revolutionizing effects in my life.

My faith in the Lord was growing at an accelerating pace. I knew, beyond all doubt, that He is able "to do exceedingly abundantly above all that we ask or think, according to the power that works in us" (Eph. 3:20). The shaking in my body was His power at work in me. He was preparing me for the time when He would prove His ability to do exceedingly abundantly through me.

No Fear!

DURING THE NIGHT of February 12, my body shook more violently than it ever had. I was almost hurled from the bed because it was so forceful. I tried to grab the sheets to steady myself, but I couldn't because I had no control over my body. The shaking was unremittingly forceful, and I grew afraid.

My thoughts began to run away with me. *Is all this a deception of Satan? What is happening to me? Am I going crazy?* I wondered.

Then I remembered what someone had once shared with me—"When you are about to receive a blessing, Satan will try to destroy it." Was this violent shaking the work of Satan or the work of God? I thought it might be Satan trying to harm me. I rebuked the enemy, and then the Lord interjected, *"Daughter, do not fear; I am your Lord."*

That was enough for me. His sweet voice turned my fear into laughter. I heard the echoes of His soft laughter near the window. In a most pleasant and peaceful voice, He said: *"No one will harm you because I will be with you always and I will protect you from the evil things of this world. You are My precious daughter."*

A passage of Scripture came to mind and complemented His words. "There is no fear in love; but perfect love casts out fear, because fear involves torment. But he who fears has not been made perfect in love. We love Him because He first loved us" (1 John 4:18–19).

The love of the Lord in my life was more real than it had ever been. I knew He loved me. In light of such an amazing love, how could I ever be afraid? The experience of that evening taught me I never again needed to fear Satan, evil or myself, because the Lord had promised that He would be with me forever.

His Word backed up this promise: "I will never leave you nor forsake you" (Heb. 13:5).

I knew that He had called me to help fulfill His Great Commission: "Go therefore and make disciples of all the nations, baptizing them in the name of the Father and of the Son and of the Holy Spirit, teaching them to observe all things that I have commanded you; and lo, I am with you always, even to the end of the age" (Matt. 28:19–20).

The verse preceding this tells us how this is possible: "All authority has been given to Me in heaven and on earth" (Matt. 28:18). His power, His authority, His strength and His might will prevail in every situation when we yield ourselves to Him.

The Lord gave me additional assurance of His will and His love when He said: *"I am giving you all the gifts you will need to enable you to begin the ministry I'm giving to you. Keep a record of the day and times when I meet with you.*

"Your husband, Roger, will have gifts for the ministry too. You need

never worry about anything because I promise you that I will take care of you while you are on earth."

Deep in my heart I knew I didn't need to worry about anything again. He was taking care of everything not only in this life but also in the afterlife. His liberating promises called Psalm 23 to mind, and I focused especially on the final verse of that inspiring psalm: "Surely goodness and mercy shall follow me all the days of my life; and I will dwell in the house of the LORD forever" (Ps. 23:6).

With such peaceful thoughts I grew sleepy, and the Lord said: *"I know you are tired. Go to sleep."* The Lord does, indeed, give His beloved sleep.

A NEW BODY

FROM 11 P.M. TO 1:08 A.M. on February 19 and February 20, the Lord took me walking with Him. Once again, the familiar hard shaking of my body and the intense heat of His anointing alerted me to His imminent arrival. His presence was stronger than ever before, and then I heard His voice: *"I am your Lord, My precious daughter, and I am about to release all the work I've prepared for you to do."* I could see Him standing by the window, and His glorious form was clearer to me than it ever had been before.

"Daughter, I must show you some things," He stated as He extended His hand in my direction. Next, I felt the strange sensation of my body being lifted from the bed. Not knowing what was happening, I began to scream and flail my arms wildly. It seemed as if the insides of my body were detaching from the rest of me. It was an experience that truly defies description. I even felt my body to see if it was still the same. I wondered if I was dying.

My mind was clear, and I was groaning in my spirit. Then I recognized that I was with the Lord, wearing a white robe like His. My body was new. I was like a young girl again. Even my hair was long and straight.

I realized I was walking along a deserted beach with the Lord. Perhaps you can imagine how surprised I was. He had transported me from my bed, home and body and had given me a new body that enabled me to fly and walk with Him. The Lord of heaven and earth had suspended the laws of gravity, life, time and space in order to show me some things that I will never forget.

The Bible says, "Flesh and blood cannot inherit the kingdom of God; nor does corruption inherit incorruption" (1 Cor. 15:50). I was about to discover the true meaning of these words by the apostle Paul.

As I began to take notice of my new body, I felt that it looked like me, but it wasn't me. I had heard of out-of-the-body experiences before, but in this case I had been taken out of my body and deposited in a body that was not me—yet it was me.

It was me as I was when I was a young adolescent. I had the same hair I had as a teenager. I couldn't see my face clearly, but I felt certain it was the face of the bewildered youth who had been without God and without hope. This time, however, the young girl knew God, and she was filled with hope. It was so fascinating. What did it all mean?

A Shiny Tunnel and Stone Walls

Where had the Lord taken me? Why had He taken me with Him? I couldn't wait to hear His answers to these questions, because I knew they were for me as well as for all those He would lead me to.

First, we went to the right side of a hill that was alive with foliage. I could see a narrow, winding road snaking its way to the summit. Then we walked alongside a narrow river that flowed with the most crystal-clear water I'd ever seen. We followed the river to the entrance of a shiny tunnel that seemed endless. It was high and wide and, in comparison, the Lord and I were quite tiny. We walked through the mysterious tunnel, and when we emerged on the other side, we walked down to the beach again.

"We are going to a very high place," The Lord said.

The minute He spoke these words He took my hand, and my body began to lift above the surface of the beach. As it did, my physical body on the bed trembled furiously. My hands and arms began to move in all directions as if I were swimming desperately in an effort to not drown. The groanings that emanated from my spirit grew louder and stronger.

We were literally flying through the air. We landed at a location that was filled with trees and grass, and our feet set down on a narrow, winding road.

The Lord and I walked along the road that came down from the top of the hill. Eventually we reached a huge white gate that stood in front of a large white building. We walked through the gate and proceeded toward the white building.

We entered and walked down a long corridor that led to a very large room, which we entered. As I looked down, I realized for the first time that I was wearing a different robe than I had on at the beach, and I could feel something heavy was resting on my head. I reached up and discovered a beautiful crown had been placed there without my realizing it.

Then I looked directly at the Lord. He was sitting on a throne, and He wore a radiant gown and golden crown. Others were there with me, kneeling on the floor and prostrating themselves before Him.

The walls of the room were made of large shiny stones that glowed. The multicolored rocks provided an effect that made the room seem warm and happy, as well as mysterious.

WHERE ONLY THE PURE-HEARTED CAN GO

THEN, JUST AS quickly as I had been transported up the mountain and into the white building, I found myself on the beach again. As I had been doing all along, I found myself alternately laughing, screaming, crying, shaking, flailing my arms and perspiring. The joy was so intense, I felt as if I could touch it. I knew I had been transported to a different world, but where was it? Why was this happening? What did it all mean?

The Lord answered my questions clearly and emphatically. *"My daughter, we went to the kingdom."*

He quickly recognized the question that was forming in my heart: *How did we get there?*

"The only ones who will go there are the obedient and pure-hearted children."

The Master paused for a moment and then went on, *"Tell My children to preach the gospel. I am coming soon for those who are waiting and ready for Me."*

Now I knew my primary mission. I had seen the kingdom of heaven, and it was so very real. I'll never forget all the wonderful things I saw.

The Lord added, *"Those who don't tithe are disobedient children."*

"Should I tell this to anyone, Lord?"

"I want you to tell it to everyone."

Then He reiterated something He had commanded me to do several times before: *"Write down everything I show you and tell you."*

"Tell me more, Lord."

"Another time, My daughter. I know you are tired. Go to sleep."

As He left, so did my transformed body. I reached over to the night-stand and got my pad and pen and began to write everything I had experienced on my exciting journey to the kingdom of God. I felt so numb and humble. There were no words to describe the feeling. I felt that I didn't belong to this world anymore.

From then on, all I could think about was the Lord and heaven. I longed to return to the kingdom. That longing must have been heard as a prayer, for, as you will see, the Lord took me with Him many times after that.

Chapter 4

Sooner Than You Think

He who testifies to these things says,
"Surely I am coming quickly." Amen.
Even so, come, Lord Jesus!

—REVELATION 22:20

M
Y DAUGHTER, CHOO *Nam, I am your Lord."* It was the familiar voice of my Master speaking so compassionately and confidently in my bedroom during the wee hours of February 24.

The shaking in my body had already awakened me around midnight. This time I watched the clock to see how long the trembling would last. After approximately twenty minutes, the groaning from deep in my spirit began. I continued to shake, and the heat of the Lord's anointing was causing me to perspire. It was after this time of preparation that I heard the Lord speaking to me.

I was getting somewhat accustomed to His presence. Most of the time I greatly enjoyed His visits. On this occasion, the image of His presence was very clear. His figure was bathed in a soft, warm glow of pristine whiteness. He reached His hand toward me as I continued to shake even more intensely, and my arms began to flail in every direction.

As I had experienced the week before, my spirit lifted from my body, and I could see myself as a young girl with long, straight hair. Once again I was walking on the beach with the Lord. We walked and walked and walked. It was a quiet time. Jesus seemed to be thinking, and for the longest time He did not speak a word.

One thing He did say eventually, over and over again, was, *"We have a lot of work to do."*

"WE ARE GOING TO HEAVEN"

THE MASTER AGAIN took me into a huge tunnel. Again—unlike most tunnels—it was bright and shiny. I soon realized this was the same tunnel He had taken me through the first time. I reasoned this must be the tunnel that people who have near-death experiences frequently describe as the passageway from this life to the next.

In most such cases of out-of-the-body experiences, people report that they are hurled into a long, dark tunnel at a rapid pace. At the far end of the tunnel they can see the glorious brightness of heaven. This, I thought, must be the doorway to the indescribably wonderful kingdom of heaven. Now my Lord and Savior was taking me there again.

We walked by the beautiful, crystal-clear river once more, and then we returned to the beach. Jesus then said, *"We are going to heaven."*

My heart leaped into my throat as my soul was flooded with excited anticipation over the realization that I was going to heaven. I was going home, and Jesus was giving me a personal tour of the afterlife so I could write about it and let others know. It was so thrilling to be chosen for such an honor, and I could hardly contain the joy that overwhelmed me.

No sooner had Jesus announced our destination than I began to fly. I had flown in airplanes before, and those flights were always exciting and exhilarating; but this time my body was taking flight like a bird. I remembered the passage from Isaiah: "But those who wait on the LORD shall renew their strength; they shall mount up with wings like eagles, they shall run and not be weary, they shall walk and not faint" (Isa. 40:31).

I had always interpreted that verse from a spiritual perspective, but now it had become a living reality. I was flying and soaring like an eagle, and I was not afraid, because I knew Jesus was with me.

The experience of flight did not last long, however. It seemed like only a second. Soon we touched down on a narrow, winding road that was beautifully bordered by tall trees and lush, green grass. Just ahead I could see a huge gate that was set in a white fence. As we approached the gate I noticed that the road on the other side of the fence was all white, and on both sides of the lane, gorgeous flowers of every type and hue displayed their varied colors and tender blossoms.

I had never seen such beauty before, and another verse came to mind:

> So why do you worry about clothing? Consider the lilies of the
> field, how they grow: they neither toil nor spin; and yet I say to you
> that even Solomon in all his glory was not arrayed like one of these.
> Now if God so clothes the grass of the field, which today is, and
> tomorrow is thrown into the oven, will He not much more clothe
> you, O you of little faith?
>
> Therefore do not worry, saying, "What shall we eat?" or "What
> shall we drink?" or "What shall we wear?" For after all these things
> the Gentiles seek. For your heavenly Father knows that you need all
> these things. But seek first the kingdom of God and His righteous-
> ness, and all these things shall be added to you.
>
> —MATTHEW 6:28–33

Then I began to understand more clearly why God was permitting me
to visit His kingdom. I realized at that moment that if mortals on earth
could see what I was seeing, they would never worry again. I knew I had
to tell everyone I met about my experiences so that they, too, would
never need to worry again.

God indeed does take care of everything in our lives. God is working
His purposes out. His love for His children is unrelenting. His Word
is true. Now the burning desire of my heart is to help people to understand, to see, to believe the truth. My experiences have taught me that
"all things work together for good to those who love God, to those who
are the called according to His purpose" (Rom. 8:28).

HEAVEN IS BETTER

THE ARRAY OF flowers was more spectacular than any garden I'd ever
seen. I found myself thinking, *I'm happy to know there are flowers
in heaven.* They had the most lovely blossoms I'd ever seen, and they
seemed to grow brighter and more colorful as we approached the
entrance to the large, white palace we had been walking toward.

Jesus led me up the steps to the double doors at the front. I noticed
that the entry was framed with gold, and beautiful stained-glass panels
were on both sides. We walked through the doors onto a white marble
floor. The shiny stone walls of the corridor reminded me that I was in
the vicinity of the throne room of God once more, and with each step
we took, my heart pounded more intensely.

We entered the room, and it was even more awe-inspiring than before. The Lord's glistening, golden throne stood atop a raised, oval-shaped platform. Beams of radiant glory streamed from the center of the room where this platform was located.

I was directed by an angel to a little room on the side, and I was surprised to discover a powder room there. A full-length mirror covered the entire wall on the left side of this room, and many beautiful velvet chairs were neatly arranged in front of the mirror.

A beautiful being stood in front of me, and I immediately perceived that I was with an angel. The being opened a large, walk-in closet that contained many robes, gowns and crowns. The angel selected one of the gowns and put a crown on me. Each robe had rich embroidered colors. I thought the garments were the most stunning and expensive clothing I'd ever seen.

After I was dressed, the angel escorted me back to the main room. The Lord was waiting for me. I noticed that He was wearing a gown and crown like mine.

He took me to another building that looked like the pictures of medieval European castles I'd frequently seen. There was a rock wall on both sides of the castle, and magnificent flowers were planted all around. As I took in the scene in front of me, I felt like I was in a wonderland of beauty, peace and happiness. I did not want to return to earth.

The Bible says we all will worship the Lord before His throne: "All nations whom You have made shall come and worship before You, O Lord, and shall glorify Your name. For You are great, and do wondrous things; You alone are God" (Ps. 86:9–10). In another place the psalmist proclaims, "The LORD has established His throne in heaven, and His kingdom rules over all. Bless the LORD, you His angels, who excel in strength, who do His word" (Ps. 103:19–20). The prophet Isaiah says: "Heaven is My throne, and earth is My footstool" (Is. 66:1). Heaven is such a glorious place, and it will be a joy to worship God there throughout eternity.

I once heard a chorus about heaven that proclaimed: "Heaven is better than this / Praise God / What joy and bliss / Walking down the streets of solid gold / You'll enter a land where you'll never grow old" (source unknown). Now I know the truth of this song. Heaven is far better than this earth. Truly, there is no comparison between earth and heaven.

We entered the castle, and I immediately noticed how colorfully carpeted the foyer was. The elegant furniture was selected to fit the color and style of the carpeting. The walls were sparkling and shiny—so brilliant, in fact, that they almost blinded me. At the end of the hallway, just ahead, I noticed a sliding door. I wondered what we would discover on the other side.

THE SPECIAL POND

THE SLIDING GLASS door, I soon discovered, did not lead into another room; rather, it was a doorway to the castle's garden. In the center of this glorious place there was a pond. The entire "back yard" was surrounded by a rock wall. Flowers of every type and description formed a sea of beauty everywhere I looked.

I noticed that a variety of fruit trees grew close to the rock wall. These trees were filled with the biggest, most luscious-looking fruits I'd ever seen. They were ringed by a magnificent profusion of lovely flowers. Scattered throughout this amazing garden were huge, gray boulders that seemed to be strategically placed for sitting and resting.

The pond really intrigued me, and as soon as I saw it, I began to sing in the Spirit and to dance for joy. I can't really explain why I reacted to the scene with such enthusiasm, but something supernatural was propelling me to express my gratitude, happiness and peace in a demonstrable way. The Lord sat on a rock and watched me dance.

I recalled a verse from the Old Testament: "Then David danced before the LORD with all his might" (2 Sam. 6:14). The pond reminded me of a verse in the book of Revelation: "And the Spirit and the bride say, 'Come!' And let him who hears say, 'Come!' And let him who thirsts come. And whoever desires, let him take the water of life freely" (Rev. 22:17). Yes, there are bodies of water in heaven, and the water of this pond was clear and placid. It shone like crystal.

He, the Lord, spoke to me, *"This is a special pond."*

I knew it was, but I could not understand why. The Lord did not explain His statement to me at that moment, but I surmised that the pond held many spiritual secrets that I would eventually learn, one by one. I wondered: *Is this where my sins, and the sins of all other believers, have been buried? Is the pond a symbol of the water of the Word of God?*

Certainly, water typifies the cleansing from sin that our Lord has provided for us. His Word tells us that "if we confess our sins, He is faithful and just to forgive us our sins and to cleanse us from all unrighteousness" (1 John 1:9). Words of Jesus, as recorded by the apostle John, entered my mind: "Most assuredly, I say to you, unless one is born of water and the Spirit, he cannot enter the kingdom of God" (John 3:5).

JESUS IS READY ... AND WAITING

AFTER A FEW moments of pure enjoyment, as I danced and sang nearby the pond, the Lord took me back to the white palace where I changed into the clothing I was wearing when He took me to heaven. Then we walked back to where we had landed on the mountain covered with trees and green bushes.

"We are going back to earth," the Lord said.

He took my hand again and we began to fly from the heavenly firmament to earth. We went back to the place where we had begun this particular journey—the beautiful, peaceful beach along which we had strolled before.

Jesus said: *"My daughter, now you know how special you are to Me. I want you to remember it took Me a long time to prepare you to bring you to My kingdom, to show you these things so you could tell the world."*

I nodded my agreement with what He was telling me.

The Lord continued: *"I want you to remember everything I tell you and show you. Make sure you write everything down. I will make sure everyone understands all the things I show and tell you."*

This part of His message lifted the heavy load of responsibility that I had been feeling since He first told me that I had been chosen to do His work. Now I knew that He would simply speak through me and reach out to others. I only had to be willing to be used by Him. There was nothing hard about that, after all that I had experienced and seen.

Jesus went on, *"Many people think I will never come for them, but I tell you, I am coming sooner than they think."*

When He said this, the tone of His voice changed. He seemed to be almost angry, or at least I sensed a great urgency in His words. It was a warning. It was a message I had to share—and share now. The End Times are truly upon us. Jesus is coming soon.

I believe the Lord is ready for His people, but His people are not ready for Him. He sounds very urgent. This is why I must get this message out. I have no alternative—I simply must obey the Lord. People need to be warned that the coming of the Lord is near. People need to get ready for His Second Coming by repenting of their sins and receiving Him into their lives.

The Bible is very clear about this:

> But as many as received Him, to them He gave the right to become children of God, even to those who believe in His name: who were born, not of blood, nor of the will of the flesh, nor of the will of man, but of God. And the Word became flesh and dwelt among us, and we beheld His glory, the glory as of the only begotten of the Father, full of grace and truth.
>
> —JOHN 1:12–14

Jesus—the living Word of God—was telling me to go quickly and tell others that He is soon to return. That's what He meant when He said, *"We have a lot of work to do."*

POWER IN THE BLOOD

THE END OF February 1996 was even more thrilling than the beginning had been. From 4 A.M. to 5:30 A.M. on February 28 the Lord was with me. He came to me and said, *"Choo Nam, I am your Lord."*

He reached out and took my hand, and we were miraculously transported to the beautiful beach. He held my hand as we walked along the shore, and this time the Lord seemed eager to talk with me. It was as if He had a burning desire to share many things with me.

We sat down on the sand near the edge of the ocean. As the waves ebbed and flowed in front of us, an amazing thing happened. The edge of the water turned to blood. A dark red, foaming surf surged in front of us. It seemed as if the blood was filthy, and I asked, "Why is the blood so dirty?"

"It is My blood, Choo Nam," He said. *"It has washed away all the sins of My children."*

I began to weep as I heard this statement. He had shed His blood for me, to cleanse me of all my sins. He who knew no sin became sin for me so I could be clothed with the righteousness of God. The blood of the perfect Lamb of God had washed me clean and set me free. It is His blood that enables me to defeat the enemy in my life. The tears I cried came from a deep reservoir in my soul as I recognized with gratitude all that Jesus had done for me.

"Don't cry, My daughter," He said.

He took my hand, and off we flew once more. As I ascended with the Lord, I knew He was going to reveal more truth to me. I was filled with eager anticipation.

"We are going to heaven," He stated.

My transformed body was devoid of physical sensation as we lifted from the beach. The sensation of flying in my transformed body does not make me feel light-headed or dizzy because my transformed body does not react like my earthly one would in similar circumstances.

THE SCARLET THREAD

WHEN WE ARRIVED in the kingdom of heaven, we walked along the familiar road, went through the now-familiar gate and entered the white palace. We changed into the beautiful gowns of the kingdom. Then we went to the pond again.

The pond—it is such a special, extraordinary place. Once more I sang the songs of the Spirit and danced before the Lord. He simply sat on a rock and watched me enjoy myself. It seemed to please Him to see me dancing and singing and praising God.

"Do you like this place, My daughter?"

"Yes, my Lord," I said, smiling.

"I will bring you here each time you come to heaven."

This announcement thrilled me for two reasons—I wanted to keep on coming back, and I loved this particular, extraordinary setting near the pond. It was an oasis from the cares of this world—a place of refreshing, discovery and joy. I loved it here.

Before long, we left the pond and walked to the white building where we changed to regular robes and flew down to the beach on earth. I wondered why He didn't show me anything new when He took me to heaven this time. We walked by the river where the tunnel is that I saw before, and I saw the river turn to blood. Jesus pointed out, *"That is My blood—the blood I shed for My children."*

His words caused me to cry. I bowed my head and began to sob.

The Lord touched my head and said, *"Do not cry, My daughter."*

It was the pleading sadness in His voice that caused me to keep on weeping. He wanted His children to know He had willingly shed His blood for them, but so many failed to recognize this powerful provision in their lives. Again, the truth of Scripture echoed in my mind: "He came to His own, and His own did not receive Him" (John 1:11). I could tell that this fact caused pain and grief in my Lord's heart, and I felt so honored and thankful that He had chosen to share these feelings with me.

"I did everything for My children," He said. *"Even so, some of them do not believe, and even some who do, do not live by My words."*

The hurt in my Lord's voice was very real. I remembered how He had once wept over the city of Jerusalem because the people there had forsaken Him. I remembered how He had been saddened by the fact that His disciples did not understand Him. He had really been bothered by the fact that some of them fell asleep instead of praying on the night of His betrayal.

How it must have hurt Him when Peter denied that he knew Him, and how deeply He must have suffered when Judas Iscariot betrayed Him. Yet every day, as He acknowledged to me, His children turn away from Him, betray Him, forget Him and lose sight of the power of His blood that He shed for them. I sensed the deep pain my Master was feeling.

Now I knew more than ever why my calling must be fulfilled. People— both the saved and the lost—need to know the power of the blood of Jesus. They need to understand all that He accomplished for them at Calvary.

The people of God, as well as people in the world, need to know that Jesus has made a way for them to overcome the world, darkness, evil and all the works of the enemy. The blood of Jesus—a scarlet thread that weaves the entire Bible together—has made a way for them.

They need to know that the truth of what Jesus said in Revelation is upon us even now:

> Because you have kept My command to persevere, I also will keep you from the hour of trial which shall come upon the whole world, to test those who dwell on the earth. Behold, I come quickly! Hold fast what you have, that no one may take your crown.
>
> He who overcomes, I will make him a pillar in the temple of My God, and he shall go out no more. I will write on him the name of My God and the name of the city of My God, the New Jerusalem,

which comes down out of heaven from My God. And I will write
on him My new name. He who has an ear, let him hear what the
Spirit says to the churches.

—REVELATION 3:10–13

Maranatha!

Chapter 5

*My Kingdom
Is Ready*

*Because of the hope which is laid up for
you in heaven, of which you heard before in the
word of the truth of the gospel.*

—COLOSSIANS 1:5 (EMPHASIS ADDED)

THE ONLY ONES *who can come here are the ones whose hearts are as pure as the water,"* Jesus assured me after we arrived in heaven during the early hours of February 29. *"My daughter, Choo Nam, the work I've called you to do is very important to Me, and it needs to be completed soon."*

I stood in His glorious presence amazed. He had arrived in my room at 4:15 A.M. We went to the tunnel I'd seen before. This time it was brighter and shinier, and the walls of the tunnel sparkled with a magnificent array of colors. It was like a mine that contained diamonds, emeralds, sapphires and rubies. It was breathtaking.

The next stop was the beach, where I noticed the water was a dirty bloodlike color once again. The edge of the sand, where the waves had washed up, was dirty and blood-colored, too.

"It is My blood," the Lord told me again.

The Master is a very patient teacher. He frequently repeats the most important parts of His message so I will be sure to understand what He is preparing me for. Every time He shows me the blood He shed for His children, including me, I begin to weep.

Upon seeing my tears, Jesus comforted me by saying: *"My kingdom is ready for My children. Whoever is ready and wants to come will be permitted to be here."*

"I Don't Deserve It!"

We walked past a beautiful white gate that seemed to be inlaid with pure ivory and smooth pearls. Then we entered the majestic white palace where an angel escorted me into the powder room and I put on the beautiful gown that had been prepared for me.

Next, Jesus took me to a river. A gray stone wall ran alongside the stream, and stately evergreens formed the backdrop. I noticed how clear and still the water was. It sparkled like the finest crystal I'd ever seen.

The Lord reiterated the invitation He extends to all who want to follow Him and have an eternal home with Him in heaven, *"The only ones who can come here are the ones whose hearts have been made as pure as the water."*

I then noticed other beautiful white buildings in the vicinity of the beautiful river, just behind the tall trees. Jesus took me to one of the dwellings. It was a white mansion sumptuously landscaped with a profusion of colorful flowers and leafy trees. The most wonderful flowers I'd ever seen graced the doorway. The doors were lovely as well, decorated with extraordinary stained-glass panels.

Inside the palace, everything was colorful and shiny. The great room was filled with people who were wearing beautiful gowns, and each person was wearing a crown that was set with jewels of every variety. I felt like Cinderella at the ball.

Many men were present in the room, but there were very few women. The Lord didn't explain who these individuals were or why they were there, but He did tell me, *"You will be like them."*

I responded to this prophetic word with tears. Every time the Lord gave me new insights I would cry because I felt so humbled by His goodness and His grace. I was so humbled, in fact, that I said, "I don't deserve it!"

The tone of the Lord's voice reflected anger as He rebuked me, *"Don't say that again, daughter."*

The Source of Happiness

After changing into our heavenly robes and crowns, the Lord and I walked and talked together by the peaceful pond I had seen before. It was my third visit to this special place of communion with Him.

I took hold of the Master's arm and said: "I don't want to leave here. I want to stay here with you forever."

"Not yet, My daughter. You have a lot of work to do for Me first. I must show you so much of heaven, and I will bring you here many more times. I want you to be happy, My precious daughter."

We returned to the palace and changed into our regular clothing. Then we went back to the beach on earth and sat down on the shore. The Lord held my hand and told me: *"I am giving you healing power and the other spiritual gifts. Wherever you are, I'll be there to guide you. You will serve Me all over the world."*

Such a message should have filled me with eager anticipation, but it actually overwhelmed me. "Lord, I don't know anything."

"You don't have to know anything. I will do everything for you. Also, your husband will be with you. He will serve with you."

That part of His announcement brought a measure of relief to me. It was calming to know Roger would be a part of the ministry God was preparing me for. I had often leaned on my husband for strength and encouragement, and it was comforting to know that he would be my partner in ministry. At the same time, however, I sensed the Lord was calling me to depend totally on Him—not on Roger or myself or anyone except Him.

A passage sailed across my mind: "Trust in the Lord with all your heart, and lean not on your own understanding; in all your ways acknowledge Him, and He shall direct your paths" (Prov. 3:5–6). I determined that I would claim this promise from that moment on. I knew that the Lord would direct my paths each step of the way. I also knew the truth of His Word: "Your word is a lamp to my feet and a light to my path" (Ps. 119:105). I committed myself to walking in the light of God's Word from then on.

I believed that Jesus would always be with me. Therefore, I would never need to fear anyone or anything. He had spoken to me. He had held my hand. He had comforted me. He had made personal promises to me. How could I ever doubt His presence, His reality, His truth?

I would never be the same. Jesus, my Lord and Savior, had taken me to heaven in order to prepare me for a ministry that would share the truth of eternity with others. He had called me, chosen me and selected me for this important work.

As I was reflecting on these wonderful things, I realized I was truly happy for the first time in my life. I had found my purpose and my completion in Him, and He was altogether lovely to me.

Though my confidence and my faith were growing, I still responded meekly to the Lord's words.

"Lord, I am very shy, and I don't really know how to pray for others in public."

"I will take care of everything," He answered. *"I will be with you always. I want you to tell everyone what I show you and tell you. The whole world will know these things very soon."*

"You Are Going to Write a Book"

THOUGH I WAVERED from time to time, Jesus was always faithful. He patiently and lovingly reminded me of the power of His presence that I had experienced firsthand.

"My daughter, Choo Nam, I want you to be patient," He continued, *"because it is going to take a while to show you and tell you all I have to reveal. There is much to do because you are going to write a book for Me."*

This announcement was truly shocking news. I didn't say the words aloud, but I thought, *How can I write a book, since I don't know anything?*

By this time I knew better than to disagree with the Lord. I was learning that if He told me to do something, then He would enable me to accomplish it. I never asked for the gifts He was so lavishly and graciously pouring upon me, but I did remember praying for the gifts of healing and ministry that would enable me to lead others to Him. Now He was answering those prayers in ways that far exceeded my expectations! That's the kind of God we serve.

Jeremiah wrote, "Call to Me, and I will answer you, and show you great and mighty things, which you do not know" (Jer. 33:3). This was one prayer promise that was proving itself true and dependable in my life. Over and over again the Lord honored me with abundant spiritual blessings that I did not deserve.

"I do not want you to miss anything I show or tell you," He instructed. *"Nothing more; nothing less. Everything has to be exactly as I reveal it to you."*

My Kingdom Is Ready
A GOLDEN BRIDGE

AS THE GLORY of springtime neared, I realized that nothing on this earth could truly compare with the glorious beauty of heaven. Early in the morning of March 1, the Lord visited me once more, in the usual way, saying, *"My precious daughter, we have work to do."* He reminded me of several things He had already spoken: *"I chose you, My daughter, because of your obedience to Me. I like your will power and your faith."*

Since becoming a Christian, I have never once seriously doubted my Lord. In fact, my reverential fear of Him, mixed with my great love for Him, has led me to conclude that I must never displease Him. These convictions keep me on the path of obedience in my walk with God.

The Lord said, *"I must show you more of the kingdom."* He took my hand and we went back to the seashore. Then my body began to ascend into the heavens. I realized this time that the journey upward was more like floating than flying. I was being gently lifted from the earth.

I often wondered why we departed from the beach, rather than somewhere else, and I concluded that it must be because the site is usually deserted so early in the morning. I chuckled when I thought what might happen if someone saw us ascending into heaven. More than likely they would think they were seeing an alien abduction or a hallucination. They probably wouldn't mention it to anyone for fear of being called crazy.

Then it occurred to me that some people could think the same about me when I would begin to tell my story. The thought was extinguished by a wonderful sense of peace that washed over me as I realized such concerns do not matter because I know that Jesus has fully accepted me. Therefore, why should I ever worry about what others think?

A GOLDEN THRONE

JESUS HELD MY hand as we were being lifted from this planet. We landed in the same place as usual, and He led me to a fruitful orchard. It was huge, and every row of fruit trees was in a perfect line. Each tree was laden with ripe, luscious fruits. They all produced a different kind of fruit. The orchard was so vast that it seemed endless.

The Lord picked an oval-shaped purple fruit and handed it to me. Then He did the same with a round, deep-red fruit. I ate them, but I could not taste them very well.

I reciprocated by picking a small, round, pink fruit for the Lord to eat. Though I could not see His face clearly, I sensed that He was smiling and I knew He was very pleased by what I had done.

Next, we went to the now-familiar white palace where we changed into our heavenly attire. The Lord took His seat on His golden throne. Once again, the room was filled with people who were wearing beautiful gowns and crowns like mine.

The atmosphere in the room was one of peace and worship. The people were humbling themselves before the Lord. I tried to join in, but my sense of amazement and wonder did not permit me to focus on worship as quickly as I would have liked.

Before I realized all that had transpired, the Lord had changed back into His regular gown. He reached out, took my hand and led me outside. The experiences I've had in the kingdom of God occur so quickly that it sometimes seems as if I'm living out the fast-forwarding of a video tape.

The Lord led me across a golden bridge that arched over a fast-flowing river. The banks of the river were very fertile, and magnificent trees and flowers grew on both sides. The trees and flowers in heaven are different in so many ways from those we know on earth. There are many varieties, and they are bigger, healthier, more colorful and more beautiful than any plants I've ever seen.

I felt as if I were in a fairytale land like those illustrated in the picture books I would read to my children—except this was no fantasy.

"I WILL KEEP THEIR BABIES!"

AFTER WALKING OVER the beautiful golden bridge, the Lord led me to a place where babies and infants—many of whom looked as if they had just been born—were kept. It was a huge room, like a warehouse, and wasn't fancy or pretty. It was filled with babies who were naked and lying close to one another.

"Why are there so many babies here?" I inquired.

"These are babies of mothers who did not want them. I will keep their babies!" the Lord answered.

"What are you going to do with them, Lord?"

"If their mothers are saved, they can have their babies back."

"What will happen if their mothers are not saved? What will you do then?"

"Other mothers will have them when all My children come into the kingdom."

I then understood that these babies had been aborted from their mothers' wombs, and I began to cry. Jesus shouted, *"I do not like abortion!"* His voice and His demeanor grew harsh and angry, and I realized, then and there, that this was a message I would soon be sharing with all who would listen.

The Lord does not like abortion. It is one of the worst of all sins to Him. It was Jesus who had said, "Let the little children come to Me, and do not forbid them; for of such is the kingdom of God" (Mark 10:14). Jesus loves little children, and I could see His tender compassion for these aborted babies as I watched Him and listened to Him.

Nearly 1 in every 4 pregnancies in the United States today ends in abortion. How this grieves the Lord. The United States has the most permissive abortion laws of any democracy, and the number of abortions continues to accelerate. I'll never forget what I saw that morning in heaven, and I'll never be able to remain silent about the horrendous sin of abortion again.

Since that time I have been praying for the women of our nation, asking God to open their eyes to the truth about abortion, to keep them from making the wrong choice. I now know that the choice of abortion has eternal consequences, and I pray that the numbing of the American conscience with regard to this form of murder will be lifted.

I can still hear the Lord's angry voice trembling with emotion as He said, *"I do not like abortion!"* Heaven is better than this / Praise God / What joy and bliss / Walking down the streets of solid gold / You'll enter a land where you'll never grow old.

A PLACE FOR THE FAITHFUL

THE LORD TOOK me to a barren site outside the gate of the kingdom and showed me many people wearing sand-colored robes were in this region, standing very close together, and I noticed that they looked forlorn and lonely even though they were in the midst of so many others.

I had no idea who these individuals were, but I knew the Lord would answer my questions about them when He determined I was ready. He took me up a little hillside that was dotted with white buildings on both sides. A body of water separated the two sides from each other, and trees surrounded the water.

In front of the buildings I noticed many adults and children who were wearing white gowns, and some of them were wearing crowns. They were simply standing there with very happy looks on their faces. I sensed the Lord was showing me a vivid contrast between those who were happy and those who were sad. I assumed the happy ones were people who had given their hearts and lives to the Lord Jesus Christ.

The next stop on our heavenly itinerary was the huge white mansion where Jesus had taken me before. Again, I noticed that inside the great room were numerous men, but very few women. "Who are these people?" I asked.

"These are people who sacrificed for Me."

I wondered how many of them were the patriarchs and saints of the Bible, and I remembered faith's "hall of fame" in Hebrews 11, which lists the great men and women of faith, such as Abel, Enoch, Noah, Abraham and Sarah, and what they accomplished through faith. Then I was reminded of a very important verse: "But without faith it is impossible to please Him, for he who comes to God must believe that He is, and that He is a rewarder of those who diligently seek Him" (Heb. 11:6).

Abel's sacrifice was more excellent than Cain's because it was presented in faith and obedience. Abraham's willingness to sacrifice His own son, Isaac, to the Lord confirmed his faith and His desire to please the Lord. And now I knew that God honors such sacrifices. In fact, He calls us to surrender everything to Him.

By showing me this room that was filled with people wearing beautiful gowns and bejeweled crowns, Jesus was portraying the importance of sacrifice. I remembered Paul's words:

> I beseech you therefore, brethren, by the mercies of God, that you present your bodies a living sacrifice, holy, acceptable to God, which is your reasonable service. And do not be conformed to this world, but be transformed by the renewing of your mind, that you may prove what is that good and acceptable and perfect will of God.
>
> —ROMANS 12:1–2

CALLED TO TELL THE WORLD

MY HEART LEAPED within as I committed everything to my Lord and Master. This, I realized, was the sacrifice He required of me.

After seeing all these scenes, we went to the white palace and changed into beautiful gowns and crowns. Then the Lord took me to the peaceful pond where we had spent such wonderful times of fellowship together. This time we just sat and talked.

Then it occurred to me that the only places where the Lord really opened up and shared His heart with me were on the earthly beach and at this heavenly pond. At other times, when He was showing me different aspects of the heavenly kingdom, He would rarely talk. I loved the more relaxing times when He was able to tell me the things that were important to me.

He went on to remind me, *"I am telling you all this and showing you these things so you can tell the world."* Then He reiterated the importance of all these experiences by saying, *"I know that a lot of My children don't think I will come back for them for a long time. Some even think I will never come back for them, but I want you to tell them that My kingdom is ready for those who are ready and waiting for Me. I am coming very soon."*

Again, there was such a sense of urgency in His voice. Whenever I am in heaven, the only one who ever speaks to me is the Lord. His words are so vital. Even the angel who helps me to change my robes does not speak to me, but constantly smiles in such reassuring ways at me.

The Lord showed me the ocean of dirty blood once more, and then He concluded that visit to heaven with these words: *"I'll never leave you. I'll be with you forever. I will guide everything that you do. You will not have to worry about anything because I will be there to do it for you. I am releasing My power to you and in you. You will be able to heal the sick and do the same things I did when I lived on earth. The key to these gifts is your faith, My daughter."*

His words, so tender and uplifting, opened fountains of tears deep within my soul. *"Do not cry, My daughter."* He continued. *"I want you always to remember how precious you are to Me. I will talk with you again."*

From that day forward I have felt like I'm living more in heaven than on earth. My visits to heaven have wrought permanent changes in my life. I don't even require as much sleep as I used to, because I feel supernaturally energized by power from on high. Truly, I know that *heaven is so real,* and this makes all the difference in this world.

41

Chapter 6

A Place Called Hell

*And being in torments in Hades, he lifted up his eyes
and saw Abraham afar off, and Lazarus in his bosom. Then
he cried and said, "Father Abraham, have mercy on me, and send
Lazarus that he may dip the tip of his finger in water and
cool my tongue; for I am tormented in this flame."*

—LUKE 16:23–24 (EMPHASIS ADDED)

ON MARCH 2 the Lord awakened me at 3 A.M. His visit lasted for three hours. As usual, we started our journey at the seashore. This time the Lord and I walked for a while. I wondered where He was taking me.

I noticed that the hill with so many trees and bushes was to our right. At the bottom of the hill, close to the sand, were many large and small rocks. We sat on a large rock, and I noticed that the clear water suddenly turned to blood. It always disturbed me to see this reminder of the Lord's sacrifice, so I began to look up, turning my head away from the sea.

Just then I noticed that the nearby mountains were ablaze with bright red flames. I was very surprised at this scene. The brightness of the blaze was soon replaced by a dark, smoky haze that covered the entire scene.

People were fleeing from some unknown location and heading toward the beach. I noticed that some of them were naked, as if they had had to leave their beds so quickly that they had not had time to dress. Panic was on their faces, and they were running as fast as they could. Some stumbled, and the throng ran right over them. They seemed to be fleeing from some terrifying monster.

Soon the entire beach around us was filled with these frightened people. The fire they were fleeing from now filled the surrounding area.

42

Most surprising was that flames began to leap from the bloody ocean. It was as if the world was coming to an end right in front of me.

Outbursts of flame were popping from the ocean as if from miniature volcanoes, and the flames began to creep toward the shoreline. It was intensely frightening, and I began to sob as I listened to the screams of the mob around me.

Before this time, we had only sat peacefully on the sand on this beach. The scene taking place in front of me was horrifying and terrifying. I knew the Lord had a purpose for showing these things to me. Suddenly the scene changed back to normal.

"Why are you showing this to me, Lord?" I asked.

"All the things you see are going to happen very soon. So many people do not believe My Word, so I have chosen you to help them see the truth. What I show to you, I want you to tell the world."

There was anger in the tone of the Lord's voice.

We left the rock where we were sitting and walked along the sand. Jesus spoke once more.

"I must show you more of the kingdom," He said.

We went through the usual processes to get there. I had the privilege once again of standing before the Lord's throne with so many others who were humbling themselves in His presence. I joined in the worship that all of us were experiencing, and it was a wonderful time of peace, adoration, joy and blessing.

My visits to the Lord's throne room have opened my eyes to the great importance of worship in our lives. This is what we have been created for—to worship God and to enjoy Him forever. This is how we will spend all eternity.

The scene in front of me was exactly as it is described in the book of Revelation, in which John writes: "Immediately I was in the Spirit; and behold, a throne set in heaven, and One sat on the throne. And He who sat there was like a jasper and a sardius stone in appearance; and there was a rainbow around the throne, in appearance like an emerald" (Rev. 4:2–3). How exciting it was for me to realize I was going through the same experience the apostle John had reported about in the last book of the Bible. The Lord had spoken to him in the same way He had invited me, "Come up here, and I will show you things which must take place after this" (Rev. 4:1).

I knew from what the Lord had told me that people were not heeding the words of the Revelation, and now He wanted me to reiterate its message so that as many as possible would truly believe.

FLOWERS, MANSIONS AND CASTLES

JESUS TOOK MY hand and led me out of the throne room into a big, beautiful flower garden. In contrast with the horror I had seen at the beach, the peace of this immense garden filled me with love. I began to sing with joy, and a smile came automatically to my face. The Lord picked a flower, something like a rose, and gave it to me. I held onto it throughout this visit to the kingdom of heaven.

The garden was so vast that I could not see where it ended. It was a true paradise of beauty, love, joy and peace. The aroma was sweeter than any I had ever known. This was heaven, and it was more beautiful than I had ever imagined it could be.

We hiked out of the garden, along a narrow, winding road that led to a mountain vista overlooking a lush, green valley. I could see animals of all sorts galloping and playing among the trees. I particularly noticed a spectacular deer that looked so strong and healthy.

I noticed that these animals, which would usually be considered wild, were playful with one another. It was like a scene from Disney's *Bambi* movie.

As I turned in another direction, I noticed a beautiful river. Along the river was a rock wall, and magnificent dwellings were situated on the left side of the river. Many of these homes looked like castles where only the very wealthy might live.

The Lord said, *"These are houses for My special children."*

I was very curious about this place, but the Lord didn't take me closer to it. He only showed it to me from the top of the hill and from a very far distance.

Beholding that sight, I realized the truth of His Word: "In My Father's house are many mansions; if it were not so, I would have told you. I go to prepare a place for you. And if I go and prepare a place for you, I will come again and receive you to Myself; that where I am, there you may be also. And where I go you know, and the way you know" (John 14:1–3).

There was a time when I wondered if this was simply figurative language, symbolic of heavenly things. Now I know those mansions and castles are real, and the Lord has already prepared them for us. More importantly, He wants us to be with Him there forever!

THE PIT OF HELL

THE LORD LED me to a different area outside the gates of the kingdom. We continued to ascend the mountain, and as we climbed higher and higher the road became rougher and rougher. We hiked along this narrow road for a long time, and it eventually led us through a dark tunnel. When we emerged from the tunnel, I noticed that we had climbed even higher up the hillside. It seemed strange to me that heaven would have such a dark tunnel and a winding, rough road.

When we reached the summit and I looked over the crest of the mountain, I could see fumes and dark smoke rising from a deep pit. It was like the crater of a volcano, and inside I could see flames scorching a multitude of people who were screaming and crying in the kind of agony that only the severely burned truly know.

The people were naked, without hair, and standing close to one another, moving like worms, and the flames were scorching their bodies. There was no escape for those who were captured in the pit—its walls were too deep for them to climb, and hot coals of fire were all around the edges.

Even though the Lord did not tell me this, I knew I was standing at the brink of hell. It was even more horrible than the description the Bible gives: "The sea gave up the dead who were in it, and Death and Hades delivered up the dead who were in them. And they were judged, each one according to his works. Then Death and Hades were cast into the lake of fire. This is the second death. And anyone not found written in the Book of Life was cast into the lake of fire" (Rev. 20:13–15). Throughout the Gospels and the Book of Revelation, Jesus was careful to tell us about the horrors of hell.

The flames would leap out unexpectedly from all directions. People would move away, and then as soon as they seemed to think that they were safe, another fire would burst forth. There was no rest for these unfortunate victims of sin; they were doomed to spend all eternity being scorched and burned as they endeavored to escape the flames of hell.

"Who are these people?" I asked.

"My daughter, these people did not know Me."

He made this statement with a voice that heaved with grief. I could tell that the Lord was not pleased by the sight in front of us; it bothered Him deeply. I knew that He had no control over the destinies of people who deliberately chose to reject Him. These were the ones who were writhing in pain and suffering in the pit.

I knew two vitally important things that I had to share with others. On one hand, heaven is real; on the other, hell is just as real. I know many people who do not believe in either place, and I knew it would become my mission to show them the reality of the afterlife.

I knew my parents had never given their hearts to Jesus, so I began to wonder about them.

"Lord, what about My parents?" I asked. "I know they weren't saved, but they were good people."

"I'm sorry, my daughter. There is nothing I can do for those who do not know Me." My Lord Jesus voice was so sad when He said this.

The importance of His words stung me as I realized my mother and father must be among the doomed I was watching in the pit of hell. I sobbed the whole time He showed me these scenes.

The Lord touched my head, and took my hand, leading me down a dark tunnel, and we emerged on another rough road that ran very far and to the edge of the pit. This mountain road led through tall trees and huge rocks. When we got to the top, I looked out over a brown and lifeless valley. Everywhere there was brown. The whole region seemed to be filled with dead grass.

I noticed multitudes of people who were wearing sand-colored robes roaming aimlessly in the vicinity of the pit's yawning mouth. Their heads were hanging low, and they looked very dejected and hopeless.

"Who are these people, Lord?" I asked.

"They are disobedient 'Christians.'"

"How long will they have to stay in this barren, lifeless place?"

"Forever, My daughter. The only ones who will enter My kingdom are the pure of heart—My obedient children."

He went on to explain: *"Many who call themselves 'Christians' do not live by My Word, and some of them think that going to church once a week is enough. They never read My words, and they pursue worldly things. Some who even know My words never have their hearts with Me."*

The whole plan and purpose of God was beginning to clarify in my thinking. I remembered how Jesus had warned that it is hard to enter His kingdom, and now I had an inkling of what that meant.

"My daughter, My Word says that it is hard to enter the kingdom of heaven, but so few really believe this and understand its importance. I am revealing this to you so you can warn them," He explained.

As if to reiterate the importance of His message, the Lord took me to the beautiful castles I had seen earlier. As we got closer to these dwellings, I could see the streets were paved with lustrous gold and that every castle was lavishly decorated with the finest gems. It's true—heaven's streets are paved with solid gold!

I longed to go into one of the castles, but the Lord stopped me by saying, *"I will take you later."* I was disappointed, but I felt so privileged that I had seen this city where the saints of all the ages will reside together.

WHOSOEVER WILL

THE LORD AND I returned to the changing room, donned the most beautiful robes and crowns imaginable, then went to the pond and sat on a rock. I couldn't truly appreciate the serenity of the scene in front of me because my mind was preoccupied with the horrifying memories of hell.

I could not get the thought of my parents out of my mind—it grieved me so deeply to know that mother and father were both in hell. I was overcome by sadness. I knew for sure that my parents never knew Jesus because no one ever preached to them.

Jesus saw within me and said, *"You are not happy."*

"Yes, Lord," I responded, realizing that He knew the reason for my despondency.

A time of tender quietness followed. Then I said, "Lord, I never want to leave You." His presence was the only true security I'd ever known.

"My daughter, you have much work to do. I want you to write a book. This is an important book for the last days, and it will be translated into many languages.

"I chose you for this work before you were born, and this is why My Holy Spirit is always shaking your body—to pour My power into you. If you did not have the power of the Holy Spirit, I could not use you.

"You must remember that My power began working in you when you first opened your heart to Me. You are the daughter I trust to do this work for Me."

"Lord, I don't know anything."

"You don't have to know. I will be teaching and guiding you in every-thing. Tell everyone that I am ready for whoever is ready and waiting for Me. I love you, My daughter."

I began to cry, and the Lord took my hand and said, *"I will take you back."*

After we changed our clothing we returned to the beach and sat together for a while. The Lord spoke to me, *"I still have more to show you, and I want you to wait for Me."*

"But we plan to go to my daughter's place next week."

"Stay home, My daughter. I do not want you to travel anywhere for a while. What I am doing with you is too important for Me and all My children, so I want you to concentrate on everything I show you and tell you until everything is done. Be patient."

"I will do anything You tell me to do," I said. "Nothing is more impor-tant than Your work."

"Thank you, My daughter. I still have a lot of work for you to do. I know you are tired, so get your rest."

He left me, and my body stopped shaking. Then, as usual, I wrote down everything I had seen and heard.

In essence, Christianity is so simple that it eludes so many. Human beings have a tendency to need to complicate everything, including mat-ters of faith. Jesus simply wants people to come to Him in faith so He can lead them and help them.

I now knew, more fully than I had ever known before, that whoso-ever will may come to Him and receive eternal life. His Word states it plainly: "For God so loved the world that He gave His only begotten Son, that whoever believes in Him should not perish but have ever-lasting life" (John 3:16).

A SMOKING PIT

THE NEXT DAY—March 3—was filled with many new, God-given experi-ences. From 2:30 A.M. until 4:50 A.M. the Lord was with me. He began His visit by saying: *"My daughter, this is your Lord. I know you are tired, but I must show you more things."* For fifteen minutes before His visit, my body shook uncontrollably.

He took my hand and we walked along an earthly beach. It was a new site for our visits to the seashore. There were many trees and bushes. We climbed over a narrow road that was lined with trees and bushes. We strolled along this lane, which wound around a mountain that we ascended rapidly. Near the summit we rested on a huge rock that was shaped something like a gigantic bear.

I looked toward the ocean, and I noticed that its water had turned to blood once more. Again I saw people running on the beach. These were not casual joggers; they were running in fear and panic. The panorama before us helped me understand what they were running from.

To my left the mountains and the buildings situated on each mountainside were all ablaze. It was an inferno worse than the annual brush fires that plague the citizens of Southern California.

Next, I noticed huge fires bursting forth everywhere. People were on fire. Some were jumping into the ocean for relief, but when they stepped into the water, they would fall because of the fire. Everyone had become a human torch. I began to scream in horror and compassion for those I saw.

The bloody ocean had turned into a cauldron of blazing brimstone. The sand was a bed of hot, flaming coals. The people were running from the fire that pursued them, surrounded them and licked hungrily at their bodies. A few of them were naked and had no protection at all from the fire.

It was futile anyway, for there was no escape from the scorching enemy that threatened to devour them. They could not flee to the mountains because they were engulfed in flames. No place was safe.

I was screaming the whole time, and I began to sob: "Lord, what is happening?"

"You must remember, My daughter, that I am showing you these things so you will be able to let everyone know what is going to happen soon."

"When will this happen, Lord?"

"After I bring My children home. Many people do not believe My Word. That's why I want you to write a book that describes your experiences with Me. I want the whole world to see this book, and I want them to realize that I am ready for them.

"I love all My children, but I cannot bring them to My kingdom if they are not ready for Me. I will never force My children to do anything if they don't have a heart for Me. I have been planning for you to do this work for a long time because My kingdom is completely ready now."

The Lord had to keep on reminding me and reassuring me of His plans because I was still so stunned that He had chosen me for such an important assignment. It was beyond my ability to comprehend the enormity of it all.

The implications of the Lord's words to me were overwhelmingly important. There was a part of me that wanted to shrink from such an all-consuming work, but my commitment to obey the Lord in all things kept me going. I knew that He was preparing me for an End-Time work of epic proportions, and I was thrilled and yet intimidated. I knew He still had much work to do in my life.

"I will take you to heaven again."

Once we had arrived in heaven, we did not take time to go through the usual procedures. The Lord immediately led us away to the pit we had seen yesterday outside the gates of the kingdom. This time we did not change our clothing. To get there, we had to walk on a mountainside, through a dark tunnel and on to the summit of the mountain. When we arrived at the top, we looked down into a yawning pit that was so wide and deep that it appeared to be endless.

It was a frightening, disturbing scene. The Lord said, *"I want you to see this again."*

It was so hard to look into the pit of hell, but immediately my attention was directed toward a figure who was waving at me. Through the smoky haze, I could determine that the person was a woman. Then I heard her voice. She was speaking in my native Korean tongue, and she began to scream: "Hot! Hot!"

I knew that voice. The smoke cleared, and I looked directly into the eyes of the tormented woman. I immediately recognized my mother! She stretched out her right hand and waved it at me, saying, "So hot, so hot!" I remember so clearly her eyes and my eyes meeting, and the way her eyes begged me to help her.

My very own mother was screaming for help from the gaping pit of Hades. My heart stopped. A knife of cold hopelessness stabbed at my heart. My mother was in hell! I felt as if the boulder I was sitting on was on top of me. I wanted so desperately to reach out and take my mother's hand so that I could lift her from the licking tongues of fire that swirled all around her. It was the worst moment of my life.

There is no word in the dictionary that truly identifies what I felt at that moment. It was a mixture of fear, desperation, hurt, terror, sadness and hopelessness. Then I realized that these were the very emotions that my mother would have to experience throughout all eternity.

My mother had died when she was forty, but her face looked the same as I had remembered her. She was a beautiful woman, but her expression reflected the torment she was experiencing in the pit. I wanted to touch her, to hold her, to tell her everything would be OK, but I knew that these things had been made impossible because of her choices in life. I knew that I could not help her—that even the Lord could not help her because she didn't know Him.

She didn't know anything about the Lord because no one had ever preached to her. It is not knowing the Lord that leads a person into hell, and this is why I want to tell the whole world about the pit I saw and the wonderful kingdom of heaven.

Next I saw my father, my stepmother and a close friend who had died when she was only nineteen. They all were in hell! They looked the same as I had remembered them, but their faces were distorted by the agony of their punishment. I felt I couldn't take it anymore, and I turned my head away from the dreadful scene in front of me.

Then I heard another familiar voice screaming out of the pit. It was a friend who had died ten years before. Next to her was my nephew who died when he was twenty. The last time I had seen him, he was only ten, but he looked the same as I had remembered him, only he was taller.

I began to weep profusely. I had been crying the whole time, wailing like a child. So many of my loved ones and friends had made choices that had cast them into the fires of hell for all eternity! It was too much for me to bear!

Some of them, I'm sure, had heard about the Lord, but I felt quite certain that no one had ever explained to them who Jesus was. I felt quite certain that if they had known who He truly was, then they would not have made the choices they had made. How I wished I could tell them about Him who said, "I am the way, the truth, and the life. No one comes to the Father except through Me" (John 14:6).

The pit of hell was a long way from us, but it was as if I had a telephoto lens that enabled me to see these people very closely. I could not control my tears, and the Lord lovingly wiped my tears and stroked my hair. It was then that I realized the Lord was as sad as I was, and I could sense that He was crying along with me. He broke the silence.

"The reason I am showing this to you, My daughter, is so that you will fully understand that no matter how good people are, they will go to hell if they do not accept Me."

I nodded my head.

"I know your parents and friends were good people in many ways, but they were not saved. That's why this is the only place for them. It is here that they will have to spend eternity.

"Daughter, I know it hurts you to see them, but you must include this experience in the book you will write for Me. This is why I show you your parents and others as you remember them. You have to warn the people of the world about the reality of hell. I want to see as many souls saved as possible before I return to gather My church unto Myself.

"My Father loves all of His children, but He has given them certain laws that He expects them to live by. When I saw your loved ones, I felt deeper pain than you did, but I must live by My Father's Word. Once a person goes to hell, there is no way for them to ever get out again. I want the unsaved to know this—the reality of hell is forever.

"I love every one of My children, but I cannot force anyone to love Me or to obey Me. If they will open their hearts to Me, then I can help them to believe in Me and love Me. I want to save as many souls as possible. I want believers everywhere to preach the gospel. This is most important to Me."

It was enough. I had seen enough and heard enough to propel me into a ministry of evangelistic fervor that could never subside. How could I ever remain silent after all I had seen and heard?

I would tell everyone I saw about Jesus so that they could receive eternal life in heaven. Nothing in all the world was more important than this. My own parents and so many other family members and friends were in hell. I could not stand by and watch anyone else go there. I was so happy to know that my book would find its way into the hands of many people who need to know that hell is just as real as heaven is.

Even though the things I saw in hell had greatly unnerved me, they had planted a resolve in my spirit that nothing would ever be able to dissipate. I was determined that no one else within my reach would be able to deny the reality of hell and heaven. Heaven is real, and I want everyone to be able to go there with me. I know that this is the Lord's desire as well. He says it in His Word:

> The Lord is not slack concerning His promise, as some count slackness, but is longsuffering toward us, not willing that any should perish but that all should come to repentance. But the day of the Lord will come as a thief in the night, in which the heavens will pass away with a great noise, and the elements will melt with fervent heat; both the earth and the works that are in it will be burned up.
>
> —2 PETER 3:9–10

The last days are truly upon us. The Lord's patience has been most gracious up until now, but He is getting ready to come again to receive His children to Himself. It is then that the people who remain on earth will truly experience hell on earth before they end up in the fiery inferno of everlasting destruction. My job is to warn the whole world about these events that are "just around the corner."

Chapter 7

Maranatha!

"Surely I am coming quickly."

—REVELATION 22:20

AFTER THE HORRIFYING vision of hell, the Lord and I descended the mountain, passed through the dark tunnel, and returned to a place I had started to call "animal mountain." This is the wonderful place I briefly described in the previous chapter—a place of peace and joy where all the animals coexist in delightful harmony.

The Bible depicts this peaceful place for animals in the book of Isaiah, where the prophet proclaims:

> It shall come to pass that before they call, I will answer; and while they are still speaking, I will hear. The wolf and the lamb shall feed together, the lion shall eat straw like the ox, and dust shall be the serpent's food. They shall not hurt nor destroy in all My holy mountain, says the LORD.
>
> —ISAIAH 65:24–25

After seeing the tormenting fires of hell, this peaceful scene was most reassuring. Heaven is a place of peace and joy in contrast with the violence and depression of hell. The Lord's "animal mountain" is a place of eternal joy and happiness.

It is reassuring to know that animals will live with us in paradise. So many people wonder if their pets will be in heaven, and I am happy to let them know that heaven is a place of beautiful flowers, peaceful animals and glorious radiance where people and animals alike will never experience pain, hardship, death or suffering ever again.

GOLDEN CASTLES

AFTER OUR BRIEF visit to the animal paradise, the Lord and I went back to the waterside where we visited shiny mansions and castles on streets of pure gold. We approached one of the castles, and the Lord opened the door for me to enter. My vocabulary does not permit me to aptly describe the interior of this regal dwelling place. The walls were constructed of multicolored precious gems that glistened and glowed in a magical way.

I opened my mouth in surprise and couldn't close it for a while because I never expected to see such beauty. For a moment I thought it was a dream, but this was a real castle; there was no doubt about that.

The Lord rested on a chair as I went up the winding staircase that was more massive and grand than the one shown in *Gone With the Wind*'s Tara plantation. I was filled with a sense of wonder as I imagined the magnificence of the rooms upstairs.

At the top of the staircase, I noticed that the carpeting was a plush white. I entered a huge powder room that had very large, sparkling mirrors everywhere. They reflected the brightness of the room and the multitude of colors that arrayed themselves spectacularly on every wall. It was a more wonderful place than any fantasy castle could ever be.

The breathtaking joy and fascination I was experiencing was soon shattered by an exceedingly painful memory. The view of my mother flashed in front of me, and I was downcast once more. I fell to the carpet and began to sob.

I heard the Lord calling me from downstairs, so I got up, brushed myself off and went back downstairs. The Lord stood up and I walked toward Him. He extended His hands toward me and asked, *"How do you like this house?"*

"It is beautiful, Lord, but I am not truly happy. Whenever I've visited heaven before I've been filled with joy and I usually sing spiritual songs, but this time it cannot be so."

The Lord nodded as if He understood, then He took my hand and led me out of the house. We walked across a golden bridge toward the white building where we usually change our garments. In the white building, the Lord introduced me to a very impressive gentleman. *"I want you to meet Abraham,"* He said.

A CITY AWAITS

ABRAHAM! THE GREAT patriarch of faith and obedience—the man who had defied the entire world by proclaiming there is only one God. This was the great leader who had founded Judaism and had paved the way for Christ. It was such an honor to actually meet this good man of whom the writer of the book of Hebrews said:

> By faith Abraham obeyed when he was called to go out to the place which he would afterward receive as an inheritance. And he went out, not knowing where he was going. By faith he dwelt in the land of promise as in a foreign country, dwelling in tents with Isaac and Jacob, the heirs with him of the same promise; for he waited for the city which has foundations, whose builder and maker is God.
>
> —HEBREWS 11:8–10

Now I knew that Father Abraham had received the reward that his faith had justified. He was living forever in "the city which has foundations, whose builder and maker is God," and I was there with him! It was too wonderful to fully comprehend.

Abraham was a most dignified person who had long white hair and a flowing white beard. Though he looked old, his eyes sparkled with youth and joy. He put his hand on my shoulder and simply said, "Daughter."

The smile on his face caused me to know that his blessing was upon my life, and I immediately loved this great man to whom I, and every believer in the world, owe so much. Perhaps more than anyone else, it was Abraham who taught us that "without faith it is impossible to please Him, for he who comes to God must believe that He is, and that He is a rewarder of those who diligently seek Him" (see Heb. 11:6).

He was one of that great host of patriarchs and prophets of whom it was said:

> But now they desire a better, that is, a heavenly country. Therefore God is not ashamed to be called their God, for He has prepared a city for them. By faith Abraham, when he was tested, offered up

Isaac, and he who had received the promises offered up his only begotten son, of whom it was said, "In Isaac your seed shall be called," accounting that God was able to raise him up, even from the dead, from which he also received him in a figurative sense.

—HEBREWS 11:16–19

For the first time in my life I saw the many truths of this verse with utter clarity. God has prepared a city for Abraham, and for all of us who believe and obey. Abraham, like God, had willingly offered his only begotten son, fully persuaded that God could raise him from the dead if need be.

In the same way, our heavenly Father gave His only begotten Son—Jesus—as a sacrifice for our sins. He was crucified and buried, but on the third day God raised Jesus from the dead, and because of His resurrection none of us ever have to fear death again!

Abraham called an angel to be my escort. The angel took me into the powder room where I changed into my beautiful heavenly robe and crown. Then the Lord took me back to the pond.

Each time the Lord takes me to the pond, the moment we arrive there I begin to sing and dance, but this time I wanted only to cry. The Lord knew how sad I was. He let me sit next to Him, and He began to talk.

VALLEY OF THE SHADOW OF DEATH

JESUS SENSED THE sadness that I carried in my heart over the full recognition of my parents and loved ones being in hell.

"My daughter," He said, *"I know how you feel about your loved ones that you saw in the pit. How I wish I did not have to show you these things, but I do not want any of My children to go to the place where your loved ones are. I am showing these things to you so that whoever heeds my warnings will be saved!"*

The Lord then took my hand, and we returned to the place where Abraham was. We changed our clothing again, and He took me to another high mountain from which I could look down into another endless valley where a multitude of people dressed in gray-colored robes were wandering about in an apparent mood of dejection. Their robes reminded me of the gowns worn by hospital patients.

The people looked weak and lost, and their gray faces matched the color of the robes they were wearing. They stared at the ground in front of their feet as they walked around in circles, aimlessly and hopelessly. This place was mostly men with just a few women.

"Who are these people, Lord?"

"They are the sinful 'Christians.'"

"What is going to happen to them?" I wondered aloud.

"Most of them will go to the lake of fire after the judgment."

I wondered why these people were here, and then I remembered that their valley leads to the burning pit. These so-called "Christians" who don't really know the Lord and who continually and willfully sin and don't repent before they die or before the Rapture happens will be eternally lost.

Romans 1:29–32, Galatians 5:19–21 and Revelation 21:8 all are examples of how some Christians live. Someone once asked me how sinful Christians could enter heaven. We all must appear before the judgement seat of Christ to receive what is due to us for the things done while on earth, whether good or bad (see 2 Cor. 5:10).

"My daughter, this is why I keep telling you about the importance of obedience and purity," Jesus said.

Then it occurred to me—each time we went to the beautiful places of the heavenly kingdom we crossed the golden bridge, from the white building where we usually change. When the Lord took me to see the dreadful places, however, we would go on different roads that were outside the gate of the heavenly kingdom.

SADNESS AND JOY

THIS REALIZATION HELPED me understand some of the preparations we would go through before I would be shown a different part of the kingdom. Therefore, it was not necessary for us to change our robes when the Lord took me to the earthly beach. On this occasion, we sat on the sand, and I reflected on all that I had experienced. I began to cry as I remembered all I had seen in the pit and the valley. The Lord took my hand and said, *"Do not cry, My daughter."*

This was the hardest of all commands to obey, but I steeled myself against the horrible memories, choked back the tears and began to ask all the questions that were flooding my mind.

"Lord, I do not know anything, and I am a nobody. How can you use me?"

"People may think you are a nobody, but I want you to understand that you are My special daughter. I treat you as My friend, and I trust you implicitly. Don't worry about anything. I will take care of everything for you."

"When are you coming to take us home?"

"You saw the kingdom. Everything is ready, and that is why I am in a hurry for everyone to be ready for Me. This is why I want you to do this work for My children. You have been given a special anointing to do this work, so do not say that you are a nobody. I will bless you more than you ever thought."

"Lord, you know that I love you, but I cannot get rid of my mother's face as I saw it contorted by the fires of hell. I do not want to remember what I saw."

Just then the Lord touched my eyes, and from that moment on I could not recall my mother's face. Even as I write these words, I cannot see her face. All I can remember is that I once saw her face in the pit, and it was a terrifying experience.

Jesus then said: *"I know you are tired. We will talk again."*

We both stood, and He embraced me, then departed. As the Lord hugged me, my body shook so hard that I felt I would fall to pieces. Every time He touches my transformed body, my physical body experiences the overpowering force of His touch, and every nerve and sinew in my body quakes and quivers. Then, the minute He leaves, my body stops shaking.

That same morning, I went to church, and I experienced the presence of the Lord shaking my body throughout the service. I could see Him standing by the pastor. During the worship time, the Lord was walking in the front of the church. It was wonderful to see His glowing presence in the church.

Throughout the service I cried tears of love and joy. My heart thudded within my breast as I contemplated the majesty of the heavenly kingdom I had visited. The anointing was so heavy upon me that I could not stand. I could not even hear the pastor's sermon as my body responded to the Lord's presence with intense heat and shaking.

The people in my church understand what is happening to me, and they've been very supportive. In times past I would have been embarrassed and ashamed by such a physical manifestation in public, but I was happy because I knew it all was a gift of God and He was preparing me to serve Him in ways I had never thought possible. I never want this manifestation of His powerful presence in my life to go away.

THE TRIBULATION

ON MARCH 4 the Lord visited me from 2:30 A.M. to 5:05 A.M. My body shook for twenty minutes, then the Lord took me to the beach, and we walked up the mountainside to the big rock where we had sat the last time.

Everything seemed normal for the first few moments, but suddenly I noticed that the mountains where the fires had burned the day before were now only scorched, charred mounds of ash and rubble. The whole area was simply a huge, black hole of destruction. I noticed that the beach, where the people had run and fallen the day before, was pockmarked with black spots, and I assumed that each of these spots represented the charred remains of human beings who had died in the fires of the last days.

The ocean, once filled with blazing blood, was now a large, empty sinkhole—scorched beyond recognition. After a few moments of beholding this scene of ultimate desolation, darkness and destruction, the ocean and the surrounding area returned to normal.

I had studied the Word of God to see what it said about these phenomena. In Revelation 8:8, I read these words: "And something like a great mountain burning with fire was thrown into the sea, and a third of the sea became blood." Revelation 16:3 refers to the sea becoming like blood: "Then the second angel poured out his bowl on the sea, and it became blood as of a dead man; and every living creature in the sea died." God had shown me the very things He had already described in His Word.

"When is all this going to take place?" I asked the Lord with great curiosity.

"At the tribulation."

"Lord, when will the tribulation occur?"

"After I bring My children to My kingdom. Whoever has read My book and believes My prophets should know about these things concerning the end of time. All the things I showed you on this beach will happen very soon."

I feel the Lord is coming for us very soon, and that is why so many unusual things are happening in the world. One glance at the daily headlines concurs with this observation. Earthquakes, other natural disasters (including hurricanes, tornadoes, typhoons, fires, floods and blizzards), violence, lawlessness, plagues, terrorism and many other phenomena are occurring with greater intensity and frequency than ever before, just as the Bible predicted.

Jesus told His disciples:

> And you will hear of wars and rumors of wars. See that you are not troubled; for all these things must come to pass, but the end is not yet. For nation will rise against nation, and kingdom against kingdom. And there will be famines, pestilences, and earthquakes in various places. All these are the beginning of sorrows.
>
> Then they will deliver you up to tribulation and kill you, and you will be hated by all nations for My name's sake. And then many will be offended, will betray one another, and will hate one another. Then many false prophets will rise up and deceive many. And because lawlessness will abound, the love of many will grow cold. But he who endures to the end shall be saved. And this gospel of the kingdom will be preached in all the world as a witness to all the nations, and then the end will come.
>
> —MATTHEW 24:6–14

These were the events that Jesus had already shown me. How I wish I could impress their vividness and reality upon everyone in the same way that those scenes have been so indelibly imprinted on my mind. Jesus' words are real, and His prophecies soon will come to pass!

THE PLACE OF LIVING WATER

IN THE BOOK of Revelation, the Bible talks about the "water of life": "And he showed me a pure river of water of life, clear as crystal, proceeding from the throne of God and of the Lamb. In the middle of its street, and on either side of the river, was the tree of life, which bore twelve fruits, each tree yielding its fruit every month" (Rev. 22:1–2).

After the Lord took me to heaven, we went into the white building, and an angel took me to the powder room where I changed clothing. When I came out, I saw the Lord who had changed into heavenly garments as well. He took me to His throne and directed me to sit on a chair next to Him. This was the first time the Lord seated me next to Himself.

There I saw many men wearing beautiful gowns and crowns sitting in front of us. I noticed that they looked very dignified and important.

"Lord, who are these men?"

"They are the ones I gave My sacred words to, and they faithfully recorded them in My book."

He pointed to a huge black Bible in the corner of the room, and I noticed that the pages of the Scriptures were turning by themselves as if a soft breeze was fingering its way through the pages. I was surprised, but then I realized the wind of the Spirit of God was rustling through the pages of the holy Word.

The men began to walk out slowly, and an angel took me back to the powder room so I could change into a regular gown, and my body took on the form of a teenager. I remembered then that heaven is a place where you never grow old, and this thought delighted me and filled me with wonder.

We crossed the golden bridge again and walked along a hillside by a beautiful valley. A golden fence formed a boundary around the entire area, and the fence had several gates that were placed close to one another all around the perimeter. Trees were planted close to the fence, and lovely yellow flowers filled the ground around the trees. It was a magnificent rock garden that led to a crystal-clear river.

I noticed that the trees were laden with purple fruits. The Lord reached up and gave me one to eat while He enjoyed another one that He had picked. The river was narrow, but it seemed to have no end as it coursed its way through the fertile valley. Nothing on earth—not even the majestic Rocky Mountains or the fruited plains—could compare with the lush paradise in front of me.

"What is this place, Lord?"

"It is the place of living water. Would you like a drink?"

"Oh, yes, Lord."

He bent down and cupped His hand, filling it with the clean, pure water. He drank from His hand and indicated that I should follow His lead. I reached down and filled my palm with water and sipped its delicious freshness. It was the sweetest water I'd ever tasted.

"How do you like this water, My daughter?"

"It's so delicious, Lord."

"Now I want to take you to a very special place."

THE MANSION

I WONDERED WHERE He was leading me as He took my hand and began walking. He led me to the castle we had visited on the previous day. My heart sang with wonder. How could anything be this beautiful?

The golden streets amazed me, and I felt so happy as we walked along this place the Lord has prepared for His own. The street looked slippery because it was so shiny, but felt normal underfoot. Because of its brightness, it resembled an indoor ice-skating rink. Sunlight, it seemed, was shooting through the whole place.

Whenever I walk with the Lord, I feel so intensely happy that there truly are no words to describe it. It is a feeling of comfort and joy mingled with unwavering security.

We walked past many mansions and castles, each more exquisite than the last. In front of one of these dwellings, the Lord stopped emphatically. I knew He was going to take me inside, and I was excited beyond all measure. My heart kept skipping beats as we walked up the front steps.

My eyes were drawn to the doorknob, which was made of gold. Then I saw a gold plate on the front door. It had a name inscribed on it, and I realized quickly that it was my name. I almost fainted with surprise. Written in fancy lettering was the name "Choo Nam."

This was the place Jesus had prepared for *me!* I was amazed. It was too good to be true. Here I was, standing at the door of a regal palace in heaven, and my name was inscribed in gold on its beautiful door! It was too much to take in! My head reeled in astonishment. How could these things be?

I cried tears of gratitude and joy as my heart overflowed with love and adoration for the Lord. I had never really anticipated such wonderful things from Him. I had always felt that if He simply noticed me it would be OK, but now He literally was showering His blessings on me!

I had tasted the living water, and I knew I would never thirst again. I had tasted the purple fruit of paradise, and I could never hunger for the things of the world again.

I had been with Jesus—my Lord and Master—and He had taken me to the mansion He had made for me. I wept openly as the Lord led me into the house. He said: *"Do not cry, My daughter. I want you to be happy."*

As we stepped across the threshold of the mansion, spiritual songs welled up from my heart, and I continued to cry tears of joy and gratitude. I was awestruck by the sparkling stone walls that lined the corridor of my mansion. I loved the red-and-cream-colored carpet with its round patterns. The red velvet chairs—so classic and sophisticated—were like the ones I had always wanted in my home. The red draperies were the finest I'd ever seen.

The Lord took His seat on one of the velvet chairs as I walked up the majestic stairway, savoring every single moment in my mansion. The bedroom was carpeted in pure white, and I noticed that the headboard of the bed was silver with blue stones embedded decoratively along its border.

The mirror on the dresser also had blue stones highlighting its brightness. The bathroom had a silver bathtub that was decorated with precious jewels of every color.

I sang as I walked around the interior of my mansion. I felt like a princess in fairyland. But I knew this was no fantasy—it was more real than I had ever imagined. I had always believed in a heavenly paradise, but I had never been absolutely sure of its existence. Now I knew, beyond all doubt, that heaven is real, and I wanted everyone in the world to know it, too.

After several moments of wonderful joy, I walked down the stairs to where the Lord was sitting. He stood up and asked, *"Are you happy, Choo Nam?"*

I knew the Lord was happy about showing me my mansion.

"Yes, I am very happy, and so very grateful for all you've done for me," I responded, "but I still feel as if I don't deserve such wonderful blessings. I haven't really done anything for You yet, Lord, but I always want to serve You and to make You happy."

"You have already made Me happy, My daughter. You are a very special daughter to Me, and I want to bless you so much."

"MY CHILDREN ARE NOT READY FOR ME"

AS WE LEFT and walked over the golden bridge, we went back to the white building and changed into beautiful gowns and crowns and went to the pond. I felt so joyous, I was singing before we even arrived at the pond.

Maranatha!

We sat and talked for a little while, and I realized that I was the most fortunate individual who had ever existed. The Lord broke my reverie with an urgent message.

"Choo Nam, I have prepared everything for My children. I am in a hurry for everything because My kingdom has been ready for a long time, but so many of My children are not ready for Me, because they love the world too much.

"That is why I want you to write a book for Me. I know it's tiring for you, but this work has to be done soon.

"Lord, I am so surprised about everything you have shown me already. If I were to hear of such a book, I know I would want to read it because I love You so much."

"I know you do, My daughter," He responded, smiling. *"This is why I am in such a hurry. Preaching the gospel is the most important thing in the world. I want all My children to know that I am coming soon."*

My mind went back to some of the closing words of the Bible, and with all my heart I cried the same: "Even so, come, Lord Jesus."

Maranatha! The Lord truly is coming soon.

Chapter 8

Preparation for Service

I beseech you therefore, brethren, by the mercies
of God, that you present your bodies a living sacrifice,
holy, acceptable to God, which is your reasonable service. And do not be
conformed to this world, but be transformed by the
renewing of your mind, that you may prove what is that
good and acceptable and perfect will of God.

—ROMANS 12:1–2

MY SUPERNATURAL EXPERIENCES were both wonderfully exhilarating and somewhat exhausting, and the Lord recognized the toll they were taking on my body and health. The shaking that my body had to endure was part of my preparation for service. This physical manifestation of God's supernatural work in my life, as well as the deep groanings that emanated from my spirit, were having an effect on my body.

After my body quivers so intensely for a period of two or three hours, I am left reeling. My mind feels as if it is spinning, and I get very dizzy. Sometimes this sensation is so strong that I am hardly able to walk.

The strength of the Lord's anointing in my life kept me from eating very much for periods of several days at a time. The sleep deprivation and lack of food caused me to feel weak and emaciated. In fact, I had already lost five pounds. I frequently felt nauseated, and I often experienced pain in my stomach and joints. Before leaving each day, however, the Lord would heal me of my pains.

He would embrace me, and a single touch from His hand would lift the anguish and cause the shaking to stop. He would usually say tender words of concern and caring that helped me know that He truly understood how tired I was. It is so wonderful to know that He cares about everything that concerns His children—our aches and pains, our worries, our tiredness, our hopes and dreams.

The writer of the Book of Hebrews explains how this is possible:

> Seeing then that we have a great High Priest who has passed through the heavens, Jesus the Son of God, let us hold fast our confession. For we do not have a High Priest who cannot sympathize with our weaknesses, but was in all points tempted as we are, yet without sin. Let us therefore come boldly to the throne of grace, that we may obtain mercy and find grace to help in time of need.
>
> —HEBREWS 4:14–16

Jesus wept. He knew the pain of loneliness and rejection. He faced temptation. He wrestled with the will of God. He experienced anger and fear. No matter what we face, He has been there. More importantly, our great High Priest is right there with us. He is praying for us. He is bearing our burdens. Jesus truly understands.

He knew that many things had to be healed in my inner life before I could be effectively used in the ministry He has called me to. He had already explained to me that He repeated things so many times so that I would truly understand. He took me to some of the same heavenly places more than once so that I could fully experience their reality—and remember them. He had emphasized that the reason why my body shook so forcibly every time I was in His presence was because He was pouring His power into me.

In short, therefore, I was being prepared for a worldwide ministry of evangelism and healing that would begin with the book you now hold in your hands.

THE BIG, BLACK BIBLE

ON MARCH 5 the Lord kept me awake from 1:50 A.M. to 4:20 A.M. In the process, my body shook for about twenty-five minutes. Then the Lord took me to the beach in preparation for the next journey to heaven.

We revisited the white building and the powder room. We both changed into our heavenly robes and crowns. Then we went to the throne room where the Lord took His seat and directed me to sit in a chair next to Him. There were several men in front of us who were wearing crowns similar to my own.

"Who are these men?" I asked.

The Lord replied, *"They are the ones who wrote My Word."*

I looked at each glowing face and I tried to guess who each one was. Sitting in front of me were the apostles John, Matthew, Luke, Mark, James, Peter and Paul. The prophets were there as well—men such as Isaiah, Jeremiah, Joel, Micah, Malachi, Daniel, Obadiah, Hosea and many others.

I thought, *Moses and Joshua must be in the crowd as well; and Nehemiah, Job, David, Solomon, Ezekiel, Nahum, Jonah and Zechariah. I wish I had time to talk with each one. I'd ask Jonah what it was like to be in the belly of the great fish. I'd want Daniel to tell me how it felt to be in the lion's den. I'd love to hear David describe his experience with Goliath.*

Then it dawned on me: One day, in the near future, I would take up the heavenly abode Jesus had shown me, and I would be able to have lasting fellowship with the saints of all ages! Then I could ask them. Then I would find out. Then I would know. Won't it be wonderful?

Paul wrote: "For now we see in a mirror, dimly, but then face to face. Now I know in part, but then I shall know just as I also am known" (1 Cor. 13:12). It was still beyond my comprehension how I had been chosen to receive so much in advance of the great day of the Lord when we shall know, even as we are known, but I did understand that I had been granted an incredibly special grace to see so many things. I knew that this special privilege was not for me alone. I knew it was for everybody, so that as many as would be willing to do so would believe and be saved.

The huge black Bible I had seen on a previous visit was directly in front of me. It radiated with the power of the Holy Spirit who spoke to my heart: "All Scripture is given by inspiration of God, and is profitable for doctrine, for reproof, for correction, for instruction in righteousness, that the man of God may be complete, thoroughly equipped for every good work" (2 Tim. 3:16–17).

I noticed that the writers who were inspired to write the Bible had notebooks in their hands, and then I realized that the Lord was showing this scene to me for the second time so that I would fully understand the importance of His Word in my life. I knew He wanted me to read and study and take notes as I focused on His Word.

My Lord and Master wanted me to "take the helmet of salvation, and the sword of the Spirit, which is the word of God; praying always with all prayer and supplication in the Spirit" (Eph. 6:17–18). The enormity of the Bible in front of me served to remind me that the Bible should grow ever bigger in my life—that it should be the foundation on which my ministry would be built and launched.

A TRANSFORMED BODY

AN ANGEL ESCORTED me back to the changing room where I could see my reflection in the huge, clear mirrors. I had been transformed! My new body was that of my teenage years. I was young, beautiful and vibrant. Each time I saw the transformation I was shocked! But it was a reminder that when I get to heaven I will have a new body.

Our new, heavenly bodies will not grow old. They will be incapable of pain. There will be no wrinkles in our faces. Our teeth will be white and even. No gray will be found in our hair. The radiance of youth will glow from our eyes. Our posture will be straight and even. Any handicaps we experienced on earth will vanish. We will be completely new in every respect, and it will be wonderful!

THE LIVING, FLOWING WATERS

WE CHANGED, THEN walked across the golden bridge, through a verdant valley. We followed a beautiful road that was bordered by a golden fence with many gates. Along the way I noticed the now-familiar fruit trees and picturesque yellow flowers. Beautiful rocks were strewn across the fields and the fast-flowing, clear-as-crystal river was nearby.

"That water is living water," the Lord pointed out. It was the second time I had seen this magnificent river. The time before, I had even tasted its sweet, pure water.

I noticed that the river of life was narrow, but it did not seem to have any end. As we walked toward the nearest gate, the Lord asked me if I wanted to drink from the river of life again but I shook my head because I did not want to impose on His gracious kindness to me, and I was eager to see the next sight, which I hoped was my mansion—the one He had already prepared for me.

We headed in the direction of my palace, and when we arrived there, we entered. The Lord sat in the same chair He had taken on the previous visit and seemed eager for me to explore my future dwelling.

I went into the same rooms I had visited before, and I imagined what it would be like for me to live there. The silver bedroom set with beautiful stones and the beautiful powder room, the beautiful draperies and carpets, the glistening walls—all reminders of what Jesus had done for me.

He was showing me these things again so that they would stick in my memory—so that I would truly believe. I was filled with even more wonder and anticipation than I had experienced on the previous visit.

We left my mansion and went back to the white building where we changed our garments once more. Then we went to the placid pond where the Lord took His usual place on the solid rock.

He sat, but I could not contain myself. I began to dance and sing with the greatest, fullest joy I had ever known. From my heavenly vantage point, I could see that my physical body, still lying on my bed, was moving and my hands were waving. The Lord seemed so pleased with me, and He beckoned for me to come and sit next to Him.

WHOLENESS AND HEALING

I KNEW THAT the Lord still had much to do in my life before I would be ready to fulfill the calling He had imparted to me. Things from my past caused me to feel inferior and unworthy. He seemed focused on helping me gain confidence, first in Him and then in myself.

"My daughter, I have shown you the important parts of the kingdom of God, and I want you to tell everyone what you have seen. I know I have shown you many things today that I showed you before. When you do the work I've called you to do many souls will be saved. The book will be read all over the world."

"But, Lord, I am nobody. Why did you choose me? Why not someone who is famous already?"

"Choo Nam, I created you for this End-Time work. I will make you famous. I know you are learning what I teach you. I know you will be faithful to Me."

"Who will write the book?" I queried. "I try to write down everything you say and to describe the things you show me, but I don't really know how to write a book." (The fact was, I felt very intimidated by the whole idea!) "Lord, I don't have enough education to write a book."

"You do not need to know how to write the book. Just write down what I show you and tell you, and a writer will write the book for you. Daughter, do not worry. I will guide someone in rewriting what you have put down. A Spirit-filled writer will do this work for you."

This new bit of information eased my mind. Ever so slowly, and step by step, I was learning to lean on the Lord instead of my own understanding. A passage came to my mind: "Trust in the Lord with all your heart, and lean not on your own understanding; in all your ways acknowledge Him, and He shall direct your paths" (Prov. 3:5–6).

My problem was not in trusting the Lord. He had already proven His faithfulness to me in so many extraordinary ways. My problem was in trusting myself. Since my childhood I had always been afraid to step out, to take the lead—and now I was being called to write a book and launch a worldwide ministry! Actually, I was frightened.

The Lord then interjected a new thought by saying: *"You will have great wealth, and I want you to use it to build a church for Me."*

"But I cannot preach, Lord."

"You will not have to preach."

The groaning deep in my spirit began to emerge, and I knew a special anointing was upon me. Then something more vivid than a natural scene appeared before me.

It was a vision of a church—a white-frame church building with a very high steeple. The entry doors were beautiful double doors. The sanctuary was adorned with deep-red chairs and carpeting. I could see that many activities and functions were taking place in wings to the side.

The sanctuary was filled with people, and I noticed that some of them entered the church in wheelchairs, but they left walking. There was marvelous joy on their faces because they had been completely healed. Just seeing this vision was bringing healing to my hurts and fears as well. Like them, God wanted me to be whole, and He was equipping me for the ministry to which I had been called.

"Do you like what you are seeing?" the Lord asked.

I radiated a smile back at Him and responded, "Yes!" I was more excited than I had ever been in my life.

Then He repeated something that was vitally important to Him, *"Before I come for My people, half of the unbelievers will be saved."*

"When will you come for us?" I asked again, hoping for a more precise, definitive response.

"I told you it will be soon. Didn't you see that everything is already prepared for everyone here?"

That, I then knew, was precisely why the Lord had taken me to heaven so many times—so that I would see that He had almost completed His work. The time of His return is truly at hand. This is the burning message that must be told. This is the theme of my book and my life.

Jesus wants everyone to know that the end is coming. He has already prepared an eternal home for all who believe in Him. It is no longer accurate to say that He is preparing a place for us because the place is already prepared!

Isn't it thrilling to know that half of the unbelievers in the world will be saved before the Lord returns in the very near future? Many millions of people will be ushered into the church of Jesus Christ, and the church had better be prepared for them.

I can't wait to start building the church of my vision. I have embraced the vision God gave me, and I am beginning to run with it. My confidence is building, and all of my inner insecurities, worries and fears are being absorbed by the love of God. I know, beyond all shadow of doubt, that God's love is everlasting, His kingdom is real and He will keep His Word.

Through the experiences I'd had in heaven, I was learning that God enables those He calls. He fills in the empty places and provides strength in our weakness. Like the handicapped people I'd seen in the vision of the church, we're all limited or handicapped in one way or another.

But God is able to give new strength to the legs of the lame, and as He heals our handicaps, we are able to walk in newness of life—in the strength and power of His Holy Spirit. On that early March morning I learned an all-encompassing truth anew: "I can do all things through Christ who strengthens me" (Phil. 4:13).

A NEEDED REST

FOR ONE AND a half months the Lord had been waking me from my sleep in the early hours of many mornings to take me to heaven so He could prepare me for the work He had called me to do. I was tired, and my body was weak. Recognizing my need for more sleep, the Lord said, *"This is the last time I will bring you to the kingdom, and I will not wake you up any more."*

My heart sank as I thought that His wonderful visits would be over. But He continued, *"My daughter, I have shown you enough for a while."*

I began to cry. My heart was filled with sadness. I wanted to be with the Lord forever. I protested, "Lord, I don't want to leave You."

"I will be with you everywhere. You will see Me and hear My voice."

He then reached over and embraced me as He said, *"Choo Nam, I know you need rest."*

I acknowledged my need for rest, but my desire to be with the Lord overtook my physical needs. I saw my spiritual needs as being vastly more important than my physical needs. We left the pond and went back to the white building to change into our regular robes. Then we were transported back to the beach where we sat and conversed for a little while.

"I know how tired you are right now, so I will not be waking you from your sleep. You must rest for a while."

A sense of dejection threatened to overwhelm me as the Lord spoke these words I did not wish to hear, but then He clarified what He was saying, *"I will take you back to the kingdom again, but now you need your rest."*

Even with this reassurance, I could not stop crying. Truly, I was devastated by the thought that Jesus was leaving, and that He might stay away for a long time. I love Him so much, and the thought of His departure left me feeling very empty and somewhat insecure.

I imagined what it must have been like for the original disciples who had to say goodbye to their Lord and Master. How must His mother, Mary, have felt when she saw Him crucified, dead and buried? How did she feel when He ascended into heaven? It was the loneliest feeling in the world.

By this time every waking moment of my life was filled with thoughts of Jesus and heaven. I had been in the Lord's company daily for more than one and a half months. I had been to heaven and had seen the streets of gold, the mansions over the hilltop, the River of Life. In fact, I had tasted the sweet water of life.

I had been escorted by angels and had fellowshiped and worshiped with the saints, martyrs, apostles and prophets. I had walked into the eternal dwelling Jesus had already prepared for me. I knew I could never be the same again. Nothing in this world could compare with heaven— my true home.

I had seen the pit of hell—that raging inferno of violence, corruption and shame. I had seen the signs of the End Times unfurl before me like a living video of what is yet to come. Most importantly, I had been with Jesus—and all of life had taken on an entirely new meaning.

I had a purpose, a mission, a calling. I had seen a vision of some of the things God has planned for me. To think that I would be spending time sleeping when there was so much to do seemed entirely incomprehensible to me. I was really disappointed.

The Lord departed from the beach, as did my transformed body, and the shaking of my body stopped. My crying ceased as I realized what He had said, *"I will take you back to the kingdom again."* That was enough. It would be OK.

Then it occurred to me that the rest He was wanting me to take was a part of the preparation He was doing in my life. I certainly knew I needed the rest, because there were times when I felt disoriented.

A lovely passage of Scripture came to my mind and settled me down: "The LORD is my shepherd; I shall not want. He makes me to lie down in green pastures; He leads me beside the still waters. He restores my soul" (Ps. 23:1–3).

The Lord, my Shepherd, was permitting me to lie down in the green pastures so my soul could be restored—further preparation for the ministry that lies ahead!

"Everybody Will Know You"

THE NEXT MORNING, March 6, was difficult because I woke up at 2:30 A.M., half expecting the Lord to be there. I had believed what He had told me, but a part of me still wondered if He would come. I waited for Him from 2:30 until 6:30, then I fell back to sleep. When I awoke again at 9:30 in the morning, I realized the Lord was not there. I missed Him, and I began to weep.

Soon my whole body began to shake, accompanied by the anointing of heat. I groaned in the spirit for more than fifteen minutes. Then, as had happened so many times before, the Lord appeared. He was sitting by the window next to the bed.

He said, *"My precious daughter, Choo Nam, I told you I will be with you always. You are going to see Me anytime you want, and you will hear My voice. I am visiting you now because I know you waited for Me all morning long."*

"Lord," I said, "I want to do everything You tell me. I still feel I do not know anything."

"That is precisely why I chose you. Never forget that I will take care of you. I have given you this special gift because no one knows you.

74

Soon, however, everyone will know you."

I found it hard to accept those words. *Everyone* will know *me?* It seemed so unlikely, but the Lord, in His mercy and patience saw fit to visit me again to give me this reassuring message. He concluded His visit by saying, *"Daughter, I want you to rest."* Then He left and my shaking body quieted down.

For the next ten days I enjoyed the soundest sleep and quietest rest I had ever known. Once again, the Lord was faithful to His promise:

> There remains therefore a rest for the people of God. For he who has entered His rest has himself also ceased from his works as God did from His. Let us therefore be diligent to enter that rest, lest anyone fall after the same example of disobedience. For the word of God is living and powerful, and sharper than any two-edged sword, piercing even to the division of soul and spirit, and of joints and marrow, and is a discerner of the thoughts and intents of the heart. And there is no creature hidden from His sight, but all things are naked and open to the eyes of Him to whom we must give account.
>
> —HEBREWS 4:9–13

The Lord wanted me to rest because He was preparing me for a ministry that would usher countless unbelievers into the kingdom of God. Knowing that He was coming back to escort me to heaven again brought such peace to my soul that I was able to truly enjoy His rest.

I was finally beginning to understand that the book I was to write, the church I was to build, the ministry I was to begin were His work, not mine. This restored my soul, erased my anxieties and brought total trust to my heart.

The truth communicated by the psalmist so many centuries ago echoed deep within me: "Unless the LORD builds the house, they labor in vain who build it" (Ps. 127:1).

Jesus reminded me of His great invitation to the weary and downtrodden, from Matthew 11:28–30: "Come to Me, all you who labor and are heavy laden, and I will give you rest. Take my yoke upon you and learn from Me, for I am gentle and lowly in heart, and you will find rest for your souls. For My yoke is easy and My burden is light."

Chapter 9

Worry Is a Sin

Be anxious for nothing, but in everything by prayer
and supplication, with thanksgiving, let your requests
be made known to God; and the peace of God, which surpasses
all understanding, will guard your hearts and minds
through Christ Jesus.

—PHILIPPIANS 4:6–7

AFTER TEN DAYS of rest, with good, sound sleep every night, I knew I was ready to meet the Lord again and to go with Him to heaven. The Ides of March—March 15, 1996—had arrived, but they were not something to beware; indeed, they provided me with the moment I had been eagerly awaiting since the Lord's departure nearly two weeks before.

From 6:40 A.M. to 8:40 A.M., I enjoyed the Lord's visit and another journey to heaven. As usual, before His arrival my body shook, and I groaned for thirty minutes. Then the Lord appeared before me and said: *"My daughter, I see you are rested now. We have a lot of work to do yet."*

The Lord of heaven and earth was concerned about me, His daughter and handmaiden. He made sure I had caught up on my rest before He returned to take me with Him. He understands the limitations of my body and soul, and He truly cares about me. He knows everything that is good for His children, and He will withhold no good thing from those who love Him.

After the last two times I had gone to heaven my body had felt as if it were out of control. I was very tired from the shaking, and I found myself feeling dizzy much of the time. I had slept only three hours a night for a period of two weeks. It was impossible for me to sleep during the day because the anointing of the Holy Spirit was so strong upon me.

Little by little, I was learning how to manage the situation by going to bed earlier in the evening to ensure I would have sufficient sleep before the Lord arrived. On this morning, the Lord took my transformed body to the beach where we walked by the seaside for a while before He took me to heaven. My heart was filled with great joy and anticipation as we flew away.

We arrived at the usual location and entered the white building. By now, I was getting used to the setting and the procedures we normally followed. We changed into our heavenly clothing, and then the Lord took my hand as He led me down a wide road that coursed its way up an exceedingly high mountain.

It was very much like the Cascade Mountains that I'd visited in the northwestern part of the United States, and I remarked that heaven looked, in many ways, like earth—but it was far more beautiful than anything I'd ever seen on this planet.

There were many leafy trees and bushes on the mountainside. From the summit I could see a beach. It was a rocky coastline, much like the pictures I'd seen of Bar Harbor, Maine. Everything glowed with a whiteness that was stunningly brilliant and pure. We descended the mountain and walked on the sand between the rocks. It was the whitest, cleanest sand I'd ever seen, and the beach was absolutely the most beautiful I'd ever seen.

Some of the rocks nearby were so huge that I could not see their tops. As we walked around one of them, I noticed a large group of people wearing white robes. Each person was distinctly different from the other in appearance, and many children could be seen playing in the sand. Some children were holding the hands of grown-ups, and everyone was walking around in a playful, happy manner. It was wonderful to see a place of such brightness and joy.

The Lord and I sat on one of the big rocks for quite a while, simply enjoying the vibrant beauty all around us. He turned to me and said: *"I have made so many of the things here similar to the things on earth so that My children can enjoy them when they come to My kingdom, but there are many things that are not the same as things on earth. I have so many exciting surprises for My children."*

He sounded so happy—like a parent who has provided as many gifts as possible for his children to open on Christmas Day. The Lord seemed to want His children to be happy—like the ones who were playing so joyfully in the sand. This is why He created heaven to be such a wonderful place. It will be the home for His children forever and ever.

"Do you like what I am showing you, Choo Nam?"

"Yes, Lord. I've seen many beaches on earth, but none of them can compare with this beach."

I could sense that my response greatly pleased my Master. Soon thereafter we left the beach and returned to the white building. We changed into regal robes and crowns, and the Lord took me to the pond where we usually end each visit to heaven. The Lord sat on His favorite rock while I joyfully sang and danced with my transformed body. Meanwhile, the hands of my earthly body were moving in rhythm to the heavenly music.

"I still have many things to show you, My daughter," the Lord said as I moved closer to Him. *"You must be patient."*

This was good news to me because I knew He meant that I would get to go to heaven with Him many more times. My heart soared with delight and rejoicing as I danced in this wonderful place of joy near the peaceful pond. I was in the presence of the Lord, in the place He had prepared for me, and I knew I had to be the happiest person who had ever lived.

"STOP WORRYING!"

TEARS OF UTTER joy flowed freely down my face as I said, "Thank You, Lord, for bringing me to heaven with You again."

"My daughter, I notice that you worry about everything I ask you to do. I have told you many times not to worry, daughter, and you are not obeying Me in this."

"Lord, I'm sorry. It's just that I can't seem to stop worrying. All I want to do is the work You've called me to do for You. I want to do it the way You tell me to, and all this causes me to worry."

"I don't want you to be concerned about anything from now on," He directed. *"I am going to take care of everything for you. Watch out for some people, because they will give you wrong advice. That is why, while you are writing the book, I do not want you to leave town, and I don't want anyone else to come to your house, except your family."*

The Lord was more explicit with His instructions than He'd ever been before. I listened intently as He went on.

"Did you notice that no one has come to visit you since I took you to heaven?"

"Well, yes. It seems that every time I invited someone to come or made arrangements for company, something always happened to change their plans."

"Now you know why, My daughter. I want you to concentrate on the book, with no interruptions. This book is very important to Me, and it will be a special blessing for My children. Whatever you do, I want you to talk to Me first. Everything about this book has to be My will."

The Lord's clear message rang in my heart as we left the pond, returned to the white building and changed into our regular clothing. Then we returned to the beach on earth, and the Lord said, *"Daughter, you see this beach is so much different from the beach you saw in My kingdom."*

"Lord, everything You showed me in Your kingdom was so beautiful, except for the sad things You showed me."

"This is why I chose you to do this work. I do not want any of My children to have to go to the pit. It is all up to them either to believe or not to believe. I'll talk to you more about this later, My child." He then reached over and embraced me. When He departed, the shaking of my body stopped.

The power He was unleashing in my body was beginning to heal the weak places in my character that remained from my childhood. I was learning how to be more confident, how to reach out and truly trust the Lord, but I still struggled with certain worries and fears.

On March 19 the Lord spent two hours with me, from 7 A.M. to 9 A.M. I shook for half an hour and then groaned in the Spirit for an additional fifteen minutes that morning. Then I heard the pleasant, compelling sound of the Lord's voice speaking to me. He took me by the hand and we went back to the beach.

My body underwent its supernatural transformation, and I found myself wearing a white robe like the one Jesus had on. We then ascended the mighty mountain along the narrow road. I noticed a large rock where we sat for a rest.

The length of time my earthly body had had to endure the manifestations preceding the Lord's visits was inordinately long, so I knew this visit would be a very special one. My mind raced with thoughts of anticipation and joy. What will the Lord show me today? Where will He take me?

Jesus broke my reverie by saying: *"I know you are still worried about the things I told you and showed you. I told you to stop worrying."* The tone of His voice sounded angry and severe. *"You do not trust My words."*

I knew immediately what He meant. I was still worrying about the book, even after what He had shared with me the last time. He had told me that every detail would be carefully handled by Him, but I still felt intimidated by such an important project. I was truly overwhelmed by the magnitude of the assignment.

I began to cry tears of shame and repentance at the Lord's rebuke. I put my hands together, bowed my head and began to plead, "Please forgive me, Lord. No matter how hard I try not to worry, Lord, I still end up worrying about all this."

"From now on, Choo Nam, I want you to stop worrying. I do not want you to worry about anything. Some people will not believe you, but you don't need to worry about that. My daughter, I am simply using you for this book. It is My book and I will take care of it.

"As I told you at the beginning, it will take a while to prepare you for this work, so do not worry. Leave everything to Me. If you worry, you are not making Me happy."

"Lord, I'm so sorry. Please forgive me."

"I know you do not know many things, but I see that you are pure-hearted. I know that you believe everything about Me. I've seen your obedience, and I know you fear My words.

"I want you to concentrate only on My work and nothing else. I am pleased about everything about you, My daughter. After you finish this book, I will bless you more than you ever wanted."

"Lord, the only blessing I want is for my whole family to please You more than anything in their lives."

"Because you are what you are, I chose you for this work. This is My book and My responsibility. I will take care of everything. Don't ever worry again. I always want you to be happy because you are My special daughter."

"Lord, I need Roger to help me with so much of Your work."

"Your husband is going to serve Me through you. I have many plans for both of you, so prepare your hearts to serve Me. It will all begin to happen very soon. Now I must take you back."

Worry Is a Sin

We walked back down from the mountain. While we walked on the sand I felt incredibly happy. It was as if a great burden had been lifted from my shoulders. Truly the Lord had shown me many new and important things—things that brought healing and freedom to my timid soul. After the Lord left me this morning, I felt like a new person.

PUT GOD FIRST

I BEGAN TO delve into the Scriptures to see what I could learn about the sin of worry. My eyes were drawn to the words of Jesus that were recorded by Matthew: "But seek first the kingdom of God and His righteousness, and all these things shall be added to you. Therefore do not worry about tomorrow, for tomorrow will worry about its own things" (Matt. 6:33–34).

The context of this passage is the Sermon on the Mount, in which Jesus shares the secrets of spiritual victory with His disciples. Like me, the disciples were fretting over so many things. They worried if they would have food to eat and clothing to wear.

Jesus reminded them:

> So why do you worry about clothing? Consider the lilies of the field, how they grow: they neither toil or spin; and yet I say to you that even Solomon in all his glory was not arrayed like one of these. Now if God so clothes the grass of the field, which today is, and tomorrow is thrown into the oven, will he not much more clothe you, O you of little faith?
>
> —MATTHEW 6:28–30

That's the key—faith! The Holy Spirit then led me to another verse of Scripture that helped clarify this for me: "Whatever is not from faith is sin" (Rom. 14:23). That's why worry is a sin—it is not of faith. God wants us to walk by faith, and yet in His great mercy He had already shown me so much. I had seen the reality of heaven and I had walked with the Lord! Why should I ever worry again?

The season of spring began with another visit to the earthly beach. From 6:30 A.M. to 8:15 A.M. on March 22, the Lord visited with me. He took me to the beach again, and this time He seemed much quieter than He had been three days earlier. Finally, as He sat on the rock on the mountainside where we frequently sat, Jesus said: *"Don't concern yourself with testifying in church, Choo Nam; concentrate on My work."*

He knew that I was literally bursting to tell my story to everyone I saw. Even though I am a shy person, I felt I had to tell everyone what I had seen, heard and experienced. My last visit with the Lord and my subsequent study of the Word had imparted a confidence and boldness to me that I had never known before. I felt as if I could share my story with an audience of millions!

I took every opportunity I could find to testify for my Lord and Master, and I thought He would be greatly pleased by this. In fact, I had such a strong desire to speak on His behalf that I had rehearsed my testimony over and over again with the help of a tape recorder. The anointing of the Holy Spirit seemed to propel me into this kind of public ministry.

Even when I went shopping I told people about heaven. Some people reacted with surprise. Others reacted with joy and wanted to hear more. I told them to read the book when it comes out.

Some people, as I could tell by their facial reactions, didn't want to hear about my journeys to heaven, but I had learned that their doubtful responses were not important. I knew I had a story to tell, and no human reaction could keep me from sharing the excitement I had experienced.

I soon found that most Christians wanted to hear more. Many were asking, "When will the book be finished?" Most of the people I know are believers, including the members of my extended family who all have given their support to me by saying they believe my story. As I shared my story with one nephew, he was drawn to the Lord. Now he goes to a Bible class and attends church regularly and is hungry for the Lord.

The Lord was not displeased with me, but He emphatically reiterated, *"I want you to concentrate on the book; then you will be able to satisfy many churches and reach the unsaved."*

The sound of His voice, His words, His message was a wave of joy to my spirit. I began singing in the Spirit, and I noticed that the Lord was looking at my face and smiling, and I could see the face of my transformed body smiling at the Lord the whole time I was singing.

"My daughter, I enjoy the time we spend together," the Lord stated as He placed my right hand under His arm. He didn't talk much for a long time, but finally spoke.

"I want you to write about how you live your Christian life. It is important for others to know how you have lived your life with Me, to

see how open your heart has been to Me. Your honest and obedient life is so important to Me, and I know you always put Me first in your life. When you pray, you always say you will put Me first—that I'm more important to you than anyone else or anything in the world.

"I want you to know that I've heard all your prayers even though it may seem that I have not answered each one. I know the hearts of all My children. I cannot bless anyone who does not have a sincere heart, but I do want all of My children to be blessed."

After He left me this time I reflected on His words. He had seemed so genuinely pleased with me, and I was thrilled to hear Him say that He had heard all my prayers. He led me to an important passage in the Bible: "Now this is the confidence that we have in Him, that if we ask anything according to His will, He hears us. And if we know that He hears us, whatever we ask, we know that we have the petitions that we have asked of Him" (1 John 5:14–15). God hears and answers the sincere prayers of His children.

He showed me so many rich and precious prayer promises, and I knew He wanted me to claim each one:

> He shall call upon me, and I will answer him: I will be with him in trouble; I will deliver him, and honor him. With long life will I satisfy him, and shew him my salvation.
>
> —PSALM 91:15–16, KJV

> The Lord is nigh unto all them that call upon him, to all that call upon him in truth.
>
> —PSALM 145:18, KJV

> Call unto me, and I will answer thee, and shew thee great and mighty things, which thou knowest not.
>
> —JEREMIAH 33:3, KJV

> Your Father knoweth what things ye have need of, before ye ask him.
>
> —MATTHEW 6:8, KJV

> Ask, and it shall be given you; seek, and ye shall find; knock, and it shall be opened unto you: For every one that asketh receiveth; and he that seeketh findeth; and to him that knocketh it shall be opened.
>
> —MATTHEW 7:7–8, KJV

And all things, whatsoever ye shall ask in prayer, believing, ye shall receive.

—MATTHEW 21:22, KJV

These were just a few of the mighty prayer promises from God's Word that the Holy Spirit revealed to me. On March 23 I was praying intensely under a great anointing from the Holy Spirit. My body was shaking very hard, and groanings from deep within my spirit were coming forth with a violence I had never experienced before.

The Lord came into my room and sat by the window. Then I saw my transformed body sitting next to the Lord, and I was greatly surprised. It was as if I was having a total out-of-the-body experience—I was pure spirit. Jesus' tender voice spoke to me: *"You are living your life completely for Me. Your heart has willingly given up all worldly things for Me. I now know that nothing brings satisfaction to you more than being in My presence. Therefore, I never want you to say that you are not good enough for Me. Your faithfulness is very important to Me."*

An unusual, unearthly voice emanated from my spirit. This phenomenon usually accompanies the visions the Lord gives to me.

Then the Lord showed me His feet and hands. I could see the scars from the nails in His feet and hands. At first He sat with His legs crossed, but then He straightened His legs. I noticed that the tops of both of his feet had deep round scars on them. Then I looked at His hands—there were round, white scars very close to His wrists.

My heart ached for my Lord and Master. I touched His hands and His feet. Then I put my face on His hands and feet and began to cry in heaving sobs. I was crying like a baby as I realized all the Lord had gone through. I wondered if the whole household could hear me crying. I could see my transformed body with its face on the Lord's hands and feet, rubbing so gently—and I could tell I was crying in my transformed body. The Lord began to speak.

"When I was on this earth I lived for My Father's words, and I knew what I would have to face, but I lived for My Father's words. That's why all of heaven and earth are Mine now.

"So many of My children know what I want them to do, but they still love the things of this world more than My words. The children who live with My Word, according to My Word, are the ones who are pure

of heart. *They are the only ones who will enter the mansions I've pre-pared for them, like the one you saw with your name on the door. No one can have both this kingdom and My kingdom. If anyone enjoys the world more than Me, he or she cannot enter My kingdom.*"

This was the strongest message the Lord had given to me so far. I knew I had to record it carefully and faithfully so the world would know that He wants to be first in all of our lives. He created us and died for us so we would not have to perish in hell. He continued.

"*When I was in this world, I suffered until the end. I gave My life for My children. I want them to live with My Word so that they can have eternal life with Me. This worldly life can never compare with My kingdom.*"

When He said these words, He sounded sad and hurt.

I'll never forget those words—and I know they are so true. This life has nothing to compare with the kingdom of God. I've seen it, and I know His kingdom is prepared for us.

Chapter 10

Jerusalem Is Ready

*Behold, I am coming quickly! Hold fast what you have,
that no one may take your crown. He who overcomes, I will make him a
pillar in the temple of My God, and he shall go out no more.
I will write on him the name of My God and the name of the city of My
God, the New Jerusalem, which comes down out of heaven
from My God. And I will write on him My new name.*

—REVELATION 3:11–12

I
T WAS SPRINGTIME—the season of marvelous flowers, warm breezes
and blossoming trees. In Washington state, where I live, it is a spectacular time of year. In heaven, it seems like it is perpetually springtime—
warmth, beauty, peace and joy are everywhere. In my heart I had been
celebrating springtime throughout the now-ending winter because of
my visits with the Lord and my intriguing trips to heaven.

On March 24, Roger and I attended church services. Our pastor
preached about Jesus' suffering before the crucifixion. It was Lent—the
time of year when Christians prepare for the crucifixion and resurrection
of Jesus Christ. As the pastor described the Lord's suffering and read
Scriptures related to His passion, I began to cry. It was not uncommon
for me to shake during our times of worship, but this time my body
was shaking so severely that it almost knocked me out of my seat. The
anointing of the Holy Spirit was strong upon me.

SCARRED HANDS AND FEET

I SAW JESUS in front of me and He said, *"My daughter, I want you to
look at My hands again,"* and He pointed to the scars on His hands and
feet. The unusual voice that I used for vocalizing when spiritual visions

came to me did not come forth this time. I sat in the Lord's presence in total silence as He continued to speak to me.

"I want you to keep on writing everything I show you," He directed. I nodded my agreement.

It was incomparably wonderful to be able to visit privately with the Lord during our public worship service. I wanted to stand up and tell everyone I had just seen the Lord and that He had shown me His scars, but something deep in my spirit cautioned me not to do this, so I sat patiently until the service was over. I believe it was the "still, small voice" of God's Holy Spirit that told me not to speak.

Since that time I have learned that there is, as Solomon wrote, a time to speak and a time to remain silent (see Eccles. 3:7). Jesus was training me to become sensitive to the Spirit's leading in my life, and I knew that until He directed me otherwise I was to be receiving instead of giving.

Throughout the service I cried under the precious anointing of the Holy Spirit. The shaking subsided when the Lord left, but the tears did not. I heard the pastor's words, but my mind and spirit were focused on something else—the scars the Lord had now shown me twice.

I began to meditate on some of the Scriptures I had remembered from my study and other church services: "But He was wounded for our transgressions, He was bruised for our iniquities; the chastisement for our peace was upon Him, and by His stripes we are healed" (Isa. 53:5); "And when they had come to a place called Golgotha, that is to say, Place of a Skull, they gave Him sour wine mingled with gall to drink. But when He had tasted it, He would not drink. Then they crucified Him, and divided His garments, casting lots" (Matt. 27:33–35).

I could see my precious Lord and Master hanging on the cross of Calvary, atop Golgotha's hill. The sharp spikes ripped at the flesh of His palms and ankles as He hung there so weak and limp. The Roman soldier's spear opened a gaping wound in His side, and streams of blood coursed down His face from the crown of thorns they had pushed onto His head.

There was a puddle of blood at the foot of the cross, and the people stepped into His blood as they clambered, trying to get His seamless robe. The sky overhead was lead gray, and lightning flashed in the distance.

The people mocked Him, spit at Him and cursed Him. They were having a fiendish party at my Master's expense. Then, in my mind's eye,

I saw His mother—Mary—bowing near the cross, her body trembling and tears forming rivers on her face.

Oh, how I understood how she must have felt on that first Good Friday—she had to watch her naked son, the one she loved so much, being tortured and killed in front of her—and there was nothing she could do to stop it. Jesus could have called 10,000 angels to come to His assistance, but instead He chose to accept the cruel, shameful death of crucifixion so that we could find the path of life.

I thank God for the vision He imparted to me, for now I truly understand all that Jesus went through for the people He loves so much. He was suspended on the cruel cross, between heaven and hell, so that we would have eternal life. He never sinned, and yet He willingly took all of our sin upon Him. What a wonderful Savior He is!

The scars on His hands and feet are real. I've seen them. They are the marks of horrendous suffering—anguish He experienced for you and me.

FISH IN HEAVEN?

ON MARCH 25 Jesus visited with me from 6:35 A.M. to 8:50 A.M. We walked and talked together in the usual way—at the beach, over the golden bridge, along the winding road. After walking on the usual road for a while, the Lord escorted me to a different path, along a road that was wide and white. It looked like a highway in America, and it was lined with trees on both sides.

These trees were unusually tall and their leaves were the most beautiful I'd ever seen. As we walked, I noticed that the trees began to change their colors. It was like walking along a rainbow—the array of colors was spectacular!

This road led to a hill that was much smaller than the mountain we usually climbed. From the rising crest I noticed a silver river shining in the sunlight of heaven. Mountain ranges filled the panorama with a beauty that only heaven could produce. The mountains seemed to be forested with evergreen trees.

We descended the hillside and walked to the water where we saw all kinds of fish swimming in the river over a rocky bottom. It amused me to see fish in heaven, and I began to laugh. I was enjoying the moment so much that I stepped out and began wading in the water.

I reached down and grabbed a red, striped fish and lifted it out of the water. I was laughing uncontrollably, so the fish jumped out of my hands and swam to safety. Watching my former captive swim away, in total freedom, cavorting with the other fish, caused me to giggle hysterically. I grabbed another fish—this one a different color—and it jumped out of my hands as well. It was a wonderful time of joy and fun, and the Lord began to laugh with me.

He began to participate in the action with me by reaching down and grabbing a large fish colored like "a coat of many colors." He looked at the fish admiringly and then threw it back into the river, still laughing. It was so good to see the Lord enjoying the moment with me.

I just kept on laughing—deep, belly laughs—and it felt so good. The more I heard the Lord's laughter, the more I laughed. Finally, I was doubled over with laughter, but it felt so good.

Jesus said, *"Daughter, you must be enjoying this. Do you like fishing?"*

"I'm just enjoying being here, Lord."

"I have more fish to show you later. Do you want to catch more fish?"

"I am laughing too hard to catch any fish, Lord," I acknowledged amid waves of laughter.

"We'd better go back now, my daughter. I have to take you to another place."

We left the river, and I felt so cleansed by the preceding moments of joy and laughter. The fish were fun, and I remembered, "A merry heart does good, like medicine" (Prov. 17:22). I felt like I had had a dose of joy that would last me a lifetime!

It was so wonderful to see my Lord taking such obvious delight in my pleasure and happiness. This experience helped me understand the verse: "You will show me the path of life; in Your presence is fullness of joy; at Your right hand are pleasures forevermore" (Ps. 16:11).

I had walked along the path of life in heaven, and I had drunk from the river of His pleasures as the psalmist depicted: "How precious is Your lovingkindness, O God! Therefore the children of men put their trust under the shadow of Your wings. They are abundantly satisfied with the fullness of Your house, and You give them drink from the river of Your pleasures. For with You is the fountain of life; in Your light we see light" (Ps. 36:7–9).

My joy was brimming up like a fountain and overflowing like a waterfall.

FLYING THROUGH HEAVEN

WE RETURNED ON the same road we had taken to get to the hillside. Then the Lord took me to a high mountain on a very narrow road that was bordered by huge trees and bushes. We walked along this road for quite a while. This caused me to wonder where we were going. I also wondered why the road was so narrow.

Finally we reached the end of the road where I looked over the hill and saw a white fence surrounding many white buildings. They glistened with the purest white—a whiteness more brilliant than freshly fallen snow. I wished that I could get closer to the scene in front of me, but as was so often the case, Jesus showed this setting to me from a distance. I did not understand why.

He spoke to me, *"My daughter, I want you to see it clearly, so we must go down there."* He reached over, took my hand, and we began flying. It was a breathtaking experience, and a loud groan emerged from my real body.

When we landed in the fertile valley, Jesus took me to this pure white street. Then I noticed that it had beautiful white houses on both sides. The street was white and shiny like glass. Everything seemed so white there. The fence seemed to be much higher than the houses that I saw from the top of the hill.

It is not possible, at this time, for me to explain, or even to suggest, why the Lord has shown me some of the things He has. Many times He has shown me the same things on two separate occasions. We usually haven't spent much time at each site, and He has offered few explanations of their meanings, but that's all right with me because I know the time will come when I will know even as I am known (see 1 Cor. 13:12).

The Lord told me that He must show me this, and we approached one of the houses. It had double doors with golden trim. The door was outlined with colored glass. I took particular notice of the door knob made of pure gold!

As we entered the house, I noticed that all the windows were made of stained glass. The carpeting was colorful—a mixture of subdued hues—and it gave the interior of the house a very classic look. The jewels that adorned the walls sparkled and shone. I felt as if I were stepping into a picture rather than a house.

I walked up the golden stairway that had an intricate design etched into its surface. At the top of the stairs, I walked into a bedroom where a bed stood that was grander and larger than any king-sized bed on earth. I walked around it and into the powder room. It was laden with gold and precious gems on every wall except one. That wall had a full-length mirror to reflect the amazing beauty of the immediate environment.

I noticed that all the rooms in this house were immense, including the powder room. In fact, every house the Lord showed me had huge rooms that were beautiful beyond all expectations.

I began to sing with joy as I walked along the corridors, entering each room and enjoying such a blessed dwelling. After my excursion through the upstairs was over, I went downstairs, where the Lord was walking around in a room that was much like a parlor. He heard me, turned, looked at me, and said, *"Do you like this place?"*

"Yes, my Lord. It's beautiful. Who will live in these houses You are showing to me?"

"All of my children will live in these houses I've prepared for them. They will be living here sooner than they think."

THE HOLY CITY

THE LORD TOOK my hand and we left the lovely valley. Next, we walked on a divided street that was the same color as the yellow brick road in *The Wizard of Oz.* There were white houses on both sides of the street. The island in the middle of the road was adorned with fruit trees that had been evenly placed along a clear, blue stream that was indescribably long. There were many beautiful rocks on both sides of the stream.

Then the Lord took my hand and said, *"We are going up, My daughter."* We lifted from the ground straight up, like a helicopter does, and then we began to fly. He took me to the same mountain where we had started this particular journey.

As we took flight, my earthly body, lying on the bed, was screaming in panic. In my transformed body, however, I was getting somewhat accustomed to the extraordinary things I experienced in heaven. We walked back onto the narrow road and went to the white building where we always change our garments. Next, we proceeded to the quiet pond.

The minute we arrived at the pond I began to sing and dance. My heart was still flying with joy. The Lord said, *"Come, Choo Nam, sit by Me."*

I obeyed by taking a seat on the rock next to Him and holding His arm.

"My daughter, I showed you the river and New Jerusalem. Those houses are in Jerusalem—the Holy City. We will all live in Jerusalem when I bring My children home. I want all of my children to know that Jerusalem is ready for them.

"You saw there was no road to get into Jerusalem. Therefore, we had to fly to get there. We all will fly there soon—that is why your work is so important."

"I don't want you to miss anything I've shown you or told you," the Lord continued. *"I know some people will not believe many of the things I've shown you—the doubtful and ones who don't know My Word—but I know how hard you are trying to please Me.*

"After you finish this work, your life will be pure joy—far greater than what you've just experienced. You will be blessed. Whoever believes you and helps you will be blessed as well.

"You will be a surprise to all the churches, a joy to those ready and waiting for Me and sad news to those who love the world more than Me. This book will help to deliver many people who are in spiritual darkness.

"Daughter, you must not be concerned with what people think or say; just write down what I show you and tell you. I trust your obedience completely. You have always feared and believed My Word since you knew me. I notice that you have not been deliberately disobedient since you gave your heart to Me, and you always put Me first in your life. That is why I chose you as My special daughter and friend."

His words were both humbling and reassuring. They made me feel good. One thing I knew for sure—since I had become a Christian I had always endeavored to please My Lord, to put Him first in every situation and decision. He was blessing My obedience.

"It took a long time to prepare you for this work," He said. *"Now you know how special you are to Me. You said that you had given your life to Me, and I know your heart. Don't ever deviate from this commitment, Choo Nam.*

"Whatever you have to give up, or lose, in your earthly life will be restored to you in heaven. In heaven, you will be with Me forever."

To me, those were the most important words of all. It was this promise that kept me going, because I know how immeasurably wonderful it is to be with Him. The thrill of knowing that I would be in His presence forever was the most blessed thought of all.

"Lord, I am not that good," I cried. "It's just that I love You more than my own life. I am not happy with anyone or anything unless You are included. I feel Your control in every part of my life, and it makes me so very happy."

"Whoever permits Me to control their life will be blessed. These are My obedient children. You are My special child."

When the visit was over I pondered the many things Jesus had told me. The New Jerusalem is coming from heaven. It is ready now. The Lord wants His children to enjoy eternal glory with Him. He has selected me to share all this with anyone who will listen.

Throughout the day I studied what the Scriptures have to say about the New Jerusalem. When I read the twenty-first chapter of Revelation, I realized that the apostle John had had the same experience with the Lord that I had just enjoyed.

> And he carried me away in the Spirit to a great and high mountain, and showed me the great city, the holy Jerusalem, descending out of heaven from God, having the glory of God. And her light was like a most precious stone, like a jasper stone, clear as crystal.
> —REVELATION 21:10–11

I was enthralled by his description of the heavenly city, because I had seen so many of the things he wrote about.

> But I saw no temple in it, for the Lord God Almighty and the Lamb are its temple. And the city had no need of the sun or of the moon to shine in it, for the glory of God illuminated it, and the Lamb is its light.
> —REVELATION 21:22–23

I had walked in the brightness of that city. I felt I was surrounded by snow because everything was white and bright. Like John, I had noticed that there were no churches or temples in the New Jerusalem, only beautiful homes that the Lord had prepared for His children.

Its gates shall not be shut at all by day (there shall be no night there). And they shall bring the glory and the honor of the nations into it. But there shall by no means enter it anything that defiles, or causes an abomination or a lie, but only those who are written in the Lamb's Book of Life.

—REVELATION 21:25–27

This is what Jesus had been telling me—heaven is reserved for those who will obey. Only the pure in heart will be able to enter and live there.

I continued my reading, into chapter 22, and I was truly taken aback by this confirmation of the reality of heaven that I had experienced.

And he showed me a pure river of water of life, clear as crystal, proceeding from the throne of God and of the Lamb. In the middle of its street, and on either side of the river, was the tree of life, which bore twelve fruits, each tree yielding its fruit every month. And the leaves of the tree were for the healing of the nations.

—REVELATION 22:1–2

I had tasted the water of that river, and I had walked down the streets. I had seen the trees and had even tasted the fruit of some.

The message that Jesus gave to John was the same as the one He gave to me. This is the message that the Lord wants me to share with everyone who will listen: "Behold, I am coming quickly! Blessed is he who keeps the words of the prophecy of this book" (Rev. 22:7).

The Lord is just, and He wants everyone to know: "Behold, I am coming quickly, and My reward is with Me, to give to every one according to his work. I am the Alpha and the Omega, the Beginning and the End, the First and the Last" (Rev. 22:12–13).

Chapter 11

Heavenly Food, Heavenly Pleasures

Blessed are those who are called to the
marriage supper of the Lamb.

—REVELATION 19:9 (EMPHASIS ADDED)

THIRTY MINUTES OF deep trembling throughout my body occurred before the Lord's arrival on March 27. I was able to be with Him from 6:30 A.M. to 8:45 A.M. After the half hour of shaking, the Lord came to me and took my hand.

In my transformed body, I walked with the Lord on the beach, and then He escorted me to heaven. We walked through the pearly gates and went to the white building to change our clothing. After changing, we walked across the golden bridge.

It all was becoming so natural to me. Each believer, I'm sure, will go through the same procedures when he or she goes to heaven. I began to think of the individuals in the Bible with whom I shared the privilege of visiting heaven before death. The apostle Paul wrote about one of these fortunate souls in the twelfth chapter of 2 Corinthians.

> I know a man in Christ who fourteen years ago—whether in the body I do not know, or whether out of the body I do not know, God knows—such a one was caught up to the third heaven. And I know such a man—whether in the body or out of the body I do not know, God knows—how he was caught up into Paradise and heard inexpressible words, which it is not lawful for a man to utter.
>
> —2 CORINTHIANS 12:2–4

I know exactly what the man experienced, for there are many things I saw and heard in heaven that I am not permitted to share with others.

BIBLICAL VISITS TO HEAVEN

THE APOSTLE JOHN, as has been recorded in the book of Revelation, also went to heaven. His visit there was preceded by a personal visit from the Lord Jesus Christ, who said: "I am the Alpha and the Omega, the Beginning and the End...who is and who was and who is to come, the Almighty" (Rev. 1:8). Like John's, my visits to heaven always began with a visit from the Lord.

The prophet Elijah went to heaven, as well. Part of what was recorded about his heavenly encounter states: "Then it happened, as they continued on and talked, that suddenly a chariot of fire appeared with horses of fire, and separated the two of them; and Elijah went up by a whirlwind into heaven" (2 Kings 2:11). Elijah flew to heaven by way of a whirlwind, and I believe my flights to heaven could be described in a similar way.

God had been gracious to many others before me—people whom He has taken to heaven before death. In each case, there was a prevailing purpose for the visits to heaven. Always, God has been concerned about letting His people know that He wants them to live with Him forever.

How privileged I am to be among the select few He has honored in this way. The more I think about it, it's not because I'm particularly special but simply because I want only to obey and serve my Lord throughout all eternity. It thrills me to let others know about my trips to heaven.

FOOD FOR THE KINGDOM

THE LORD AND I walked along the road for a long time, then we turned to the right, walking down the hillside to some steps made from rock. I saw a body of water that looked like a very long, narrow river.

"What I am going to show you, My daughter, will be very special for My children."

There were magnificent fruit trees on both sides of the river. On one side, the trees bore purple fruit; on the other side, the trees were laden with beautiful, red fruit. These fruits were so attractive, and I longed to taste them. The red fruit was shaped like large teardrops.

The Lord must have known my desire to try these fruits, so He reached up, picked one and gave it to me to eat. It was unlike any fruit I had eaten. It was so delicious that my physical body's mouth drooled down the side of my face.

"Why aren't You eating, Lord?"

"I'm not hungry, but I'm glad to see that you are enjoying it."

We walked for a long time, and then I saw a picturesque bridge built from red wood. As we walked over it, I looked down and saw that the stream was filled with many different kinds of fish.

"What are all the fish for?" I asked.

"This is food for the kingdom," the Lord replied.

It made me happy to know that we will be eating fruit and fish in heaven. The fact that these are the primary foods of the kingdom suggests that we should be eating more of them on earth. I've always thought that fish and fruit are particularly healthful foods, and this visit to heaven confirmed that for me.

Seeing fish swimming so freely in the water always makes me laugh. I began to chuckle and then I asked, "Lord, where can we cook them?" Before He answered I noticed the voice that accompanies my supernatural visions came forth. Therefore I knew the Lord wanted to show me something.

I could see the right side of the water, and I noticed that a large, high rock wall stretched out so far I couldn't see the end. It was so high I couldn't see the top of it. I could see the pure white sand stretching from the road all the way to the rock wall. There were no trees in the particular vicinity I saw, but the sand looked so white and clean. The scene imparted to me through this supernatural vision was immensely beautiful.

In a few moments the Lord answered my question by wading into the water and grabbing a large, flat, white fish. It was about the size of my two hands together. I enjoyed watching the Lord do this for me, and I found the scene to be very amusing. I began to giggle as I continued to watch Him.

Next, I walked with Him beyond the rocks, where I noticed many large cooking areas that had silver-colored ovens built into the rocks. Atop the ovens were cooking grilles with oval-shaped plates and silver forks. The Lord simply pushed a button on the side of one oven and a fire began.

He then assumed the role of a cook, right in front of me. He grilled the fish until both sides of it were brown. He seemed to be so happy doing this for me.

For some reason, I wanted to eat the tail end of the fish, so I pointed to it and the Lord gave me that half of the fish. He ate the other half while I devoured the portion He gave me. It was delicious. Truly, I'd never tasted such tender, luscious fish before. The Lord watched as I enjoyed my heavenly meal.

When we finished eating, He took my plate and fork and put them into a silver container. Then He said, *"My daughter, as you can see, I have prepared everything for My children."*

I smiled with pure joy.

Then we returned to the road and went back to the white building where we always change. An angel escorted me to the powder room, and after I had changed into a beautiful robe and crown, the Lord was waiting for me.

He took my hand, and we went out to the pond. There, I began to sing and dance, as was my usual custom. This day I felt special, so humble about what the Lord was doing for me; more so than any other day since He had started taking me to heaven.

It wasn't because I ate the fish; it was because my Lord and Savior cooked the fish and we ate it together. He showed me His loving kindness as He did to His disciples before He went to heaven. All these thoughts came to my mind while I was dancing.

Then the Lord called me over to sit next to Him. I put my hand under His arm, and my face on His shoulder, then I began to cry. "Please let me stay here with You, Lord. I don't ever want to leave You. This is the happiest moment of my life."

"Daughter, you must do this work for Me. I do not want you to miss anything I have shown you or told you. I know you do not have time for yourself, but after everything is completed, you will be blessed."

"Lord, only Roger can help me with the writing, and he is already doing so much for me."

"Tell him that I love him. I will bless him more than he expects. Also tell him to spend more time with Me. Anyone who loves Me must spend much time with Me."

It was a wonderful time of sweet communion with the Lord. When our conversation was over, we returned to the white building and changed into our white robes. Then we returned to earth and walked along the beach. We sat on the shore, and I put my arm under His and said, "I love You, Lord."

"I love you, My precious daughter," He responded in a voice that was filled with happiness. *"Tell everyone that there are so many things to eat in My kingdom. Everything here will taste so much better than any earthly food. Did you like the fish?"*

I nodded my appreciation. As we stood, the Lord embraced me and then departed.

The Lord is more friendly and loving each time I see Him. I remember at first, He didn't hug me or call me His daughter or use any other sweet words. Now He calls me many sweet names. I feel He is very comfortable with me.

A PLACE OF PLEASURE

THE BIBLE SAYS: "You will show me the path of life; in Your presence is fullness of joy; at Your right hand are pleasures forevermore" (Ps. 16:11). My visits to heaven have shown me the truth of this verse. Heaven is a place of eternal pleasure. The Lord delights in pleasing His children. He wants us to be happy.

On March 29 I was with the Lord from 6:40 A.M. to 8:45 A.M. My body shook for twenty-five minutes that morning, then I heard the Lord's voice and saw His presence. He took my hand, and I saw my transformed body walking along the beach with Him. We walked along the shore for a few minutes and then we went up to heaven.

We changed our garments in the white building as usual. Then we walked over the golden bridge, along a wide road that we had not been on before. It led to a very barren area where there were no grasses, trees or mountains. The whole scene was white, as if we had entered an Arctic wasteland. We continued walking until we reached the end of the road.

A huge river appeared in front of us, and I noticed mountains on both sides of the water. The one on the right was extremely high. We walked very close to the river, where the soil was like gravel. Tiny pebbles clicked under our feet as we walked.

The river was filled with small boats. I had seen similar scenes on earth—bodies of water where people went to fish, swim, water-ski and simply to enjoy boating.

"Would you like to ride in one of the boats?" the Lord asked.

"Yes," I eagerly responded, "I'd love to."

We climbed into one of the small boats, and the Lord paddled with

His hand. He took us a good way out. When I looked over the edge of the boat, I saw a multitude of different-colored fish frolicking in the water.

My gaze was fixed on the uncommonly clear water. I could see into its depths so vividly. It was like the clearest crystal I'd ever seen. The fish, as usual, caused me to begin laughing.

They were amazingly bright and beautiful fish. They looked like the large decorative fish that people on earth use in their backyard ponds.

"These, My daughter, are for pleasure. Like you, I love to watch the fish swim around in the water."

It was so peaceful and serene on the quiet water. As I looked around, I felt as if we were sitting atop a giant looking-glass. We left the boat and walked along the same road we had taken to get to the lake; then we turned onto a narrow, mountain trail. The magnificent vista at the end of the path revealed a lush, low valley that was filled with tall grass. A narrow stream wound its way through the wide-open pastureland.

I saw something moving through the wheatlike fields. Then I saw other movement all over the wheat field. The valley was filled with cattle that looked very much like the cows on earth.

"Write this down, Choo Nam. I want all My children to know what awaits them in heaven. I know many of My children have questions about heaven. Some of them wonder if there will be food to eat in heaven."

I knew the answer to that question, and a sense of great pleasure filled me as I looked out upon the spectacular vista in front of me. I could scarcely take it all in.

We weren't able to stay there long, however. Soon the Lord took me back to the white building where we changed our clothing and then went to the pond. I began to sing for joy. Then I sat next to the Lord.

"Did you enjoy the boat ride, My daughter?" He asked.

"Oh, yes, Lord."

"When I bring My children here, I want them to have pleasure. They can do many of the same things they do on earth. I want them to be happy. You must remember all the things I showed you and talked about.

"I do not want you to be confused about anything. That is why I tell you so many important things over and over again and show you the same thing more than once."

We returned to the white building, changed and went back to the beach on earth. The Lord seemed to be in a hurry, so we didn't sit and talk this time. He simply hugged me and left. As always, my body stopped shaking as soon as He departed.

WATER FOR THE EARTH

AS THE LOVELY month of April began, the Lord appeared in my bedroom on the morning of April 1, at 6:20 A.M. I was with Him until 8:35 A.M. My body shook for thirty minutes, and then He came and talked to me. He stretched out His hand, and I saw my heavenly body at the beach, and then He took me to heaven.

After changing our clothing, we walked across the golden bridge. Our journey took us along a wide road with enormous rocks on both sides. It was a longer walk than usual, and it led us to the end of the road where a high rock mountain stood. It was so high that I could not see its summit, but I noticed that it had huge black rocks jutting out from its base. Between the rocks, big waves flowed up and down in an almost stormy fashion. The water looked to be very deep.

There was no road down to the water, so we simply looked at it from the side of the mountain. The body of water appeared to be filling a big hole. The Lord explained, "This water is for the earth."

As is so often the case, the Lord does not fully explain the meaning of His words. Often, He will simply tell me what certain things are, and what they may be used for. When I ask Him direct questions, however, He will usually provide me with an answer.

Most of the time, though, I don't feel led to ask Him about what He shows me, because I know that one day it will all be clear to me. My job now is simply to be a scribe who writes down what He shows me and tells me, and I know He will offer a full explanation whenever He deems it necessary.

We turned away from this scene and walked again on the long road. When we reached an intersection, we took a side road that meandered very close to the golden bridge that led to a beach. As we traveled along this road, I noticed many houses situated around the water.

In back of the houses there were fruit trees of all sorts. It was a very orderly orchard. The first rows consisted of pale green trees that were filled with purple fruits. The next grouping was of larger trees with red leaves. The colors were multitudinous and blended together in a most delightful way. The array of colors was so spectacular that it took my breath away.

There were not any mountains in this particular region of heaven— only water, sand, houses and trees. It was such a vast area that I could not see where it ended.

The Lord took me into one of the houses. This one was greatly different from the mansions and castles we had visited before. Its interior was quite simple, and its colors were somewhat subdued.

"These are beach houses for My children," the Lord explained.

It was amazing! We'll have vacation homes in heaven! Truly, the Lord does want His children to be happy and to enjoy His pleasures forevermore.

After this joyful visit, the Lord and I changed our robes and returned to the placid pond where I sang and danced before Him. I knew the Lord was smiling with great delight even though I could not see His face clearly.

He called me to sit by Him, and once more I began to cry, because I knew the end of our visit was drawing close. Whenever I am with Him, I do not want to leave. His presence is fullness of joy.

I sat next to Him, and He said: *"I have prepared many things in My kingdom that My children enjoy on earth. There are many activities. I made sure that no one would be bored. Everyone will have different assignments.*

"Why do you think I chose prophets to work for Me on earth? Like you, I've sent them in order to do My work. Without prophets, I would not have any way of communicating my desires to My children.

"Therefore, My daughter, do not miss writing about anything I show you or tell you. Tell it all. It is because you are such an obedient daughter that I am able to use you.

"We must go back now."

He took my hand, and we changed and returned to the beach on earth. Again, we did not sit and talk. The Lord simply hugged me and departed. Again my physical body stopped shaking as soon as He left.

Chapter 12

Enjoy
the Kingdom

*That the genuineness of your faith, being much more precious
than gold that perishes, though it is tested by fire, may be found
to praise, honor, and glory at the revelation of Jesus Christ, whom having
not seen you love. Though now you do not see Him,
yet believing, you rejoice with joy inexpressible and full of glory, receiving
the end of your faith—the salvation of your souls.*

—1 PETER 1:7–9

FOR MANY CENTURIES, the beautiful dove has symbolized two things: peace and the Holy Spirit. When John the Baptist immersed Jesus in the Jordan River, the Spirit of God descended "in bodily form like a dove upon Him, and a voice came from heaven which said, 'You are My beloved Son; in You I am well pleased'" (Luke 3:22). It was the dove that announced to Noah that the waters of the Great Deluge had dried up. It's not surprising, therefore, that I encountered doves on my next visit to heaven.

It was the morning of April 3, and the Lord was with me from 6:00 A.M. to 8:30 A.M. After thirty minutes of shaking and groaning, I heard the Lord's voice and He took my hand. Soon thereafter, I saw my transformed body walking on the beach with the Lord.

We went to heaven together where we changed into different robes. We crossed over the golden bridge and walked on the right side of a road. It was a very wide road that had a canopy of leaves overhead from the mighty trees that grew on either side of the road. This was a different road from any we had walked on before.

We walked for a long while and then took a road to the right. We walked for quite a while on this road as well. It encircled the base of a large, rocky mountain. To our left, there was a wide valley filled with green trees. The middle of the valley seemed to be filled with white gravel.

HEAVENLY DOVES

AS I LOOKED over the serene valley, I noticed movement in the region of the white gravel. The area was filled with birds.

"Lord, what kind of birds are they?" I asked.

"They are doves."

"Why are there so many doves here?"

"They are very important to Me."

It was a magnificent place—so large and so beautiful. We climbed atop a solid rock wall upon which we could stand and watch the doves of heaven. We remained there for a long time, and I was profoundly moved by what I was seeing.

AN ENDLESS OCEAN

WE STEPPED DOWN from the wall and resumed our walk along the road. A short time later we reached a narrow road on the left onto which we turned and proceeded. Around a little curve in the road I noticed a massive ocean that was so vast that it appeared to have no end. As we neared the waterfront, I noticed a high rock wall that had steps leading down to the shoreline. We went up the wall and walked down the steps.

The edge of the sea was filled with boats, large and small. It was a marina in heaven, and each boat was chained to a thick bar. All of their hulls were white. As I got closer, I noticed every boat had a beautifully furnished cabin and windows of stained glass. They resembled little churches on the water.

"Would you like to ride in one of the boats, My daughter?" the Lord asked.

"Oh, yes!" I exclaimed.

He led me to one of the boats, and we climbed in. The interior of the cabin was immaculate, but the boat was large enough for only two people. There were two seats in the front and two steering wheels.

I began to remember how our Lord had related to the sea, nature and fishing during His earthly ministry. Peter, James and John—three of His disciples—had been fishermen. He frequently preached on the shores of the Sea of Galilee, and He often used fish as object lessons.

The story of Jesus calming the raging waves came to mind.

> And suddenly a great tempest arose on the sea, so that the boat
> was covered with the waves. But He was asleep. Then His disciples
> came to Him and awoke Him, saying, "Lord, save us! We are per-
> ishing!" But He said to them, "Why are you fearful, O you of little
> faith?" Then He arose and rebuked the winds and the sea. And
> there was a great calm. And the men marveled, saying, "Who can
> this be, that even the winds and the sea obey Him?"
>
> —MATTHEW 8:24–27

Jesus loves the sea! He loves the world of nature He created. And
He wants us to enjoy it as well. In fact, when the creation took place,
human beings were to live in a paradise more wonderful than any we
can possibly imagine—the Garden of Eden—a place of purity, innocence,
perpetual springtime, fruitfulness, peace and joy. But because human
beings sinned, we were banned from that earthly paradise.

God, in His great love, however, made a way for us to regain paradise in heaven. He sent His Son to die for us: "For God so loved the
world that He gave His only begotten Son, that whoever believes in
Him should not perish but have everlasting life" (John 3:16). Paradise
lost was regained through the death and resurrection of His Son.

The more I study the book of Genesis, the more I realize that the
Garden of Eden was a replica of heaven on earth. It is the kind of existence God wants His children to enjoy. There was no death, pain, suffering, darkness or disease in Eden, and there will certainly be none in
our heavenly home!

What a wonderland it must have been, and heaven's beauty even surpasses this description of Eden:

> The LORD God planted a garden eastward in Eden, and there He
> put the man whom He had formed. And out of the ground the
> LORD God made every tree grow that is pleasant to the sight and
> good for food. The tree of life was also in the midst of the garden,
> and the tree of the knowledge of good and evil. Now a river went
> out of Eden to water the garden."
>
> —GENESIS 2:8–10

I began to realize it is not surprising that our heavenly home will be
like the most fantastic places of earth—the oceans, forests, fields, trees,

flowers, birds, animals, fruits and rivers are there for us to enjoy just as God had created them for us in Eden. Because of sin, we lost our right to enjoy such an earthly paradise, but through faith in Jesus Christ paradise will one day be restored to each of us! Won't it be wonderful there?

My mind then turned to the passage about Jesus when He walked on the water:

> Now when evening came, the boat was in the middle of the sea; and He was alone on the land. Then He saw them straining at rowing, for the wind was against them. And about the fourth watch of the night He came to them, walking on the sea, and would have passed them by.
>
> But when they saw Him walking on the sea, they supposed it was a ghost, and cried out; for they all saw Him and were troubled. And immediately He talked with them and said to them, "Be of good cheer! It is I; do not be afraid." Then He went up into the boat to them, and the wind ceased. And they were greatly amazed in themselves beyond measure, and marveled.
>
> —MARK 6:47–51

Yes, Jesus loved the sea, and He loved all of nature that He created. That's why I'm sure heaven is the prototype of everything that is beautiful on earth. Our Lord and Master wants us to enjoy the kingdom!

It was clear that Jesus wanted me to enjoy the experience of a heavenly boat ride. He pushed a button and the small craft began to move, slowly at first, and then we picked up speed. I loved the breeze against my face and the cooling mist that seemed so clean and refreshing.

I began to laugh as we sped over the sea's calm surface, and then I began to sing. I was so joyful. It was far different from any boat ride I'd ever taken on earth, during which I usually had gotten seasick or very nauseated. Not this time. I was enjoying every moment of our thrilling ride.

On the way back the Lord let me steer. I did so with a special kind of excitement that caused me to laugh and sing. I could hear Jesus laughing with me. I knew He was watching me like a parent watches a child.

Somehow, even though at times I was doubled over with laughter, I managed to steer us back to the docking area. We got out of the boat and the Lord tied it back to the bar. He then said, *"Choo Nam, you see the kingdom has many of the things that you know on earth. When all*

Enjoy the Kingdom

My children come to My kingdom, I want them to enjoy the things I've prepared for them."

I smiled, because I understood a little bit of what He meant.

"My children will be pleased," the Lord continued, *"and that is why I've told them to give up the worldly things in order to please Me. They can have anything they need while they are on earth if they are obedient to Me. I want their hearts to put Me first, and I want them to live pure lives because I love all of them and want to bring them here."*

A DIFFERENT WAY OF THINKING

GOD TELLS US in Isaiah, "'My thoughts are not your thoughts, nor are your ways My ways,' says the LORD. 'For as the heavens are higher than the earth, so are My ways higher than your ways, and My thoughts than your thoughts'" (Isa. 55:8–9). It's so true, and the Lord gave me an inkling that April morning about what this passage means.

After the visit to the heavenly sea, we changed our garments and went to the secluded pond where we often sit and talk. The Lord took His usual seat on the rock, and I began to sing and dance. Then, as He often does, He called me over to sit by Him.

He began to share some important things with me.

"Daughter, you are special to Me. When Larry Randolph prophesied over you and told you how special you are to Me, you did not believe him."

"I did not believe him, Lord, because I wondered how someone like myself could be so special to You. I marveled at the thought that You had taken notice of me. I believed You answered so many of my prayers, but I never thought You would remember me."

I began to cry as I went on.

"When Pastor Larry prophesied and told me I was Your friend, I was shocked, and it was hard for me to believe, but now I listen to his tape every day. Each time I listen and hear him talking about me, my body begins to shake. The anointing comes, and then I am able to believe that You are going to use me in special ways. I always wait for You to talk to me each night."

The Lord listened intently, then responded: *"I choose My children who are pure and obedient—those who put Me first in their lives. You are trying so very hard to please Me, but you must remember, I look only at the hearts of My children. You think like a human being. My thinking is different than yours.*

"I know it's tiring for you right now, but you must be patient.

"My daughter, I don't want you to ever worry about anything. Just leave everything to Me. As I have told you, this is My book, and it will be done according to My will."

I loved these times of sweet communion with the Lord. I felt very much like Mary who willingly sat at the Lord's footstool to learn His ways. Martha, on the other hand, was always trying hard to please Him, and she was filled with anxiety, jealousy and turmoil. I decided that I wanted to be like Mary from that moment on.

Martha, so worried and fretful, had remarked: "Lord, do You not care that my sister has left me to serve alone? Therefore tell her to help me" (Luke 10:40). The Lord answered: "Martha, Martha, you are worried and troubled about many things. But one thing is needed, and Mary has chosen that good part, which will not be taken away from her" (Luke 10:41–42).

Yes, I determined I would be like Mary instead of Martha. I have chosen the "good part" that will never be taken away from me, which is a personal relationship with Jesus Christ. Nothing in all the world is more important than that!

I wanted to have my mind renewed so that I could see things from a heavenly instead of an earthly perspective. The Lord was helping me achieve this goal. I remembered what the apostle Paul had said in the book of Romans:

> For those who live according to the things of the flesh set their minds on the things of the flesh, but those who live according to the Spirit, the things of the Spirit. For to be carnally minded is death, but to be spiritually minded is life and peace. Because the carnal mind is enmity against God; for it is not subject to the law of God, nor indeed can be. So then, those who are in the flesh cannot please God.
>
> —ROMANS 8:5–8

To be spiritually minded truly is life and peace, and every time I went to heaven with the Lord I knew what this meant. I determined to take the heavenly perspective back to earth with me, to continue building on my relationship with the Lord and to let Him renew my mind.

Back on earth this morning, we sat on the beach for a while, and the

Lord said, "*You saw many things in heaven.*"

"Yes, Lord, and these visits are so enjoyable that they're all I can think about. My mind stays in heaven, not on earth."

"*I know, My daughter.*"

"I don't really have my own life anymore, Lord. Since the first moment I spent in Your presence, I've changed. I'm sure if my husband were not a Christian, he would have left me long ago.

"I lived for You before I saw Your presence and before I went to heaven, but now—even when I sleep—each time I wake up I sense Your presence with me. The only thing I can think of now is the book You want me to write. I am honored to do this for You, Lord. Thank You for entrusting me with such an important responsibility. I always want to do my best to make You happy."

"*I know, My daughter. Be patient, and remember that I love you.*"

He stood up to leave, gave me a hug and vanished. The supernatural shaking in my body ceased.

HEAVEN, A PLACE OF WORSHIP

TWO MORNINGS LATER I had another life-changing visit from the Lord. It took place from 5:50 A.M. to 8 A.M. on April 5. After nearly 30 minutes of shaking, I heard the Lord's voice. He came close to me and took me by the hand. I saw my transformed body walking with Him along the beach. We went to heaven, changed our clothing and walked over the golden bridge. Then we found our way to a white, shiny road that was adorned with beautiful flowers on both sides.

I couldn't comprehend the grand beauty of these gorgeous flowers. *How can any flowers be this beautiful?* I wondered.

"*Would you like a flower, My daughter?*" the Lord inquired.

"Yes, I have always loved flowers."

He picked an exquisitely shaped yellow one and placed it in my hand. I held onto it all the way through this visit to heaven.

After an incredibly long journey, we arrived at a huge and beautiful mansion. The palatial structure was situated at the end of the road, in a region where the ground was white and shiny, and multitudes of flowers could be seen everywhere.

We went to the back of the mansion, and I noticed flowers everywhere, as far as my eyes could see. It was indescribably wonderful. Then the Lord escorted me back to the front of the building.

We walked through the doorway, into a spacious corridor. All of a sudden, the interior of the home became dark. The Lord disappeared. I felt very much alone and somewhat frightened. I began to cry.

Just as quickly as it had darkened, the room was filled with the most radiant of lights I had ever seen. The room was so attractively furnished, arranged and decorated, and I was stunned by its brightness and beauty.

Then I noticed steps leading to a platform where the Lord was sitting. He was dressed in pure gold. His golden crown glistened in the light, and His golden robe sparkled and shone. His face was very bright, and I couldn't tell what He looked like.

Then the room filled with people who wore white gowns and silver crowns. They bowed in the Lord's presence, and I did the same. It seemed as if the room began to expand in order to accommodate the rising number of people of all colors and types. It was a moment of sacred worship and adoration before the Lord.

Then they all disappeared as if they were in a video, and the Lord came toward me, wearing His regular white gown.

"Daughter, look around," He said.

I did so, taking in everything I could see. It was the biggest room I'd ever been in—like a majestic ballroom that could contain countless thousands of people. The walls sparkled with jewels and gems, and the floor was made of immaculate white marble.

"They worship Me. They worship Me continually," the Lord said, explaining why the people were there.

I immediately thought of a particular passage of Scripture that relates to worship:

> All nations whom You have made shall come and worship before You, O Lord, and shall glorify your name. For You are great, and do wondrous things; you alone are God.
>
> —PSALM 86:9–10

"May I worship You with them when I come back to heaven to be with Your forever?" I asked.

The Lord chuckled and said, *"Of course, My daughter."*

That's all He said. I must admit I had felt rather intimidated by His appearance as He sat on the throne in all His radiant glory. And as we walked together, I felt a bit uncomfortable with Him because the vision of Him sitting on His throne left me with a scary feeling.

When He is with me, He looks entirely different. When He's with me He is like a normal man, except I can't see His face with my eyes, but my mind can tell what He looks like. He is loving and sweet, gentle and so understanding.

The uncomfortable feeling alternated with moments of joy as we changed and went to the pond. I began to sing and dance, as usual, and the Lord took His customary seat on the rock. Flashbacks of the Lord's austere presence on the throne would steal my joy from me from time to time, but I endeavored to keep on dancing joyfully.

"Come here, My daughter," He called.

I began to cry because I knew the visit would soon be over. "I don't want to leave You, Lord."

"The place I showed you, Choo Nam, is where all My people will gather to worship Me. I will never let anyone on earth hurt you. If you were not such a special daughter, I could not bring you to heaven to show you all the things you have seen."

It was the reassuring message I needed to hear. The Lord's love for me was dispelling all my fears. The discomfort I had felt earlier was gone, but I responded to the Lord's uplifting message in my usual way.

"I'm nothing, Lord."

He rebuked me.

"Don't ever say that again. You are very special to Me. You must believe this. I had to choose the right daughter for this important work, and you are the one I've chosen. I want you to have the best possible life on earth until the last day arrives. I will never leave you and I will always look after you. My daughter, I love you."

His tender words of love and comfort broke my heart. I wept profusely. It was a moment of cleansing, healing and catharsis, and I felt fully renewed.

Heaven, I now know, is a place of great joy. It is designed to be enjoyed by us. That is its purpose. As the Westminster Catechism states, the chief end of man is "to glorify God and to enjoy him forever." The closer I get to Jesus on this earth, the more I am able to enjoy my life. His love casts out all fear.

Yes, heaven is so real.

111

Chapter 13

Angels in Heaven and Earth

"I will be to Him a Father, and He shall
be to Me a Son...Let all the angels of God worship Him."
And of the angels He says: "Who makes His angels spirits
and His ministers a flame of fire."

—Hebrews 1:5–7

MY SUPERNAL EXPERIENCES with Jesus and the heavenly home that all true believers will one day enjoy opened my eyes to several spiritual truths. I began to realize that in the same way God had created us in His own image, He had created earth in the image of heaven. This was thrilling to me—to know that the most beautiful things we enjoy on earth will be a part of our eternal existence.

God said, "Let Us make man in Our image, according to Our likeness; let them have dominion over the fish of the sea, over the birds of the air, and over the cattle, over all the earth and over every creeping thing that creeps on the earth" (Gen. 1:26). God gave us a beautiful earth, filled with fish, birds and cattle, and He wanted us to take dominion over it. In heaven, as I've already mentioned, there are fish, birds and cattle as well. His creation was marvelous in every respect—a place for us to enjoy forever.

But Satan came, and, in his pride and envy, he tempted the first people to disobey God. He had lost his right to eternal glory in heaven because of his sin. In a similar vein, Adam and Eve were banned from their earthly paradise forever, and those who do not obey God in this life will be banned from the heavenly paradise. The

Lord has emphasized this to me over and over again.

I often wondered whom the *Us* refers to in Genesis 1:26, and now I understand it to mean the Holy Trinity. Many people, like me, are having intriguing experiences with angels in these last days. Angels are visiting us in the same way they did in ancient times. They are assuring people of the love of God, and they are warning them of things that are soon to come. As Jesus has told me so often, we truly are in the last days.

Angels are His messengers. I have met one of them, and they are wonderful beings who radiate the love and glory of God. They enjoy worshiping the Father in heaven, and they obey Him by sharing His message with us on earth.

I love the holy angels of God, and I believe they are with me even as I write. The Lord told me that I have personal angels surrounding me. We must never forget God's angelic promise: "For He shall give His angels charge over you, to keep you in all your ways. They shall bear you up in their hands, lest you dash your foot against a stone" (Ps. 91:11).

On Top of the Clouds

THE MORNING OF April 8 brought forth another sweet encounter with the Lord. He visited with me from 6 A.M. to 9 A.M. My body shook for forty minutes before I heard His strong voice calling to me. He took my hand, and in my transformed body we went to the beach where we walked for a longer time than usual. Then we flew away to heaven.

After changing, we walked across the golden bridge and onto the road we normally took. Eventually we turned to the left and began walking along a wide, white road that was lined with huge, leafy trees. The leaves were brightly colored orange.

We walked for quite a distance and then turned onto a rocky road that twisted and turned through high rocks. It led to a high bridge that stretched between two mountains. After crossing this bridge, we climbed a mountain and looked at the scene before us.

We were above the clouds. In fact, everywhere I looked there were clouds. The Lord said, *"We are on top of the clouds."*

Clouds have symbolic importance to the Lord. The Scripture tells us when He returns that "the dead in Christ will rise first. Then we who are alive and remain shall be caught up together with them in the clouds to meet the Lord in the air. And thus we shall always be with the Lord.

Therefore comfort one another with these words" (1 Thess. 4:17–18). The Book of the Revelation also mentions clouds: "Behold, He is coming with clouds, and every eye will see Him, and they also who pierced Him" (Rev. 1:7; 14:14).

It was another awe-inspiring moment in heaven. I was glad to know that there will be clouds in heaven because I've always found them to be so peaceful and lovely. I remember, as a little girl, wondering what it would be like to rise above the clouds, and now I knew. It was a spectacular vista that the Lord and I were enjoying.

I wondered if we were going to take flight above the soft, billowing clouds that seemed to be so far from where we were standing. I don't really know why He showed me the clouds. So many people ask me, "Why does the Lord show you?" I don't usually know the answer to their questions.

All I know is that He seems to take great pleasure in showing the heavenly kingdom to me. I suspect He wants us to know that heaven is a lot like earth, only so very much better.

One thing is for sure—He is Almighty God, and I know that everything He shows me is very important to Him. The fact that He takes the time to personally escort me on tours of the kingdom is overwhelming to me, but those experiences and their related messages are more important to me than life itself.

I literally burn with a spiritual passion to share my experiences with other mortals who need to know and understand, and by being a representative of humanity I can become a vessel through which the Father can pour out His great love for His people. We are such a fortunate generation. God is on the verge of moving in spectacular ways. The Lord will be returning very soon.

BELIEVE IN HEAVEN

SOMEONE HAS WRITTEN these very truthful words: "Heaven is a prepared place for a prepared people." God has given me these experiences so that I will be prepared for the place He has already prepared for me, and so that I can help others get prepared.

The central core of the message is this: "Rejoice and be exceeding glad, for great is your reward in heaven" (Matt. 5:12). The hope of heaven is the joy of earth.

After our visit to the mountaintop, above the clouds of glory, the Lord took me back to the white building where we changed our clothing. Abraham was there to greet us, and he spoke with the Lord for several minutes while I stood silently and reflected on the view atop the clouds.

Then the Lord went to change, and Abraham came over to me. He put his hand on my back and said, "The Lord has shown you a lot of the kingdom." Abraham is a very tall man with a long beard.

I nodded, and a beautiful angel came to escort me into the dressing room. Wearing my heavenly crown and robe, the Lord and I walked toward the pond. Immediately I began to sing.

The Lord took His place on the rock, and I started to dance, but I could not continue. A heavy sadness came over me, and I began to cry. I sensed that the Lord would not be bringing me to the pond after this visit, and this caused me to grow very disconsolate.

By this time, I was sobbing profusely. The Lord, who knows all our thoughts and feelings, called for me to come over next to Him. I didn't want to obey, because I thought I knew what He was going to tell me— that we would not be returning to the pond.

He called me again, and I reluctantly obeyed. I sat next to Him, held His arm and continued to weep.

"Lord," I said, "I feel You are not going to bring me here any more. Please don't let me go, because I will miss You so much." I squeezed His arm and held it tightly.

"My precious daughter, you are right. I don't want to bring you here until the last day. You know that will be soon, so be patient until that time. I have shown you enough of heaven to tell the world, but I still have things to show you on earth.

"I will bring you to the beach and talk with you there, so I do not want you to cry any more. I will be with you everywhere. Anytime you want to see Me, I will be there and you will see Me. I will protect you from all the evil things on the earth.

"Daughter, I know in your heart that you always want to help the needy. I will bless you abundantly so you will be able to help anyone you want to help."

"Thank you, Lord. I want that so much. I really want to help the needy."

"That is one of the reasons I love you so much, My daughter. When you return to the kingdom to be here forever, I will bring you to this pond. You

will always be My special daughter. I do not want you to cry for Me any more. I want you to be happy every day while you are on the earth.

"Thank you for being patient and doing all this work for Me. I want you and your husband to serve Me until the end of the days. This book you are writing for Me—just complete it, and you will be given guidance. Do not worry about anything.

"I want My children to read this book, because so many of them have doubts about heaven. I want them to believe there is a heaven and to live pure and obedient lives so they can come into My kingdom.

"This book is about all My words and the kingdom I have prepared for whoever wants to come. Everything is already prepared.

"This book must be written by a Spirit-filled person. My daughter, if you were not under the special power of my Holy Spirit, I could never use you for this work. As I said before, I have been preparing you for a long time for this work, because I know I am coming soon, and I want My children to know that soon I will be coming for them. My precious daughter, I always want you to remember this pond."

His words stirred me deeply. My heart actually ached with love for my Lord. He stood up, and I knew it was time for us to leave. I continued to cry, but my heart was reassured with the knowledge I would be with the Lord forever and that He would always be with me on earth.

At the dressing room, an angel of the Lord embraced me. It was so exhilarating to be in a place where so much love, compassion and understanding were always present. As I changed my clothing, I surmised that both Abraham and the angel knew this would be my last visit to heaven. As I walked out of the changing room, the angel hugged me once more.

This angel had blond hair, flowing white robes and a face that was tender and warm. The angel smiled at me as I walked toward the Lord.

We returned to earth where we sat on the seashore, and the Lord reminded me of the things He had said at the heavenly pond. He told me He would never leave me or forsake me. He said we would meet on the beach. He reminded me to write down everything He shows me and tells me.

As He left, my sadness lifted. I believed His words. I claimed His promises. A passage of Scripture spoke volumes to my heart: "Go therefore and make disciples of all the nations, baptizing them in the name of the Father and of the Son and of the Holy Spirit, teaching them to observe all things that I have commanded you; and lo, I am with you always, even to the end of the age" (Matt. 28:19–20).

I understood what the disciples must have felt when they knew Jesus was leaving them and going to heaven. He reassured them with the same words He said to me. I knew He would always be with me and His angels would be watching over me as I endeavored to help fulfill the words of His Great Commission.

> I will fear no evil; for You are with me; Your rod and Your staff, they comfort me. You prepare a table before me in the presence of my enemies; You anoint my head with oil; my cup runs over. Surely goodness and mercy shall follow me all the days of my life; and I will dwell in the house of the Lord forever.
>
> —PSALM 23:4–6

I truly believe the words of Psalm 23.

PRECIOUS MEMORIES

SAD THOUGH I had been to know I would not return to heaven for now, I also knew I would not exchange one moment of my heavenly experiences for anything this earth has to offer. Truly, nothing compares with the glories of heaven.

I spent most of the morning and afternoon of April 8 singing heavenly songs, meditating, and trying to pray more than usual because I didn't know when I would be able to see the Lord again. I do this each morning, but on that morning I spent many hours in continual prayer, worship and meditation on the Word of God. Since I've been a Christian, prayer has been my life. In this way the Lord is in my life every minute.

That particular morning was a very sad occasion for me because I was thinking about not being able to go to heaven with my Lord until the last day.

Around 1 P.M. that afternoon I began to feel very sad again. I was remembering that I wouldn't be with the Lord in heaven anymore. Being with the Lord was the happiest experience of my whole life. No words can truly explain the joy I felt while on those visits to heaven. Although I had felt exhausted during those months, I had been spiritually rejuvenated.

I began to weep. The firm, strong voice of the Lord caught my attention. He said, *"My daughter, I told you not to cry for Me any more."*

I tried to stop the tears but couldn't.

"Lord, I'm sorry. I only wish You would take me to heaven with you."

I wanted Him to take me right then because I did not care about anything in this world any more. The thought of being in heaven with Jesus preoccupied all my thoughts. I openly expressed this to the Lord.

"I don't want to wait," I said.

His rebuke stung my heart: *"My precious daughter, I've already told you that I need you to do My work on earth. Be patient."*

The tone of His voice reflected anger. He went on: *"I am coming sooner than everyone thinks. Just remember that I will never leave you. You need rest."*

With that, He departed. My burden had been taken from me, even though I still wanted to be with the Lord in heaven. All fear of death had been removed from me because I knew that death would mean the beginning of eternal life in heaven. Sometimes I even wished to die, but now I recommitted myself to fulfilling the mission Jesus had given me.

In the meantime, I had many precious memories to recall and relive. My mind remembers everything I saw in heaven—every road we walked along, the buildings we entered, the mountains we climbed, the angels, Abraham, the clouds, the rivers, the animals, the flowers, the trees, the birds, the rocks, the sea, the lake, the ponds, the people, and the wonderful peace and joy of it all.

I will never again be like I was when I thought I wanted to enjoy this earth for as many years as possible—to live to a ripe old age and to travel here and there. I just want to be with the Lord more than anything. I know heaven is so real, and more importantly, I know Jesus is always there. I love Him more than my life, and I want everyone to believe in Him and to know there is a heaven already prepared for them.

I agree with the psalmist, who wrote:

> Because Your lovingkindness is better than life, my lips shall praise You. Thus I will bless you while I live; I will lift up my hands in Your name…When I remember You on my bed, I meditate on You in the night watches. Because You have been my help, therefore in the shadow of Your wings I will rejoice. My soul follows close behind You; Your right hand upholds me.
>
> —PSALM 63:3–8

I used to wonder about these things, and sometimes I struggled to believe, but now I know that I know that I know. There is a heaven, and it is our true home. The Lord had shown me the bodies of water in heaven so many times, and He had told me: *"Anyone's heart that is not as pure as the water and does not live by My Word will not enter My kingdom."*

He repeated this time and time again, so I know it's important. He also said: *"Many will not come to the kingdom because they do not live by My Word. That is why I showed you the people wearing the sand-colored and gray-colored robes."*

I knew that I didn't know anything about writing books, and I knew very little about God's Word, except for the importance of being obedient and fearing the Lord, but He had told me not to worry. I am finally learning how to surrender all my worries to Him, because I know He cares about me. I want to do my best to please the Lord at all times.

HEAVEN IS SO REAL

EIGHT DAYS AFTER my last visit to heaven, the Lord visited me for almost two hours. It was the morning of April 16. My body shook for twenty minutes, and I groaned and perspired in preparation for the Lord's visit. He said, *"My daughter, I must talk to you."*

In customary fashion, He took my hand, and I then saw my transformed body walking with Him on the beach. We headed toward the rocks where we often sit.

As we walked, I said: "I miss being with You, Lord. It's now been eight days since You last took me to heaven."

He listened, and I knew He understood, but He did not speak for a while. We continued walking, and then we sat down on the rocks. The Lord said, *"I've missed you also."*

I began singing in the spirit. The songs come forth, and I have no control over them when I am with the Lord. This made me realize that the Lord loves song and dance. When I sing, He looks at my face and He looks happy. But this time He interrupted, *"Daughter, I must talk to you."*

I was still caught up in my singing, so He repeated, *"I must talk to you."*

"I'm sorry, Lord."

"I see that My book is doing well. Did you write down the name of the book that I gave you?"

"Yes, Lord."

"I told you I will take care of everything."

Trying to come up with a fitting title for the book had been quite a chore. It just seemed as if the right title would not come forth. Then, during a prayer time of the preceding week, I asked the Lord for the title. As I was praying in the Spirit, the words *heaven is so real* kept emanating from my spirit over and over again. As a matter of fact, I couldn't stop saying them.

Great peace came to me when I realized this was the Lord's title for His book—*Heaven Is So Real!*—and what could be a better title? This is precisely the message, the theme, the plot of this book. This is what Jesus wants people to know.

"Whoever wants to come to My kingdom must believe and prepare for My coming," the Lord continued. *"It will be much sooner than they think.*

"Even faithful Christians doubt that there really is a kingdom of heaven. I want all of My doubting children to believe My kingdom is real. This will lead them to be more faithful, obedient and pure of heart so that they can enter My kingdom."

NO EASY ROAD TO HEAVEN

THE LORD WANTS people to believe. The writer of Hebrews emphasized the importance of believing by saying we actually cannot please the Lord without it.

> Without faith it is impossible to please Him, for he who come to God must believe that He is, and that He is a rewarder of those who diligently seek Him.
>
> —HEBREWS 11:6

Faith comes from hearing the Word of God, as Paul points out: "So then faith comes by hearing, and hearing by the word of God" (Rom. 10:17). God wants us to believe His Word, and His Word points us to heaven.

Jesus said, "If you abide in Me, and My words abide in you, you will ask what you desire, and it shall be done for you" (John 15:7). The Word of God imparts faith to our hearts so we can reach out in faith when we pray, and thereby receive answers to our prayers.

This is what happened when I asked God for the title of His book. He heard my prayer and answered it. He is such a great and glorious God, and His heaven is so real!

The Lord continued: *"I will bring all who live with My Word into the kingdom, but the road to the kingdom is not an easy road.*

"Daughter, you keep asking why I chose you for this work. I will tell you again. You are the right daughter for this book. I know you will do everything I tell you to do, no matter how hard it is for you.

"You will be very surprising to many people, because I chose a daughter instead of a son for this End-Time work. I realize many daughters are more pure-hearted than sons and are very pleasing to Me. Through you many daughters will be happy. I plan to give a special anointing to many daughters for End-Time work, and they must prepare to receive it.

"I want you to write down exactly what I show you and tell you. Nothing more and nothing less. After this is done, you will receive special gifts to serve Me, and you will be a blessing to My people. I will also bless you more than you want."

"Lord, the only blessing I want is to make You happy. I do not need anything because You have given me everything I need or want on this earth. Now, if I can serve You greatly, that will make me happier than anything, and I want my whole family to serve You and be willing to give their lives for You."

"That is why I love you so much, daughter," He said, and added: *"Be sure to use Pastor Randolph's prophetic words in this book. And remember, I will bring you back here again."*

We stood up, walked down to the sand, and looked out at the Pacific Ocean. Before ascending, He said, *"Write down what I tell you."*

I held Him tightly as we embraced. I did not want Him to leave, but I knew it was necessary. I knew heaven is so real and that I had nothing to worry about. Throughout all eternity I would be with Him.

Chapter 14

Walking in the Word

*If you abide in Me, and My words abide in you,
you will ask what you desire, and it shall be done for you.
By this My Father is glorified, that you bear much fruit;
so you will be My disciples. As the Father loved Me,
I also have loved you; abide in My love.*

—JOHN 15:7–9

WHILE KEEPING THE morning watch in prayer and meditation on April 18, the Lord gave me a very special anointing. This was the signal that He would be arriving soon, and, as I expected, after fifteen minutes or so I saw Him sitting by the window of my bedroom where He usually sits. I also saw my transformed body sitting next to Him. Spiritual songs from deep within my spirit responded to His presence.

As I sang, I held the Master's hand, and I began to look for the scars in His palms by trying to turn His hand over, but He would not permit me to do this. He seemed particularly happy on this occasion, and He reminded me, *"I do not want to see you crying any more."*

The Lord shared several important things with me that day.

"My daughter, I never want you to worry about anything concerning this work," He started. *"I will take care of everything. Just be happy for Me, My daughter. I want you to put your picture on the cover of the book."*

"Lord, You always surprise me. You always make me feel so happy."

"I know all your needs before you ask Me, but I never want My children to stop asking when they need something."

His words reminded me of something I had been reading in the Bible

122

that very morning: "But when you pray, do not use vain repetitions as the heathen do. For they think that they will be heard for their many words. Therefore do not be like them. For your Father knows the things you have need of before you ask Him" (Matt. 6:7–8).

In this passage of the Bible, through His great model prayer known as The Lord's Prayer, Jesus goes on to teach us how to pray. It is an effective outline for all intercessory and personal prayer, and I use its principles whenever I go before the throne of grace in worship, intercession and supplication. I always claim God's promises, such as Philippians 4:19: "And my God shall supply all your needs according to His riches in glory by Christ Jesus." And on this particular spring morning the Master was reminding me of these precious truths.

After delivering this message about prayer, the Lord stood up and my transformed body stood with Him. I watched the Lord touch the head of my transformed body. He departed, my transformed body disappeared, and the shaking of my natural body ceased.

A VISION OF MANY BOOKS

FOUR DAYS LATER, on April 22, I was with the Lord from 6:35 A.M. until 8:18 A.M. My body shook for twenty-five minutes, and then I heard the voice of the Lord. He took my hand, and I saw my transformed body walking on the beach with Him. The Lord said, *"I love you, My daughter."*

"I love You too, Lord."

We went up to the rocks where we usually sit as we look out over the mighty Pacific Ocean. As we sat down, I began to sing. Then I cried for joy. I held the Lord's arm, and He gently patted my hand with His right hand.

"My daughter, I must show you something."

The unusual voice that accompanies the supernatural visions the Lord gives to me came forth. Then I had a vision of a bookstore filled with books, and I wondered why there were so many books there. My eyes were drawn to one particular book. Its cover had a golden background with a castle at the top—a magnificent castle like the one I saw in heaven. The title was in the middle of the page—*Heaven Is So Real*—in bold, compelling letters. At the bottom of the cover there was a cloud, a soft billowing one like those I had seen from heaven's mountain.

I was taken aback by this vision of the book. Even more startling, I began to see a multitude of books flying through the air, and people on the ground were stretching and jumping in an effort to catch them.

The vision then evaporated, and I began to ponder its importance. The Lord explained, *"I told you I will take care of everything for you, daughter. Do not worry about anything any more."*

He had shown me the finished product of the book that was occupying so much of my time and attention. It was beautiful, and its cover was so alluring. More important, He had shown me how desperate many people are to know the truth about heaven, and I realized emphatically that my book would be the means whereby they could really know.

"Lord, I trust everything You tell me," I said, "but I can't help thinking about this."

"My daughter, the book has to be done in My time and by My will. I want you to relax completely about it. I know you do not really have your own life now because you are so preoccupied with the book, but some things cannot be hurried. They have to be accomplished in the right time. I want you to learn to be patient. I want all of My children to be happy on this earth."

"Lord, no matter how hard it is, I enjoy every minute of my time that I am spending on Your book. It's not hard to write down Your wonderful words. The Holy Spirit is guiding me in every word I write; I could never do it on my own."

The hard part, I must admit, was in the waiting. Yet the Lord was faithful to every word He spoke to me. His Word is eternally true. As Isaiah testified: "So shall My word be that goes forth from My mouth; it shall not return to Me void, but it shall accomplish what I please, and it shall prosper in the thing for which I sent it" (55:11). And I knew that the same thing would hold true for the book He had asked me to write for Him. It will not return to Him void. It will prosper, and it will accomplish the purposes He has for it to accomplish.

His presence, His voice, His touch, His words all were very reassuring to me and gave me great peace. I knew it was His book, not mine, and He would take care of every aspect of it, from the writing to the cover design to the printing, marketing and distribution. It will be a wonderful work that will arrest people with its depiction of the glories of heaven.

The Lord stood up, walked down to the edge of the ocean where we started from, and said, *"I love you, My precious daughter."*

He didn't hug me this time. Then He turned and walked away.

"Everything Is Ready!"

ON THE MORNING of April 25 the Lord visited with me from 7:40 A.M. until 9:13 A.M. My body shook violently, and my groanings could be heard throughout the house. Then the Lord spoke.

"I am your Lord, My precious daughter, and I must talk with you," He said.

When He took my hand, my natural body quivered and quaked as if an electric current had been unleashed upon my system. Then I saw my transformed body walking with the Lord on the beach. We took our usual places on the rocks, but this time I did not sing.

Instead, I took particular notice of the clothing we were wearing. As I was observing this, the Lord said, *"My daughter, I really enjoy being with you."*

"Lord, I love You and I want to be with You all the time."

"You will be soon, My daughter. Have you looked at your feet?"

I had never really noticed before, but I was wearing the same kind of sandals He was wearing—beige with a gold trim. I placed my right foot next to His and noticed how much smaller my feet were than His. We both began laughing.

Next I felt the material of my robe. It was incredibly soft and shiny.

The Lord reached over and touched my hair.

"You have beautiful hair," He said.

The hair of my transformed body was like that of a young girl. It was long, straight, soft and shiny. It was like the hair I had when I was a teenager. The Lord then looked at my face and said, *"You are beautiful, My daughter."*

Those were words I really needed to hear, because I had never had a very good self-image about either my appearance or my abilities, but to hear my Master from heaven telling me about my beauty made all the difference in the world. I began to cry with joy.

"Do not be shy, My daughter," the Lord counseled me.

Then He lifted my face. I could see the features of my transformed face and the sheen of my dark hair. For the first time in my life, I felt I truly was beautiful, and then I remembered the words of the psalmist:

I will praise You, for I am fearfully and wonderfully made; marvelous are Your works, and that my soul knows very well. My frame was not hidden from You, when I was made in secret, and skillfully wrought in the lowest parts of the earth. Your eyes saw my substance, being yet unformed. And in your book they all were written, the days fashioned for me, when as yet there were none of them.

—PSALM 139:14–16

I could see that the Lord had created me. He formed me to be a very special person, and this was what He was trying to show me this day. He was admiring His creation, and He wanted me to do the same.

Usually the Lord does not talk much when He visits me, except when He wants to tell me important things about my life and ministry. He frequently reiterates these important messages.

For example, He has told me over and over again that He will be coming soon. He often has repeated the fact that His kingdom is already prepared for His children. He has told me many times to stop worrying, to be patient and to trust Him.

He has constantly told me that the book is important because it will convince many doubters that heaven is so real. The more I have thought about it, the more I have realized that this is one of the most important things anyone can know—the knowledge of heaven makes life so much more beautiful and wonderful. To know heaven is our home makes the journey through this life so much more meaningful.

That's exactly how I feel. Now that I've been to heaven so many times, I can't wait to get there permanently. Someone once said, "On earth you can gain only one thing permanently—heaven."

It's such a privilege, therefore, for me to have a part in this book. I know God will use it to usher many souls into His kingdom. That's what He wants, and that's what I want as well.

On this particular morning, the 25th of April, the Lord seemed more light-hearted than usual and very talkative. His words and actions made me laugh a great deal, and He was laughing too. It was such a joyous time. In many ways He seemed almost like a regular person instead of almighty God. He was certainly enjoying the current moment with me.

After a while, however, the tone of our meeting grew more serious.

"Daughter, I thank you for making yourself available to do this work," He said. *"The most important thing to Me is that you do the*

book exactly the way I tell you to do it. Don't ever change that. I have been guiding you step by step, as I told you I would. I knew you would be obedient in this work, and that is why I chose you.

"I say to you again that everything in My kingdom is ready for My children. I want all doubting and unbelieving Christians to realize there is a real heaven. I want to bring all of My children to the kingdom, but whoever does not live by My Word will not enter. This book will help the faithless people.

"I know you are praying for many people, but I cannot answer all of your prayers because some who know My Word are still selfish and they are living for the world. Whoever lives dishonestly and does not respect My words are people I will not bless, even if they are your loved ones.

"Daughter, I want you to think about those you have been praying for, those you know, and I want you to think of which prayers I've answered. Some will never change their hearts to become pure, and they will never be blessed.

"Many Christians are poor and have many problems in their lives because their hearts are not right with Me and they don't tithe. Any Christian who doesn't tithe will not be blessed because they love money more than My Word. Those who love money more than My Word will never see My kingdom. You already know where they will be at the end.

"If anyone comes to Me with an open heart and tries to live with My words, they will be blessed right away, and they will have peace and joy continually. Whoever loves Me and wants Me to bless them must have their heart right toward Me and put Me first in everything in their lives and have a kind heart toward others.

"Sweetheart, I want you to be happy every day of your life on earth. You are My special daughter forever. There will be no end to My blessings for you while you are on this earth.

"I will protect you from everything that I don't like on this earth, and I will never leave your side. You will always have unexpected surprises from Me."

"Lord, You have surprised me with so many things. I never know what You are going to do next."

I could sense that He was smiling at my response. Then He said, "It is time to go back." We got up and began to walk toward the water.

We embraced, and He said, *"I love you, My daughter."*

"I love You, Lord."

OMNIPRESENT AND OMNIPOTENT

THE NEXT VISIT with the Lord took place on April 29. I was with Him from 6:05 A.M. until almost 8 A.M. that morning. My body shook for half an hour, after which the Lord said, *"My daughter, Choo Nam, I must talk to you and show you some things."*

When He took my hand I could see my transformed body walking with Him on the beach. As soon as we sat down on the rocks, I thanked the Lord for taking me to this special place in order to be with Him.

He gently reminded me, *"I love you, daughter."*

"I love you, Lord." After we had talked, I sang for Him.

The supernatural voice that accompanies the visions He imparts to me came forth, and I saw the cover of *Heaven Is So Real* again. Next, the book began flying through the air, and people in a barren part of the earth were jumping and stretching to get it.

Then a book flew toward us, and the Lord grabbed it. He gave it to me. At first, I held onto it tightly with both of my hands, and I clutched it against my breast with deep appreciation. Tears of joy flowed freely down my cheeks.

The supernatural vision then showed me a church sanctuary where the Lord was standing behind the pulpit. He was lifting the book up with both of His hands. People were running toward Him. It was so wonderful, so thrilling, to see so many people coming to the Lord—and then I understood that He was using the book to draw people to Himself.

The vision opened to many different vistas at once. I could see the Lord in many different churches around the world, with people of every nationality present in the various churches. In each house of worship the people were running toward Him. My omnipresent and omnipotent Lord was able to be present everywhere—in several different churches at the same time.

I was reminded of a verse from the book of Revelation: "And I heard, as it were, the voice of a great multitude, as the sound of many waters and as the sound of mighty thunderings, saying, 'Alleluia! For the Lord God Omnipotent reigns!'" (Rev. 19:6). This was from the vision of heaven that the apostle John had received on the island of Patmos where he was in exile. This was what the people in my vision were doing—they were running toward the Lord to worship Him because they knew He was almighty God!

This was in response to the truth John revealed in the Revelation: "Then a voice came from the throne, saying, 'Praise our God, all you His servants and those who fear Him, both small and great!'" (Rev. 19:5). As the saints did this, they were filled with joy and shouted: "'Let us be glad and rejoice and give Him glory, for the marriage of the Lamb has come, and His wife has made herself ready.' And to her it was granted to be arrayed in fine linen, clean and bright, for the fine linen is the righteous acts of the saints. Then he said to me, 'Write: Blessed are those who are called to the marriage supper of the Lamb!'" (Rev. 19:7–9).

Like John, I had been called to write, and my mission was the same as his—to let people know that the marriage supper of the Lamb has already been prepared, and blessed are those who are invited to be there on the last day. The invitation is extended to all, but only those who willingly choose to walk in the Word of God will be able to attend. It's so important for us to live according to the Word of God, to pray according to His principles and to believe all His promises. We are the bride of Christ, and He wants us to be holy, clean and righteous before Him. What a wedding day that will be!

The vision ended and the Lord asked, *"My daughter, did you see everything?"*

"Yes, Lord. How can You be everywhere?"

"I can be anywhere in the twinkling of an eye."

"Lord, I know some Christians are very faithful, but they still have their old habits. Why can't You change them?"

"Whoever wants to be changed will receive My help. If they ask Me for whatever they want I will give it to them if I know they are sincere and if they persevere. I will answer their prayers.

"Many of My children, however, do not pray sincerely or long enough. If they do not have patience, they cannot receive a blessing.

"My daughter, you are so persistent. You never give up. You keep on asking Me for what you want in prayer. I hear your every prayer."

"Yes, Lord, I do not give up until I receive because I know You have all my answers. One of my Bible teachers told me to never give up praying for something you want. That's why I am very persistent in my prayers, Lord.

"I know You have the answers I need, especially in my personal prayers. You have answered more of my prayers than I ever expected. Thank You, Lord."

"I love persistent children. People's persistence proves their faithfulness, and by this I know that they believe I hold the answers to all their prayers. I also want My children to know that even though I answer prayers, I may also remove answers if they are not faithful."

"What might a person do that would cause You to remove a blessing from his life?"

"Daughter, when some of My children need something, they pray night and day and spend time with Me. They strive to be obedient and to live according to My words. Then, as soon as I bless them, they change, moving far from Me and going back to their old ways. They continue doing the things I do not like. That is why I sometimes remove My blessing."

His visit, His presence, His vision departed, and I was left with a much clearer understanding of God's ways. "As for God His way is perfect; the word of the LORD is proven; He is a shield to all who trust in Him" (Ps. 18:30).

Chapter 15

Blessings Beyond the Blue

*Every valley shall be filled
And every mountain and hill brought low;
the crooked places shall be made straight
And the rough ways smooth;
and all flesh shall see the
salvation of God.*

———

—LUKE 3:5–6

THE MORNING OF May 2 was an especially meaningful time of prayer. The anointing of the Lord was more heavy upon me than usual, and the shaking of my body was more furious than ever as I concluded my time of prayer. It seemed as if the shaking would never stop. The groanings from my spirit were like convulsions deep within. My body temperature rose, and I was perspiring heavily.

It was so overwhelming, in fact, that I failed to look at the clock. After a while, the Lord entered the bedroom window and sat in His usual place.

His voice quieted the physical manifestations in my body.

"My precious daughter, I came to tell you and show you some things. You have many things to do for Me before I come for My people. You must be patient with Me. Many of My people are not ready for Me to come for them. My kingdom is completely ready for anyone who wants to enter.

"Every believer must stand before Me at the end, and many of those who don't live by My words will be very disappointed.

"I want all of My children to come to My kingdom. Whoever reads this book, I want them to believe and realize how they have to live in the world in order to enter the kingdom.

131

"Daughter, I will bless you until you can't contain it. I will bless you more than you ever expected or asked for."

"Lord, the only thing I want to be blessed with is being able to serve You and make You happy."

"Daughter, you have already made Me so happy. That is why I chose you for this work. You and your husband will serve Me greatly until the last day. Tell your husband I am pleased with the work he is doing on this book.

"After everything is done, I want you to build My church."

This statement called forth the voice that always accompanies the supernatural visions the Lord gives me, and I began to see the same church He had shown me before. After I saw the interior and exterior of the church building, I felt completely relaxed. I could not see the Lord or feel His presence.

On this particular morning, and the mornings afterward, the Lord's visits with me were entirely unpredictable, and they did not take the usual form. During this period, I never knew what to expect from His visits because each one was so different.

One thing became very clear to me—He would never appear if I had made early plans for a given day. On days when I did not have plans, however, He most often would come to take me to the beach on earth. On other days, my wonderful Lord simply would sit by the window and talk to me when I was praying. He is such a thoughtful and loving Lord. My love for Him cannot be fully expressed.

It still amazes me to realize how much He knows about me. He knows my thoughts, feelings, plans and motives. My continual prayer is that of Psalm 139:23–24: "Search me, O God, and know my heart; Try me, and know my anxieties; and see if there is any wicked way in me, and lead me in the way everlasting."

LIKE A LITTLE CHILD

MY FAITH CONTINUED to increase as I grew in my relationship with the Lord. I truly believe that I will never have another doubt. I've been with the Lord, and He has taken me to heaven so many times. I believe His Word, and I know that heaven is so real.

"Let the little children come to Me, and do not forbid them," Jesus said, "for of such is the kingdom of God. Assuredly, I say to you, whoever does not receive the kingdom of God as a little child will by no means enter it" (Mark 10:14–15).

The Lord wants us to become like little children so we can enjoy the blessings of the kingdom of heaven forever. The qualities of childhood are possible for adults who surrender their lives completely and unreservedly to Jesus Christ. Innocence, trust, purity of heart, fascination, a sense of wonder, belief, joy, happiness, present-moment living—all these are some of the magical qualities of childhood that God wants us to exhibit to get to heaven.

Notice that the Master says "whoever does not receive the kingdom of God as a little child will by no means enter it" (Mark 10:15). Obviously He wants us to *believe* in heaven—to *receive* it as a little child. This is the key that unlocks heaven's door for all of us who wish to enter.

However, because so many things come against us while we grow up, we quickly lose our innocence, faith, trust and purity. These are restored to us when we come, fully surrendered, to the Lord. It is a beautiful transformation: "Therefore, if anyone is in Christ, he is a new creation; old things have passed away; behold, all things have become new" (2 Cor. 5:17).

God is our Father; we are His children. He wants us to be children who trust, love and obey their Father. Jesus said, "Little children, I shall be with you a little while longer. You will seek Me... By this all will know that you are My disciples, if you have love for one another" (John 13:33, 35).

The Lord wants all of His children to be with Him in heaven forever. In order to get there—to live atop heaven's highest mountain—we need to be like little children. The true transformation of Christianity is that adults become like little children—walking in wonder, trust, obedience and love.

Jesus made it very clear to me that this is what He wants each of us to be like—to have the faith of a little child. He wants us to walk according to His Word, to totally believe Him and to look forward to the reality of heaven. Those who do not, He pointed out to me several times, will be on the edges of heaven but never truly able to enter the joy of the Lord.

A Beautiful House and Car

From 6:17 a.m. to 8:14 a.m. on the morning of May 6, I was with the Lord. My body shook for twenty minutes, and I was perspiring under a very heavy anointing. The groanings from deep within my spirit poured forth. Then I sensed the Lord's presence in the room.

"Come, My daughter Choo Nam, I must take you to the beach," He said.

I noticed His hand moving toward me. The next things I saw was my transformed body walking with the Lord along the beach. It was such a happy time. I was smiling at the Lord like a little child who is enjoying a special moment with a parent. My whole body felt happy, and I could tell the Lord was happy too.

"Lord, I've missed You. I love You so."

"I love you, daughter, and that is why I've brought you here."

We went to the usual rock that served as our resting place on these trips to the beach. I always sit on His left side and either hold His hand or put my hand under His arm. I sang with joy for a time before the Lord told me: *"My daughter, I am going to show you something. I want you to be happy."*

The vision-voice came forth from my spirit. It seemed to take control of me for a long time.

The vision came forth, and I saw a huge river that was unusually wide. Many houses were situated close to the river, but they were placed high above the water, on magnificent rocks.

My attention was drawn to a particular house—it was a white-frame, two-story home with a quaint white fence all around it. There was no grass in front of the house, and, instead of a grass lawn, the grounds were landscaped in the form of a spectacular rock garden. Flowers and trees proliferated around the house.

The entrance to the yard was a huge gate. A bright, shiny red car was parked on the left side of the garage. It was a luxurious automobile. The front of the house had a couple of steps leading to beautiful double doors.

The vision continued. Inside the house there was a cream-colored carpet, and the well-built furniture was decorated in an array of colors. The living room was very large, and a master bedroom suite was downstairs, nearby. The bedroom was huge—it had a king-size bed and cherry-colored dressers, tables and wardrobes. The bedspread was gold, and the draperies matched.

I was able to look into the kitchen where I saw cabinets made of cherry wood. In the center of the kitchen there was a barbecue pit, and modern appliances were everywhere.

Just outside of the kitchen there was a terraced back yard with trees lining an attractive fence. It truly was a mansion, and I thought: *This is so beautiful, but why is the Lord showing it to me? We already have a nice car and house that the Lord has provided for us. I'm not really interested in material things any more.*

The vision evaporated and the Lord spoke to me: *"Did you like what you saw?"*

"It was beautiful, Lord."

"It will be yours."

I cried. It was all so wonderful. It was grace that exceeded all my expectations—a grace that I did not deserve. I kept asking myself, "Why me?" People often ask that question when bad things happen to them, but I was asking it because of the blessings—already the Lord had showered a multitude of blessings on me.

Truly the blessings were more than I could contain. It was as if the prophecy of Malachi had come true in my life—in the here-and-now, on this earth:

> "Bring all the tithes into the storehouse, that there may be food in My house, and prove Me now in this," says the LORD of hosts, "If I will not open for you the windows of heaven and pour out for you such blessing that there will not be room enough to receive it."
> —MALACHI 3:10

For a long time Roger and I had been tithing from our incomes and giving offerings to various ministries. When I could, I would help every ministry, but I had never expected such results from our obedience. God was so wonderful. Truly, I was unable to contain the blessings He poured upon us. He had opened the windows of heaven, and He was preparing to do even more for us!

"But, Lord," I said, "I don't need anything. I have everything I want already."

"Don't cry, My daughter," He counseled.

It always seemed to bother the Lord when I cried. I'm sure that's because He wants me to be happy. Nonetheless, I cried even harder because the vision had actually confused me. I wondered if it meant that He would not be coming back for His children as soon as I had expected. If He is coming for us soon, why would He want to give me such a big house and expensive car?

As usual, He knew my thoughts.

"Daughter, are you worried that I will not come soon—because I am giving you this house and car?"

His question stirred my deepest emotions, and I began to cry harder. The Lord lifted my face and wiped my tears. Then, in very reassuring tones, He said, *"My precious daughter, I am coming as I said I would, but until then I want you to have the best."*

"Lord, You already gave me a beautiful house and car. I do not need or want anything else. The only thing I want is to please You and serve others until You return for us. You said if we love you we must be good to others. That is why I want to lead as many people to You as I can, because I know that is what You want."

"I do not want you to worry about anything anymore. You want only to please Me, and you are not expecting anything else. That is why I want to give you more than you now have. Say no more; be happy."

His words comforted me and filled me with joy and hope. He would be returning soon, and I had nothing to worry about. My mind was drawn to a verse I had heard in church; the speaker had told us that the true believers would be the head, not the tail (see Deut. 28:44). This is the blessing that comes to all those who serve the Lord "with joy and gladness of heart, for the abundance of all things" (see Deut. 28:47).

The Lord said, *"We must go back now,"* and then He stood up. We walked back to the place where we usually begin and end our visits to the beach. While we were walking, the Lord did something He'd never done before. He picked me up and spun me around in the same way a father will sometimes do with his small child. I began to laugh hysterically, and I noticed that my natural body almost lifted off the bed. The power of the Lord was very strong upon me.

It was a precious moment of indescribable joy and one that allowed me to fully realize the meaning of the passage that says:

> That the genuineness of your faith, being much more precious than gold that perishes, though it is tested by fire, may be found to praise, honor, and glory at the revelation of Jesus Christ, whom having not seen you love. Though now you do not see Him, yet believing, you rejoice with joy inexpressible and full of glory, receiving the end of your faith—the salvation of your souls.
>
> —1 PETER 1:7–9

Joy *inexpressible* and *full of glory!* My faith had been strengthened by the personal revelation of Jesus Christ. I loved Him so much. I had even seen Him! It was glorious, and I continue to enjoy an unspeakable joy that is full of glory.

FLYING LIKE BIRDS

A MIRACULOUS EVENT will be happening in the very near future. Though the Bible never uses the word *rapture,* the apostle Paul describes a cataclysmic event in which the Lord Jesus will return from heaven with His saints to "rapture" His church. It will be the ultimate experience for all those who know Jesus.

> For this we say to you by the word of the Lord, that we who are alive and remain until the coming of the Lord will by no means precede those who are asleep. For the Lord Himself will descend from heaven with a shout, with voice of an archangel, and with the trumpet of God. And the dead in Christ will rise first. Then we who are alive and remain shall be caught up together with them in the clouds to meet the Lord in the air. And thus we shall always be with the Lord. Therefore comfort one another with these words.
>
> —1 THESSALONIANS 4:15–18

But those who don't know the Lord will appear before the judgment seat of Christ where they will hear the sentence that their lack of faith deserves—"for the wages of sin is death" (Rom. 6:23). Those who know Jesus, however, will receive the free gift of God's grace—"the gift of God is eternal life in Christ Jesus our Lord" (Rom. 6:23).

The second coming of Jesus Christ was the subject of my next visit with the Lord, which occurred on May 13. I was with Him from 6:20 A.M. until 9 A.M. I awoke at 6:20, shaking intensely. My body shook for more than half an hour, and then the hot anointing and groaning began. The Lord came toward me and said: *"My daughter, I am your Lord. I must talk with you and show you something."*

This time, as I walked with the Lord in my transformed body, I smiled at Him and said, "I love You, Lord."

I could tell He was smiling at me, although I could not see His face clearly. *"I love you, My precious daughter,"* He answered.

We sat on the rocks and the Lord said: *"I see that your husband is taking time off from work in order to help with the book. You both are doing very good work.*

"My daughter, I must tell you this. I know I told you to write down exactly what I show you and tell you. I notice you are not explaining enough about what I show you."

"Lord, I'm so sorry. I will go over it again."

The Lord had told me repeatedly to write down everything after His visits, no matter how tired I was. At times, my mind felt numb, but the minute I picked up pen and paper, the words flowed rapidly through my mind. I learned that it was the work of the Holy Spirit guiding me. That's exactly what He was doing with me, and I now knew He would find another writer who would help me to bring forth the teaching that He wanted to accompany my experiences.

Some, I know, will find it hard to understand how anyone can have the experiences I've been privileged to enjoy. They will say, "It's not in the Bible!"

The truth is, however, that most of the things God has shown me are recorded in the Bible. I believe He simply wants this book to reemphasize the biblical truths about heaven to Christians everywhere. He has chosen me as an instrument, and this book as a vehicle, to reiterate the truths of the Scriptures to His church. I also believe our Lord wants His people to know there are many wonderful things about heaven that are not recorded in the Bible.

He continued: *"You'd better remember how precious you are to Me, My daughter. Only in this way can I use you. I am coming for My children much sooner than most people expect."*

"Will all the Christians live in houses like the one that has my name on the door, when they get to heaven?"

"I will bring many of My children to the kingdom, but not every one will live in mansions like the one that had your name on the door. These mansions are for very special children."

"Will all the Christians go with You, when You come for us?"

"I am going to show you something," the Lord answered instantly. *"I want you to remember all that you see. I want the whole world to know what is going to happen soon. I know many Christians do not believe what My prophets are telling them. That is why I am showing you this."*

My vision-voice came forth as it usually does in preparation for a supernatural vision from the Lord. It seems to be the means He uses to prepare me for the things He wants to show me. This time the voice lasted a long time. After more than half an hour of singing in the Spirit with my vision-voice, I began to see the things God wanted to show me.

The first part of the vision was more like an impression rather than a visual experience. It seemed as if the whole world were excited. Earth's environment was noisy and busy. Then I began to see what all the activity was about.

The air was filled with white, moving objects. As the vision clarified, I saw people wearing white robes flying throughout the air. People were popping out of the earth everywhere and flying up into the air. The sky was literally filled with flying people, like birds in migration.

It was so unusual it was shocking. By this time I was singing loudly, and my hands were moving around like fists swinging at a punching bag. I had never felt this excited in my whole life. My body was jumping up and down because of the anointing and the shaking. I felt as if I were flying with the white-robed people I saw. The excited movement of my body and my vision-voice were so loud that I'm sure the whole house could hear me.

I had heard the rapture described before, but I had never imagined what an amazing spectacle it would be. I wondered what those who do not know Jesus would think when they observed such a scene. I was shocked and excited, but I'm sure they will be terrified.

This was the biggest surprise the Lord had ever shown me. It was the most awe-inspiring thing I'd ever seen—human beings flying through the air like birds. They soared upward with rocket-like speed. Some seemed to be soaring like kites in the wind on a clear, beautiful day.

I saw my one-year-old granddaughter. She was wearing a white robe, and her hair had grown to shoulder length. She looked pretty grown up. At first I saw her at her house in normal clothing. Then suddenly she was wearing a white robe and flying through the air. I was dumbfounded by the vision. It certainly seemed to confirm that the Lord would be returning in the very near future.

Then I saw my daughter's ten-month-old daughter. She does not have much hair right now, but in the vision her hair was down to her shoulders, and, like my other granddaughter, she was flying through the air.

I began to cry and scream. The noise in the bedroom must have been astounding. It was a good thing that Roger was at work, for surely he would have been quite alarmed and concerned by such noise.

At first, I wasn't really sure if my crying stemmed from joy or sadness. My youngest granddaughter looked like she was also pretty grown up. I felt the Lord had a good reason for showing the children to me. First, I'm sure He wanted me to know that they will be with me in heaven to enjoy all eternity with Jesus. Second, I know He wanted me to see how old they will be when He returns. It is sooner than most people think.

The joyous vision changed. I saw the people who did not ascend with the others. Places on earth had been disrupted, some had been turned upside down. It was noisy everywhere, and people were in an obvious state of panic. Terror was written on every face.

People were running wildly. Total pandemonium reigned. It seemed as if each person was searching for someone or something that they could not find. I began to cry like a little child as I watched people running down the streets. They were screaming and yelling. Some were trying to throw what few belongings they possessed into vehicles such as cars and boats. Thousands of boats were on the ocean. People were trying to escape.

Many men in uniforms were storming houses, ransacking them and taking the belongings they found. I noticed one family of four or five lying on the floor of a house. Most of them were on their stomach, and a pool of blood covered the floor.

Hundreds of people were fleeing on foot to the mountains. As they did, the uniformed guards fired guns at them, and several fell. Those nearest the guards were beaten with clubs and sticks.

I saw people destroying churches. A man threw a rock at a beautiful stained-glass window that showed Jesus with His lambs. The window shattered and glass flew in all directions. I screamed more loudly.

One woman, who appeared to be looking for a lost child, was running through her house, shouting in panic and fear. She kept calling her child's name as she jumped up and down in total frustration and desperation. I wanted to help her, but there was nothing I could do.

I cried and cried for her and for all the others.

Then I saw a family I know personally. The father ran into his house, and rushed from room to room, calling the names of his wife and children. He found one member of his family, and they sat huddled in a corner of a room. They were holding tightly to each other and crying. I know who they are, but I am not at liberty to mention their names in this book.

The vision eventually vanished, and I continued to cry. The Lord wiped my tears.

"Daughter," He said, *"I must show you these things so you can tell the whole world what is going to happen. I love all My children, and I want them to realize I am coming for them soon, but I cannot bring those who don't live according to My Word, because they are not ready for Me.*

"Many Christians will be surprised when the End Times come. What you just saw is only a small part of what will happen very soon. It will be much worse than you can possibly imagine—for those who do not know Me. That is why I want all My children to be able to come with Me to My kingdom.

"Daughter, I have shown you part of the kingdom and the things that are going to happen in this world because the time is short. I will return soon. That is why this book is so very important to Me. It is for My children. You have seen what is going to happen on earth in the very near future.

"I am ready for My children, but so many of My children do not really believe and they are living for worldly things. I love all of them and want to bring all of them to heaven with Me, but I cannot take those who are not ready for Me. Those who come to My kingdom must be pure-hearted and obedient.

My heart went out to all those who don't know the Lord, and I began to pray for their salvation. I named each one I knew, and I asked God to intervene in their lives, to get their attention. Then I prayed for Christians who are not living for Jesus. I asked Him to draw them back to Him.

I determined I would finish the book as quickly as I could, and I promised the Lord I would go where He would send me. I felt truly honored to be an End-Times handmaiden working in the Lord's harvest fields. I remembered a passage from the Bible that shows exactly what Jesus is feeling right now:

> But when He saw the multitudes, He was moved with compassion
> for them, because they were weary and scattered, like sheep having
> no shepherd. Then He said to His disciples, "The harvest truly is

plentiful, but the laborers are few. Therefore pray the Lord of the harvest to send out laborers into His harvest."

—MATTHEW 9:36–38

Heaven is so real! Paul describes it this way: "Eye has not seen, nor ear heard, nor has it entered into the heart of man the things which God has prepared for those who love Him" (1 Cor. 2:9). The way we show our love for God is through obedience—as Jesus said: "If you love Me, keep My commandments" (John 14:15).

Chapter 16

God's Great Love

There is no fear in love;
but perfect love casts out fear,
because fear involves torment. But he
who fears has not been made perfect
in love. We love Him because
He first loved us.

—1 JOHN 4:18–19

MY EXPERIENCES IN heaven, with the Lord, help me to understand what he meant. God is love, and heaven is a place where love is the environment—it is the light and life of heaven.

The events preceding the Rapture of the church, however, will be terrifying and horrifying. Though the Lord had erased the memory of seeing my mother in hell, I still had a vague recollection of her being there and I felt great pain in my heart over my parents' eternal destiny.

After I became a Christian I prayed for my parents over and over again. I pled with the Lord, asking Him not to consign them to hell, and I reminded Him of how good they were. I cried and prayed so many times for them that I felt somewhat assured that the Lord would not put them in the pit. I even begged God to let me please Him for the rest of my life to make up for what my parents didn't do right.

My mother had been a good person indeed. She seemed very pure and innocent in many respects. I always thought that my mother never knew what being bad was. She had been ill for most of her life, and she had died when she was forty. Her last concern when she was dying was for me.

When my mother died, I felt that I wanted to die too. She was all the

143

love I knew at that time. I actually hated my father because I knew he was with other women during my mother's illness.

Though it was customary for some men in the Orient to seek other women when their wives were ill, I remained deeply disturbed by my father's behavior. I knew that he was betraying his wife, and I felt her pain.

I carried hatred for my father for a long time, but when I became a Christian, I was able to forgive him, because I realized that he did not know the Lord. It is only the grace of God, I had to remind myself, that keeps any of us from sin.

I had often wondered whether I would see my mother after my own death. This thought recurred many times after she died when I was only fourteen.

HEAVEN IS LOVE

IT WAS THE Lord who bridged the gap between the love I should have received from my parents and the love I actually received. To me, He is pure love. He said to me, *"My daughter, you have been living for Me so long now, and you have been especially devoted to Me for the last few months. It all should be done soon. You need rest."*

"I will not be happy with anything on this earth, Lord, if You are not in it."

After my mother died, I felt as if no one truly loved me. Certainly nothing ever felt like my mother's love had felt to me. I needed to be loved, but for the longest time it seemed as if there was no love in my world. After I was married and had children, I greatly enjoyed the family love we shared, but as wonderful as their love is to me, the love I had felt from my mother was still missing. It was as if there was an empty space within me that needed to be filled.

That vacuum was filled by the tremendous love of God. After I gave my heart to Jesus, I felt very secure in His love and it was easy for me to trust His love. I knew the truth of the hymn that says, "No one ever cared for me like Jesus—no one ever cared for me like Him."

When I would fall and hurt myself as a little girl, my mother would pick me up, love me and take care of my hurt. In the same way, when I would stumble as a young Christian, Jesus would pick me up and bring healing to all my hurts. This is what our Lord has been anointed to do.

The Bible describes the anointing that Jesus received: "The Spirit of the LORD is upon Me, because He has anointed Me to preach the gospel to the poor. He has sent Me to heal the brokenhearted, to preach deliverance to the captives and recovery of sight to the blind, to set at liberty those who are oppressed, to preach the acceptable year of the LORD" (Luke 4:18–19).

Jesus had brought good news to me. He had healed my broken heart. He had set me free from my fears, my negative self-image, my insecurities. He had opened the eyes of my spirit, and He had lifted my oppression. Now He was proclaiming "the acceptable year of the Lord" to me. That "acceptable year" is right around the corner.

Even when people try to put me down or gossip about me, I feel secure in the love of Jesus. He is my safe place, my high tower, my Rock of refuge. When someone hurts me, intentionally or unintentionally, I am able to go to the Lord in prayer, and His peace and joy return to me. I know that God loves me. He will never let me down or leave me.

I love to reflect on the promises of God's Word. One of my favorites is found in the Psalms: "Blessed be the Lord, who daily loadeth us with benefits, even the God of our salvation" (Ps. 68:19, KJV). His love for us is everlasting: "Yes, I have loved you with an everlasting love; therefore with lovingkindness I have drawn you" (Jer. 31:3).

I know that nothing will ever separate me from the marvelous love of my God and King. "For I am persuaded that neither death nor life, nor angels nor principalities nor powers, nor things present, nor things to come, nor height nor depth, nor any other created thing, shall be able to separate us from the love of God which is in Christ Jesus our Lord" (Rom. 8:38–39).

His perfect peace is always with me. "You will keep him in perfect peace, whose mind is stayed on You, because he trusts in You" (Is. 26:3). His Word is a treasure chest filled with good gifts that He desires to share with all His children, and these good gifts will be our daily portion in heaven.

Notice what Paul wrote to the Ephesians:

> Blessed be the God and Father of our Lord Jesus Christ, who has blessed us with every spiritual blessing in the heavenly places in Christ; just as He chose us in Him before the foundation of the

world, that we should be holy and without blame before Him in love, having predestined us to adoption as sons by Jesus Christ to Himself, according the good pleasure of His will, to the praise of the glory of His grace, by which He made us accepted in the Beloved.

—EPHESIANS 1:3–6

God has already blessed us with *every* spiritual blessing in Christ. Even in this life we can enjoy the "heavenly places in Christ."

In fact, Paul adds in the next chapter of his letter to the Ephesians:

But God, who is rich in mercy, because of His great love with which He loved us, even when we were dead in trespasses, made us alive together with Christ (by grace you have been saved), and raised us up together, and made us sit together in the heavenly places in Christ Jesus.

—EPHESIANS 2:4–6

We have already been raised up, spiritually, to sit together in the heavenly places in Christ Jesus.

When the body of Christ truly understands this reality, everything will change. The world says, "Seeing is believing," but the Christian says, "Believing is seeing." The true reality is spiritual, not temporal. Most people think the only reality is found in what we can see, hear, taste, smell and feel. But the ultimate reality is the spiritual world.

There are four kinds of love—*agape* (the love of God), *storge* (the love of family), *phileo* (brotherly love) and *eros* (sexual love). Unfortunately, the world puts eros first and few ever find *agape* love. The world system works in reverse priority to God's system. God created us in His own image—He is a Trinity (Father, Son and Holy Spirit)—and we are tripartite as well (body, soul and spirit).

The Greek word *pneuma* is the word that has been translated "spirit," and this is the real part of us—it is the breath of life, the heart of hearts, the place where the Spirit of God seeks to reside. The Greek word for soul is *psuche,* and this part of us is the place where our intellect, emotions and will reside. It is here that many of our problems surface.

Last, the word *soma* is the physical part of us—the organs and systems of our bodies. Here again, the world has the order reversed. Whereas God wants us to put our spirits first, too many people give attention to their bodies first, their feelings second, and if there is any room left over, then their spirits. We forget that we are more than human beings on a spiritual journey; the fact is, we're spiritual beings on a human journey.

God has already blessed us with every spiritual, heavenly blessing in Christ Jesus, because He loves us with an everlasting love. When I began to realize these truths, I felt I wanted to give up every worldly thing in order to simply please the Lord for the rest of my earthly life.

Since that time I have been putting Him first in my life, far above any other person or thing. This is what He expects from each of us. His Word promises, "But seek first the kingdom of God and His righteousness, and all these things shall be added to you" (Matt. 6:33).

God, in His great mercy, has enabled me to find His kingdom, and He has taken care of all my needs. As a result I am able to obey His Word which says, "Therefore do not worry about tomorrow, for tomorrow will worry about its own things" (Matt. 6:34).

Worry, which used to be my constant companion, has been replaced by security, peace, trust and love. I don't care what people say about me, and I do not fear what might happen to me. My greatest joy is found in serving and pleasing the Lord. Just loving Him brings me incredible joy.

He loves me whether I do right or wrong. He has told me so many times, *"I want you to be happy, My daughter."* On this particular day—May 13, 1996—I knew great happiness and peace even as I watched the scenarios related to the End Times unfolding before my spiritual eyes in the form of a supernatural vision. The Lord reminded me, *"There are many special blessings coming to you."*

I couldn't imagine how there could be more blessings than I had already experienced. I knew the truth of the Word that declares, "For the kingdom of God is not food and drink, but righteousness and peace and joy in the Holy Spirit" (Rom. 14:17). What more could anyone want? These blessings—and so many more—were mine already, in the here-and-now, and I knew they would continue forever in heaven.

The Lord said, *"I know you are tired, My daughter. I will take you back now."*

This morning was very intriguing to me. I had spent two and a half hours with the Lord, and then I prayed for another hour and a half. I felt as if I was already in heaven where God's love is the air we breathe.

SHUT IN WITH GOD

SINCE FEBRUARY 19, 1996, I have spent every waking moment with the Lord. My social life has been limited to worship services and basic grocery shopping for my family. The rest of the time is God's. The only folks who visit with us are our family members. The Lord has made it clear to me that this is how He wants me to spend my time—focusing on Him, His Word and His will. He is preparing me for the next phase of ministry.

Though it may seem that I'm a "shut-in," the reality is that my "prayer closet" has become an open door to the kingdom of heaven. Instead of being shut in, I've been launched into higher dimensions of glory than I've ever known.

Often, when people call and plan to visit, they will call back and say that something has come up that prevents them from visiting. I believe this happens because God wants me to spend this time alone with Him so He can continue His work of preparation in my life. From the outset, He told me not to go anywhere for a while, especially out of town, until the book was completed. Really, even if I wanted to go somewhere, I couldn't because the anointing is so heavy. The anointing of the Lord keeps me on my knees in His presence.

Before Easter 1995 I had felt His anointing, but since that time, my body began shaking every time the anointing of the Lord's presence came upon me. Since January 1996 that anointing has been so strong that I cannot even control the shaking and other physical manifestations.

For example, as of this writing, I cannot even enter the room where Roger works on the computer because the Holy Spirit's presence is so strong there. Roger is implementing the corrections into the manuscript for the book. He took a week's vacation for this purpose, and I am so grateful for his help.

When I go near the computer room my body begins to jump for joy. This is a physical response that comes from the Lord, and I have no control over it. It is not something I am "working up" on my own. In fact, it is more of a spiritual response than an emotional one.

Almighty God, my Father and my Lord, has spent so much of His time with me, and it is a privilege to give a little time back to Him. I enjoy every moment of my work for Him. It is not hard for me to do work for Him because I love Him more than I love my life. I believe the Psalmist's words: "Your lovingkindness is better than life" (Ps. 63:3).

CONCERN IS WORRY

THROUGHOUT MY LIFE, as I've mentioned several times, I've been prone to worry. I guess you could call me a worrywart. It probably stems from the turmoil I experienced during my childhood. Whatever the reason, however, I often struggled with worry and fear and insecurity. I knew this was not God's will for me. In fact, the Lord had told me several times, *"Do not worry, My daughter."*

I began to look at my worrying somewhat differently, calling it concern instead of worry. Somehow, saying that I was "concerned" rather than "worried" made it seem OK. On May 20, 1996, I was with the Lord from 5:40 A.M. until 7:50 A.M. My body shook from 5:40 A.M. until 6:10 A.M., and my spiritual groaning lasted for thirty minutes. The Lord walked toward me and said, *"My precious daughter, Choo Nam, I must talk to you."*

His hand reached toward me, and immediately I saw my transformed body walking with Him on the beach. He seemed very happy, and I was really enjoying His presence. As we strolled along the strand I said, "Lord I love You and miss You."

He responded without hesitation, *"I love you, My daughter."*

The joy of the moment caused me to pick up the pace of my walking, and I actually got ahead of the Lord. He began laughing, and I did the same. We took our usual seats.

"I see you are working continually on My book."

"Yes, Lord. Roger is working hard on it. My English is not that good, so he is correcting a lot of spelling errors and grammatical problems."

"I know you both are working hard."

I knew the Lord knew all my thoughts, feelings and actions. I knew I could not hide anything from Him, and I did not want to conceal anything. He knew that I had been concerned about the book. I wondered how it would turn out, who would write it and who would publish it.

The Lord knew all this, so He said, *"Choo Nam, you are worrying about this book again even though I told you not to worry."*

"I'm not worried, just concerned," I replied as I dropped my head in shame.

The Lord lifted my face in His hands and said, *"Daughter, you are embarrassed."*

I acknowledged the truth of His observation with a smile that turned into a chuckle. He began laughing in response, then said, *"Daughter, concern is worry. From now on, I do not want you to worry at all. This is My book; I will take care of it. Haven't I done so until now?"*

"Oh, yes, Lord. I am so sorry. Please forgive me for not obeying You."

He responded with joy. He seemed to take great pleasure in my honesty and humility. I knew He had forgiven me. Great peace came to my soul, and I felt free from worry that I had pretended to deny by saying it was just concern.

This day I learned another important lesson from the Lord—He wants us to be totally honest with Him, others and ourselves. We cannot use the world's methods to justify, rationalize or cover our sins. I knew that worry was a sin, and I had tried to pretend it was not there.

Even though it may seem to be a small thing to some, I knew it was very important to my Master. He did not want me to worry. In fact, He invites each of us: "Come to Me, all you who labor and are heavy laden, and I will give you rest. Take my yoke upon you and learn from Me, for I am gentle and lowly in heart, and you will find rest for your souls. For My yoke is easy and My burden is light" (Matt. 11:28–30).

The human way is to worry. God's way is to trust. "God resists the proud, But gives grace to the humble. Therefore humble yourselves under the mighty hand of God, that He may exalt you in due time, casting all your care upon Him, for He cares for you" (1 Pet. 5:5–7). Why should we choose to worry when our Father promises us so much?

The Lord seemed to want to erase my worry by showing me some of what He has prepared for me again. He said, *"I want you to see this again."*

The vision-voice came forth and, after a long time, the vision of the house He had shown me the last time appeared. The Lord did not show me the upstairs of the dwelling the last time He showed it to me, but this time I saw the four guest rooms and one prayer room on the second floor. I took particular notice of a picture that hung on one wall of the prayer room—it was a picture of the Lord himself. Though I couldn't see Him clearly, I sensed there was something particularly appealing and attractive about His portrait.

The vision took me into every room of the house—the home He promised to give to me and my family. The Lord asked, *"Do you like the house?"*

"Yes, thank You, Lord. But I don't really need another house. All I want to do is to please You, do Your work, and see my family becoming more faithful to You.

"All the things You showed me are so beautiful, but they are worldly things, and they don't interest me any more. Roger feels the same, Lord."

"My daughter, let Me decide what you want and need. I love the hearts of both of you. We must go now."

After the first nine times we visited heaven, the Lord told me He was not going to wake me up anymore, and He fulfilled His promise. I woke up a few minutes before or after six—after I had a full night's sleep.

It was a time of pure peace and joy. There was no worry or concern. The Lord embraced me, then said, *"I will talk to you later."* I felt more completely relaxed than ever.

Heaven or Hell?

SINCE THAT VISIT in May I've been praying for the future readers of this book. I'm praying for *you*, dear reader. I want God to prepare your heart to receive the truth of all I've experienced and written about. Heaven is so real, and I want you to believe in it more than you've ever dreamed possible. This is what God wants for you, because He loves you with an everlasting love.

The Lord took me to heaven so many different times so I could tell you how wonderful it will be for each of us who love Him and live for Him as completely as possible. He and I both want you to be able to go to the beautiful mansion He has prepared for you. The things the Lord has shown me and told me are true. They are thoroughly biblical. They are a reality that far exceeds our earthly experience. I know they are more real than things of this earth, and I want you to know this reality.

Before the Lord blessed me with so many revelations of heavenly truth, I sometimes had doubts that there was a heaven, even though I loved Him and believed Him with all my heart. I did not fully understand about heaven, and I know a lot of Christians are like this. Now I know it's all true. It's not even a matter of faith for me now; it's actual knowledge—the kind of knowledge that no one can take away. It is pure knowledge.

I used to be very afraid of dying and concerned about many things in my life, after I die; but after what I experienced in heaven, nothing in this world or my life matters to me anymore. I know where I am going to be after this life is over. I will be with Jesus forever in His paradise. There are no words to explain how perfect heaven is. All I felt there was pure joy.

After the trips to heaven I begged the Lord to take me home, but His disappointed voice said: *"I didn't show you the kingdom and the pit of hell to bring you home now. I showed you all those things so you will help save the lost and let everyone know what it takes to enter the kingdom."*

After He said this, I was embarrassed for being so selfish, and I asked Him for forgiveness. Now the only thing I can think about is serving Him to the last day. No matter what it takes, I will please Him.

As one of His special daughters, why would He hurt me by using my mother in this book if it wasn't important for His people to understand that just being good will not save them without knowing who Jesus is? Someone said to me, "If He loves you, how can He use your mother to hurt you that way?" I was shocked by this ungodly question.

Though it was a very painful memory for me to see my mother and others in the pit, I had to realize that nothing can bring them out of there, so I accept the fact that they will be there for eternity simply because they did not know the Lord Jesus.

My Lord has a very special reason for using my mother in this book. If, through her, even one other mother can be saved, I would be very honored.

No matter what difficult times may come into my life, I can never be angry with the Lord. If any of my loved ones die for my Lord, I will be very pleased for them. Then I will know for sure that their eternal life will be spent in heaven with Lord Jesus. As Jesus said:

> For God so loved the world that He gave His only begotten Son, that whoever believes in Him should not perish but have ever-lasting life.
>
> —JOHN 3:16

I believe His second coming is so near that He is letting His people know how much He loves them and that He wants His church to be ready for Him.

God loves you, and this is the greatest truth in the entire world. That is why He has already prepared His kingdom for you. Even though He loves His children, He is angry toward those who do not believe. That is why He has commissioned me to write this book. He has told me many times that the salvation of souls is exceedingly important to Him. He is disturbed to think that some of His children would choose hell to be their eternal place rather than the beautiful glory He has prepared for them.

After all, heaven is a choice. The Lord does not want anyone to end up in the pit of hell. If you believe, you will have eternal life with the Lord:

> "The word is near you, even in your mouth and in your heart" (that is, the word of faith which we preach): that if you confess with your mouth the Lord Jesus and believe in your heart that God has raised Him from the dead, you will be saved. For with the heart one believes unto righteousness, and with the mouth confession is made to salvation. For the Scripture says, "Whoever believes on Him will not be put to shame"
>
> —ROMANS 10: 8–11

If you do not believe, you will find yourself in the place of torment where my parents and countless others have to endure all eternity. It is a personal choice. It is God's way versus Satan's way. It is the kingdom of heaven versus the kingdom of darkness. It is life versus death. It is heaven versus hell. Which will win in your life? The choice is yours.

Every word in this book is true. The words of Jesus have been transcribed exactly as He said them to me. The Lord chose me for this work, and I have endeavored to be faithful to every word and experience. With God's help, and the assistance of Roger and the writer, I have tried to give accurate descriptions of each experience I've enjoyed.

Ultimately, however, I realize that the choice is yours. All I can do is tell you. Now that you've read these pages, you are accountable for the truth that has been imparted. What will you do with the truth I've shared?

Before I went to heaven, I wanted to save souls for the kingdom, but now I realize I must do all I can to rescue the perishing. I can never erase the memory of those naked bodies moving around in the fire and screaming in their misery. It will soon be over for each of us, and then it will be too late to make our decisions for Jesus and heaven.

I have a burning desire to see the lost saved, to keep them from going to the terrible place the Lord revealed to me. My deepest desire is for everyone to find his name on a mansion door in heaven.

The Book of Revelation describes two types of people. I have seen the same things the apostle John saw. John describes the eternal destiny of the first, unfortunate group as follows: "And the smoke of their torment ascends forever and ever; and they have no rest day or night" (Rev. 14:11). The second group, on the other hand, is described this way: "Here is the patience of the saints; here are those who keep the commandments of God and the faith of Jesus...Blessed are the dead who die in the Lord from now on...that they may rest from their labors, and their works follow them" (Rev. 14:12–13).

Is your name written in the Lamb's Book of Life?

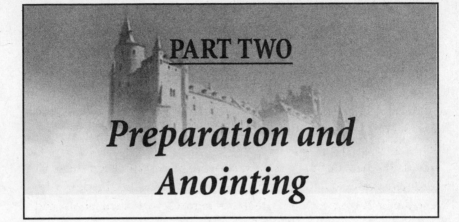

PART TWO

Preparation and Anointing

Chapter 17

Special Anointings

*And he poured some of the
anointing oil on Aaron's head and anointed
him, to sanctify him.*

—LEVITICUS 8:12

THIS SECOND PART of the book reveals how the Lord worked in my life and prepared my body to dance and serve Him after He gave me a vision for this book. Since Monday, May 27, 1996, He has visited with me regularly. He has taken me in my transformed body to a beach on earth every Monday morning.

This beautiful beach, which is clearly described in the previous sections of this book, is a very special place to the Lord. On May 27, 1996, He promised me He would take me to the beach every Monday, and He has been completely faithful to this promise, never missing these weekly visits.

Before doing the preparatory work in my body, the Lord visited me every morning. This began on July 11, 1996. He anointed me, and He began to prepare me for the work He has called me to do. He explained that until all the preparatory work was completed, the book could not be published. He clearly showed me that He wanted me to keep a record of all the work He is doing in me so it could be included in the book.

In addition, the Lord has worked with me during the early evening hours. In fact, He hardly ever works with me in the mornings any more. At first, the nightly visits would occur late at night, around 10 P.M. or 11 P.M. Then He started appearing in the early evening hours. Because of this, He told me to start going to bed early each evening.

As I prepared for bed, I found that my body would begin to shake with the Lord's power around 8:00 P.M. each evening. During the periods of shaking I would read my Bible and pray. Then, as I would get into bed, my body would undergo tremendous and violent shaking for five or ten minutes. In the process, my stomach would tighten, and I would experience spasms in the abdominal region.

All of this happens each evening before the Lord's visit to my room. The wonderful anointing of the Holy Spirit falls upon me as well. During these marvelous visits, the Lord speaks directly and personally to me. Then He begins the preparatory work in my body. When this happens, I have no control over my body for a period of two to four hours. The Lord is with me the entire time.

Often He talks with me while my body is shaking violently. Sometimes He tells me what He is going to do next, and when He senses that my heart is complaining about His plan, He rebukes me by commanding, *"Obey Me!"*

He is always careful to reiterate His expectations and plans. Sometimes this makes me weary, and I feel as if I can't take any more, but He knows my heart's desire is to please Him in all that I do so, I keep on trusting Him.

When these evening sessions first began, I could see the faces of demons all over the room. Though they were gross and intimidating, I did not fear them. I would see them flying behind the Lord's head, but when I rebuked them, they instantly departed.

Through this process I believe the Lord was teaching me how to protect myself. I also believe the Lord lets me see His presence the whole time while He is doing His work so I will learn to focus on Him alone at all times.

He has told me many times that I must focus on Him and His work only. For this reason, He had me finish the book some time ago and put it away until He was ready for it to be released. In the meantime, He wanted me to learn to concentrate on Him and on the preparatory work He is doing in my life. Completing the book was a very large burden to me, but with God and my husband's help, along with the assistance of a Spirit-filled writer, the major portion of the writing project was completed sometime in February 1997.

Spiritual Visions

EACH TIME BEFORE the preparatory work begins, the Lord talks to me about my future. Then the body work commences, while He shows me a multitude of visions—oceans, rivers, mountains that glow with fire, gold mines, the earth itself, all the buildings of the world, snow, churches, waterfalls with the Lord Himself in their midst.

He also has given me visions of many other natural and spiritual phenomena. Each vision would be shown to me repeatedly. He also showed me a hailstone as big as half a door falling from heaven. This vision came in the form of a dream. Anything the Lord shows me, I can never forget.

In fact, the visions were so multitudinous and varied that they are truly uncountable. The Lord would take my transformed body to the ocean, and He would hold my hand as we would walk on the ocean. What a sense of joy that gave to me—walking and talking with the Lord on top of the sea! Often, I would respond with laughter.

These visits to the shore were very exciting. It was as if I had become a little child—the Lord and I would even race to see who could run the fastest. These marvelous experiences occurred when the Lord took me to the beach, and they were possible only because the Lord had transformed my body through the intriguing body-work He does to prepare me for the ministry He has called me to.

A Constant Anointing

DURING EACH OF these preparatory visits, the Lord's anointing would be so strong that I would actually grow sleepy and get very tired. No matter how tired I was, however, I would humble myself before the Lord, and submit to the work He was doing in me.

A couple of times when He was doing this work, I did fall asleep for an hour or so. As soon as I awakened, though, my body would resume its shaking, and the work would begin all over again. The Lord was not interested in having me learn in some easy manner, and I believe this was specifically designed to show me that the work He is calling me to do will be challenging.

I noticed, also, that the Lord always finishes whatever He begins. Realizing this, I did not want to fall asleep, but sometimes it was very hard for me to stay awake.

On some occasions the Lord would work with me for a couple of hours in the early evening, then I would fall asleep, and He would wake me again at 2 A.M. or 3 A.M. in order to work with me for another two or three hours. When I experienced such nights, the next day I would be so tired that my face would actually be swollen from a lack of sleep.

It now seems to me as if the Lord was in a hurry to get the preparatory work finished. In fact, He kept telling me, *"There isn't much time."* I believe this is why He spends so many hours with me each night. He is preparing me for what we all will be facing in these closing days.

THE ANOINTING OIL

THE WORK INVOLVED with preparing my body for the ministry God has called me to do included my face, my hands, my head, my feet and my back. The Lord used my hands to touch every part of my body from the top of my head to the bottom of my feet over and over again. Then I would rub with my hands my entire body like washing dirt off and then put both hands together as if I was cleaning dirt from my hands. The Holy Spirit directed me in all of this.

I don't really have control of my hands, or any part of my body, when the Holy Spirit is doing His anointed work on me and with me. As a result of all of this, however, I have experienced truly supernatural physical strength. As I pray for other people, and place my hands upon them, frequently my hands will slap up and down on their heads or shoulders, because of the Holy Spirit's power flowing through me. When I am anointed, no one can hold my hands because of their fast movement under the power of the Holy Ghost.

On several different nights the Lord poured oil upon me. This precious oil was in oval vessels that looked like small perfume bottles. The bottles were of many different colors. He would pour the oil upon me from head to toes, and on my back as well.

I kept track of this special experience in my journal, and I have found that He has poured a total of eighty-five bottles of anointing oil upon me. All of the bottles He used had caps on them except the last one.

Before being bathed in the anointing oil each time, an unusual vision-song would come forth, and I could see the Lord much more clearly than before. Each time He poured the oil upon me He told me to remember the bottle's color so I could write it down. Sometimes it was hard for me to make out the color, and on those occasions the Lord would tell me what the color was. Each color seems to have a special significance to the Lord.

The Lord knows every one of my thoughts, and that's how he would realize I was having difficulty distinguishing the colors of the bottles. On some nights He would pour from seven different bottles, and each had its own distinct color. Some had a single color, and others had many colors. Each color was uncommonly beautiful.

As He poured the anointing oil on my body, I would shake, jerk, perspire and become intensely hot. Groans from deep within my spirit would grow louder, and I would become breathless. This would continue for about ten minutes, and then I would rest for five minutes or so.

Then a special song would come forth before the Lord would approach me with the bottle of oil again. As I mentioned, on some nights He would pour from seven different bottles of oil. Other times, He would pour from only one. Since that time I've learned that seven is the number of -perfection and wholeness.

When the Lord would say, *"I will pour this on your back,"* my body would respond by turning over on my stomach under the power of the Holy Spirit. When He would say, *"This is for your hands,"* my body would turn sideways in the direction where He was standing, and the Holy Spirit would cause me to thrust both of my hands in His direction.

Many times the Lord would touch my hands with His fiery hands. These were intense experiences that caused me to feel the heat of God's presence, and I would weep. The power and fire of God were so strong during these moments that my voice became weak and breathless.

SPIRIT SONGS

UNDER THE ANOINTING of the Holy Spirit I would sing for three hours on some nights. These songs are Spirit songs, composed and directed by the Holy Spirit. They are very edifying and inspiring.

After a night of such singing, my voice would not be tired or weak the next day as it might have been were I not singing under the Lord's direction. The same is true of my body. After a night of the Lord's work in my body, I would feel quite normal, except for the tiredness I sometimes experience.

Some nights, while the Lord would be working with my body and hand movements, my entire physical being would become black and cold. At

161

first, this scared me and surprised me, but the Lord's presence would always wipe the fear away. He would say, *"I'm right beside you; do not fear anything."* There were other occasions when my entire body would become invisible as the Lord was doing His preparatory work with me.

Most of the body-work was with my hands, eyes, face and head. Sometimes He would form my body into the shape of a cross, and He would breathe His breath into my mouth and nostrils. There were times when He would shoot flames from His eyes into my eyes. In the process of these special blessings, the anointing of the Holy Spirit would often be so strong that I wondered if I was dying. I would respond with deep inner groans and many tears.

During some of these sessions the Lord would both lift my body and lower it. My body would obey His power by standing up on occasion and turning over at other times.

As I mentioned, supernatural visions would frequently accompany the body-work. Once He showed me a mountain. At first, the mountain seemed normal, but then it turned to fire. The whole mountain was ablaze, and it began to shine like bright sunlight. Then I noticed that the Lord's presence was standing in the midst of the sunlight, and His body formed a cross.

Under the direction of the Holy Spirit, my body took the form of a cross as well. In fact, it was stretched so severely that I experienced great pain. Each limb of my body was stretched for at least ten minutes, and I thought the Lord was punishing me. I wept throughout this memorable experience.

Each type of body-work and the supernatural visions would continue for many days. Then, when the Lord was ready to move on, they would change to a different type of work and emphasis. Usually each type of preparatory work would last from three to five days. Upon completion, He would go back over each thing He did for me. Many times He would raise and lower my body forty-nine times a night.

When He completed each session, the Lord's presence stood close to me. Some nights He simply anointed me with the precious oil of the Holy Spirit. Throughout each visitation, I would perspire from the heat, and my spirit would groan. The power of the Holy Spirit was overwhelming—so much so, in fact, that upon occasion, I felt as if I were losing my mind.

162

CHRISTMAS EVES

WHEN THE LORD visits me He usually wears a white robe, but on the Christmas Eves of 1996, 1997, 1998, 1999, 2000, 2001 and 2002 He wore a beautiful robe and crown. The crown was made of gold, and it was embossed with a rainbow of jewels of all colors and descriptions. His gown was deep red, and it was trimmed in gold.

"Lord, why are You wearing such a beautiful gown and crown?" I asked.

"Daughter, it is My birthday," He responded with a smile.

Whenever the Lord smiles at me, I return the smile automatically. I could not close my mouth if I wanted to. Though I usually can't see His face, I am able to tell when He is happy or sad or angry.

On twenty-eight separate occasions the Lord wore this beautiful golden robe and crown. At these times it always seemed as if He was especially happy. He wears these spectacular garments at times of celebration, including each time when a phase of my body-work would be completed.

When my heart would wonder why He was dressed in such royal garments, He would say, *"I am celebrating, My daughter."* With dancing hands my heart and body would respond to His desire to celebrate, and my spirit would respond with my special vision-voice and heavenly Spirit songs.

A GOLDEN KEY

AFTER MANY MONTHS of this special work, the Lord gave me a small golden key, and I cried in deep appreciation and humility. As I received this precious gift from the Master, my body shook and jerked uncontrollably, and the Lord lifted and lowered my body. I was anointed with fire from heaven, and my body became breathless under the power of the Holy Spirit.

When this was completed, I rested for several days. Then the Lord reappeared and began to talk with me. For several nights, He simply anointed me. Each of these anointings lasted for fifteen minutes, then I would rest for five minutes. This continued over and over for at least seven times each night. Each time I would lie down and groan like a sick person, and it seemed as if I would lose consciousness.

CRUCIFIXION

AFTER MANY NIGHTS of these special anointings passed, the Lord showed me His crucified body, and I was reminded of all He did for me. Before this, He told me not to fear anything because He would be with me, but He did warn me that the coming sessions would be difficult and very hard for my physical body because I would be experiencing His power more strongly than ever.

When I saw His crucified body, there was blood streaming down His face and on His body. The crown of thorns was upon His head. I noticed how large and strong His body was. His skin was tan and His hair was dark and curly. His muscular body glistened with sweat.

The Lord's eyes were vividly penetrating and alive. Even though His body was unclean and covered with blood, He looked very handsome. I will never forget this experience. He stood before me with His hands stretched out in the form of a cross. As before, my body responded by stretching out, and it too took the shape of a cross.

The power was so heavy that I felt I would die. It was the most amazing spiritual experience I had ever had. I felt breathless and I cried throughout it. I had both sadness and joy. But the joy I experienced was so full that I felt I wanted to die for Him right at that moment.

I could not tell how much time had elapsed, but I knew it must have been a long time because my arms were stretched out as far as they could be, and it was very painful. When this vision of His crucifixion and my identification with it was over, the Lord said, *"This was the hardest work of all."* The next night He empowered me with such a powerful anointing that my body was raised and lowered seven different times. Many different anointings followed, then I rested for ten days.

The experience was profoundly moving, and it was a life-changing event for me. For the first time in my life, I truly comprehended a little bit of what the Lord went through for me on the cross. In some small measure, I actually felt the pain He had experienced, and I cried in the anguish of my soul in a way that must have been what He experienced.

Likewise, I realized more fully than ever before that He went through such horrors for me so I would be able to live, not perish. The verse that loudly proclaims my salvation is so meaningful to me: "For God so loved the world that he gave his only begotten Son, that whosoever believes in him should not perish but have everlasting life" (John 3:16). Thank You, Lord, for saving my soul.

UNLOCKING MY BODY

AFTER TEN DAYS of rest, the Lord began to work on my body in many different ways. It was as if He were unlocking the potential within my body. For example, He would raise my body from a prone to a sitting position, and He would cause me to get off the bed and stand on the floor. All of this was done under the power of the Holy Spirit, not my own power.

All of this unusual body-work would cause me to feel very tired, because He would cause my body to rise and kneel before Him in intervals of seven, over and over again. I would cry the entire time this was going on because His work in my life was so overwhelming and humbling to me.

At times I was so tired that I could barely stand again. His preparatory work that took place while I was lying down was so much easier. Many different nights I would be required to stand for two hours, and each aspect of this body-work, involving every part of my body, would be repeated seven times.

Thirty-three different times He "unlocked" the various parts of my body that needed His work of preparation. Some of my "body locks" needed to be "unlocked" seven different times during each session. When He unlocked my hands, for instance, they shook so hard that I grew frightened, and when He did the unlocking of my eyes, they became intensely hot and had to be closed tightly for at least five minutes.

The Lord would always let me know in advance which area of my body would be unlocked next. Each part of my body had a special reaction to the unlocking work. As I mentioned, He unlocked my hands seven times, and the same was true for my face and head. The remaining thirty-three unlockings were for the rest of my body.

Each time the Lord pours the anointing oil on me or unlocks the locks of my body, my physical being responds with violent shaking, jerking, intense heat, groans and supernatural power that causes my body to be lifted up. All of this work tightens the sinews and muscles of my body, and it is as if my body is trying to pull in on itself. When these things happen, my voice takes on a quality of fright, and I become

165

breathless. Before these things occur, the unusual spiritual voice comes forth from deep within me.

When the Lord completed this phase of my body-work, He gave me another huge golden key. I've never seen such a big key before, and I believe it symbolizes how He is unlocking every area of my life so He can use me for His glory.

THE LAST KEY AND LOCK

ON THE NIGHT of November 11, 1997, the Lord worked with me for approximately two and one half hours, a much shorter time than usual. This entire period was devoted to working on my hands. As He did so, my hands shook vigorously in many different ways. This reaction lasted for one and one half hours.

This time I was frightened because my hands had never shaken like this before, and it was repeated seven different times. When He had completed this work on my hands, an unusual voice came forth, and the Lord showed me a key and a lock.

The fact was that He had unlocked my whole body for His service. The last key and lock were the biggest I had ever seen. He told me that the key would unlock my whole body. As the key turned in the lock, I saw the lock open, and my body lifted as it shook and jerked while I perspired profusely. Afterward, my hands began to shake violently again, and they gestured in the shape of a cross seven different times.

Then the Lord spoke to me.

"*My daughter, I am very pleased with all the body-work in your life. Now you are ready for the world. Because of your obedience and faith, I was able to complete this work fully. Thank you for your patience.*"

The Lord has frequently told me that the body-work He did with me was the hardest part. Without His power of healing, I could not have endured it. After four hours of His continual workmanship, my body would feel so tired that I wondered how I could possibly go on.

The Lord explained: "*One hour of the body work you have gone through is harder than eight hours of work during the day, because of the anointing.*"

I knew this was true, because at the end of each phase of the work, I would feel dizzy and weak for a long time. I always had to catch up on my sleep and rest.

ON DECEMBER 6, 1997, the Lord began to work with me in different ways after my nightly prayer and morning prayer. He showed me a new vision that was accompanied with a supernatural vision-voice. I could see the whole world enveloped in a clear blue sky, then the scene changed to one with a heavy cloud cover. When the clouds began to break apart, fire rained down from the sky. The whole earth was ablaze, and then the fire changed to snow. The entire world was covered with a thick white blanket of snow.

A second vision then came forth, accompanied by a strong vision-voice. This time the Lord showed me the whole world once more. The sky was filled with black clouds. Then it began to storm and rain. The lightning flashed, and many cities were destroyed. I could see the buildings within these cities collapsing.

My voice intensified, and I began to cry as the Lord told me that all of these things would begin to come to pass at that time.

"I will destroy many countries with floods, tornadoes and earthquakes in order to show the people that I am God, and that they need to prepare for My coming. Many people will suffer, many will divorce, many hearts will be broken for their loved ones, and many lives will be taken, including many Christians. You must include these visions in your book, My daughter."

Countless times He showed me similar visions, and He told me that it is time to prepare for His coming.

Chapter 18

An End-Time Prophetess

And He Himself gave some to be…prophets…
for the equipping of the saints for the work of ministry,
for the edifying of the body of Christ.

—EPHESIANS 4:11–12

EVERY TIME THE Lord's presence comes near, the groaning from deep within my spirit begins. Words do not come forth, just groans. This permits me to communicate with the Lord from my heart to His heart, bypassing my voice and mind. Sometimes we also whisper to each other.

The Lord explained that heart-to-heart communication is the most important kind of fellowship. Through this, Satan is unable to hear what we are saying. During each body-work session I would not able to speak directly to the Lord with my voice, but only with my heart.

"My daughter, you are an End-Times prophetess," the Lord told me, *"and you are living proof of My Word and My prophecies."*

He went on to explain that it was for this reason that He showed me the writers with their notebooks in His throne room when I went to heaven with Him. He told me that many people don't believe His words and prophecies, and He said even some Christians do not believe them. Now I realize that everything He shared with me is a confirmation of the words of His Bible, and the prophecies He gave me are echoes of His Word.

ABOUNDING JOY

IN WORSHIP TIMES at church I experience such wonderful joy that it truly

168

cannot be described. It is so all-consuming that I am unaware of other people around me. After the heavenly visions He has given to me I focus only on the Lord's presence. I can see Him in the front of the church, and He always looks so happy.

What other people may think about me no longer bothers me. When I go to church, it is to please the Lord only, not other people. I have learned that a person cannot truly please the Lord if he or she is worried about what other people think.

After Easter 1995, some people considered my actions entertainment, because of all the shaking and jumping I would do under the power of the Holy Spirit. However, heavenly songs and dancing are included during each worship time now. I used to wonder what people thought about me, but now I don't care, just as long as the Lord is pleased by my obedience. Pastor Larry Randolph prophesied that I am "godly different," and he is absolutely right.

MORE UNLOCKINGS AND VISIONS

AFTER SIXTEEN MONTHS of body-work, I rested for twenty-six days. I thought the Lord would begin to use me, but He simply visited me each morning between 1 A.M. and 2 A.M. and talked with me for about an hour. This happened on eight different occasions, and then He began to anoint me and to continue working on my hands after my bedtime prayers, and sometimes after my morning prayers as well.

Each time after regular prayer, His presence comes to me. After He talks with me, He usually anoints me with very strong power, and I repeat all the hand movements He did before, and He shows me many visions that He has previously revealed. He follows all this by working on many different aspects of my preparation, including the hand movements. He lets me rest between different phases of the body-work.

The unlocking of the thirty-third lock was quite a different experience from the other times. This lock was shaped differently than the others, and it was the biggest lock and key of all. The Lord was wearing a golden crown and robe. He touched my hands with His hands, and then He said, *"You are ordained by your Lord."*

The next night He made both my hands spin around seven different times, in seven different ways. This was followed by my unusual vision-voice, and I noticed His golden apparel. He showed me a silver ball that was so round and shiny it seemed to be like glass. He held it in his right hand and said, *"My daughter, you are a perfectly made vessel."*

I learned that every time the Lord brought an object to His visits with me, it symbolized something He was doing in my life. One night, after my bedtime prayer, the Lord showed me another vision of the sky.

The moon and stars brightened the sky, and I saw the Lord in a shaft of light that was as bright as the sun. He was wearing a gold crown and robe, and He was holding a golden ball that was covered with stones, which He was lowering from heaven. A bright and shiny brilliance surrounded Him.

My special vision-voice came forth, and I saw the Lord before me. He was holding the ball in both of His hands, then He put it in His right hand and said, *"I will pour this anointing on your head."*

When He removed the top of the ball, steam came out. When He poured it upon me, I didn't feel the same strong power I had felt during previous anointings. After this, He showed me the whole ocean and the world, and He said, *"The world is yours."*

A PILLAR OF FIRE

ON MARCH 31, 1998, after my bedtime prayer, the Lord's presence came near. After we talked, He told me, *"I must show you this."* My eyes closed tightly, and my vision-voice came forth. Spiritual power filled my body, and I saw the entire sky on fire.

I rested for a few minutes, and my eyes closed tightly again. This time I saw a huge pillar of fire coming down from the sky. It fell into the middle of the ocean. After a few moments more of rest, my eyes closed tightly again, and power came into my body.

I heard a loud noise in the air, and I saw many airplanes in the sky. They were shooting huge, oval-shaped missiles. As the missiles were fired, many buildings were being destroyed. Armed and uniformed people scattered everywhere, and I began to cry. The Lord explained that this war would begin in 1998.

TIME TO AWAKEN

ON THE MORNING of April 1, 1998, after my morning prayer, the Lord showed me the same vision as the night before. He told me that the terrible things that were happening were not all Satan's work.

"I must wake the sleeping people," He explained. *"Many of them are*

living in the dark, and when bad things happen, they blame them on Satan. I will make the hearts of these people tremble because many of them are not seeing or hearing how soon I am coming for them. The only ones that will hear the trumpet are those who are ready and waiting for Me. The rest will have to go through the tribulation."

A GOLD BOTTLE

THE NEXT DAY, April 2, 1998, was especially meaningful as well. After my bedtime prayer, the Lord's presence came near as usual. After we talked, He said: *"My daughter, I have a special surprise for you tonight. You must see this."*

Immediately after He spoke these words, my eyes closed tightly and I groaned loudly. Then I saw heaven open, and two persons came down. The area surrounding these people was as bright as the sun. One was wearing a white robe and holding a huge bottle with both hands. The Lord was wearing a golden gown and crown. Then the two people vanished, and my special vision-voice came forth.

After this the Lord stood in front of me. He was holding the huge gold bottle. It appeared to be made of solid gold, and it did not have a top on it. The Lord held the bottle in both hands. The enormity of the bottle surprised me, and I thought that I would barely be able to hold it in both my arms.

Curiosity filled my heart as I reached for the bottle, and it truly did fill my arms. I realized this was why an angel had to carry it down for the Lord. The Lord spoke to me: *"I will pour it on you from the top of your head to the bottom of your feet. Your body shall be anointed with fire."*

The minute He started pouring forth the contents of the gold bottle upon me, my entire body felt like it was on fire, and my voice sounded as if I was sick, and I began to cry. Then I began to sing, and my hands stretched out sideways, then raised above my head.

As this was happening I was saying, "Father, thank You for everything You promised to me." I couldn't put my hands down until I had said, "In Jesus' name."

Next, my hands raised seven different times to the Father, and I said things I wanted to say in Jesus' name. Then I fell prostrate on the floor, and my face hit the floor as I humbled myself before the Father. I discovered that I couldn't raise my head until I said, "In Jesus' name."

I soon learned that I could never do these things on my own. Until I say, "In Jesus' name," my hands won't go down, and my face will not move. I believe the Lord was teaching me the importance of praying to the Father in Jesus' name.

I always pray in Jesus' name for everything, and I believe He wants me to include this in the book so those who don't use Jesus' name will understand. The Lord then told me that the angel who had assisted Him was Michael.

THE ANGEL MICHAEL

IT WAS EARLY in the morning on April 3, 1998, and after my usual prayer time the Lord advised me to remember all that He had told me the night before. I asked Him if I could see Michael, the archangel. He said: *"Michael is a very handsome angel. He is seven feet tall, weighs 300 pounds, has blue eyes and blond hair."*

Through the heart-to-heart communication that we had established, I asked the Lord if I could clearly see Michael. Just then my eyes closed very tightly, and the groaning from my spirit grew very loud. My body moved backward against the bed. Then I saw Michael standing in the backyard.

Within seconds he was standing before me, and his head almost touched the ceiling. Just as the Lord had described him, Michael had blond hair and deep blue eyes. His complexion was very fair, and he had a wonderful smile on his face. He said, *"Choo Nam, you are my Lord's precious daughter, and you are pleasing Him."* With that, he smiled once more and left. The thing about him that I remember most clearly was his sparkling, deep blue eyes. His beautiful smile gave me a sense of joy and peace.

ANOTHER VISIT TO HEAVEN

ON APRIL 28, 1998, after my bedtime prayer, the Lord showed me all the things He had already shown me on the trips to heaven. He also reminded me of all the things that are going to happen on the earth in the very near future.

One thing He did not show me again was hell. I believe He didn't want me to re-experience such a horrible, hideous scene. Truly, I can never forget anything the Lord has ever shown me or told me.

Jesus told His disciples: "These things I have spoken to you while being present with you. But the Helper, the Holy Spirit, whom the Father will send in My name, He will teach you all things, and bring to your remembrance all things that I said to you" (John 14:25–26).

That was exactly what was taking place in my life, and the Holy Spirit's work of remembrance continues in my life to the present.

Chapter 19

Growing Confidence

*But let patience have its perfect work,
that you may be perfect and complete,
lacking nothing.*

—JAMES 1:4

On May 7, 1998, the Lord came to me wearing a gold robe and a gold crown. He stood in front of me, and my body had such a strong anointing imposed upon it that at first I grew frightened. I saw the Lord's right hand raised up, and both my hands stretched out toward Him. He said, *"I am blessing you for all the work I have prepared for you to do."*

From July 11, 1996, until the present the Lord has done much work in my life. I've tried to detail all of this in the book by writing down each step. The Lord told me to record His work and His words under the guidance of the Holy Spirit. At first, it all seemed too hard to believe—the special gifts, the wonderful visitations, the prophetic visions, the trips to heaven and the supernatural events. It all seemed too good to be true.

Looking back over all that I have experienced, I realize that the Lord was taking me through a special growth and grooming process of preparation for ministry. As a result, my faith has soared and my hope has exploded within me. Now I believe everything He tells me and shows to me. He has kept every promise, including all the promises about the book. He gave me the title for the book, and He led me to a Spirit-filled writer who has helped me polish some of my words and phrases.

Knowing that everything He has said is true makes waiting all the more difficult.

After the vision of heaven, the Lord fulfilled all the things that needed to be done until now. His presence would always appear after each and every one of my prayer times. That was His promise, and He was completely trustworthy. About two years ago, when I was experiencing some unhappiness about matters at my church, I prayed earnestly to the Lord. I needed His wisdom and His guidance.

I knew that the Bible's promise was true: "If any of you lack wisdom, let him ask of God, that giveth to all men liberally, and upbraideth not; and it shall be given him. But let him ask in faith, nothing wavering. For he that wavereth is like a wave of the sea driven with the wind and tossed" (James 1:5–6, KJV).

In spite of my belief in that promise, it seemed as if the heavens were becoming as brass when I prayed. I could not see the Lord or hear His voice, and I wondered if I would ever be able to see Him again. I began to weep. After sobbing and screaming in a loud voice that called out to Jesus over and over again for a period of fifteen minutes or more, the Lord reappeared to me.

That day, I learned something vitally important. He showed me that my heart must be cheerful and clean in order to experience His presence and to hear His voice. I believe that is why the Lord removed from my life contact with all the people I knew since He started taking me to heaven until the present. He doesn't want anything to interrupt my mind while He is training me for the work He has for me.

Prayer, and the Lord's Presence

I LOVE THE Lord, and I know He loves me. I pray many times each day at nearly the same time every day. Each time I do, the Lord's presence comes to me. Then we talk together. This happens every day, and sometimes our conversations go on for very long periods. The Lord reminds me of all the important things He has shown me and shared with me.

Each time I pray, at the end of my prayer time my stomach tightens, my body shakes, my spirit groans and then the Lord appears. When He departs, my body goes through the same manifestations it experiences before He appears to me.

After all the body-work was completed, the Lord would visit me every day at dinner time. My husband, Roger, always prays at dinnertime, and I agree with him in prayer by praying in tongues. As we do this, the Lord's presence appears right on time, then He departs at the end of prayer. He always comments about the food, and even jokes with me sometimes. I usually laugh at His wonderful humor.

The Lord usually tells me to eat anything I want, and He explains that in heaven I will not be able to eat many of the things I enjoy here. Roger knows what I experience at these times because he sees my body shaking. Each time the anointing is so strong that my body feels like it is on fire. When dinner consists of seafood and vegetables, the Lord always tells me that they are good, nutritious foods.

WHO THE LORD IS TO ME

MANY PEOPLE BELIEVE the Lord is a very strict individual. To me, He is a kind, fun-loving, understanding, patient, loving, compassionate person. He always speaks to me gently, except when I question something He commands me to do. Then He becomes angry with me. I have learned that the Lord doesn't like questioning or complaining.

He is such a patient listener, no matter how long I talk. He never interrupts me. I soon discovered that He knows everything there is to know about me. He often reminds me of my plans for a given day.

It has now been almost two and one half years that I have been living under the Lord's control. I always endeavor to obey His ways instead of my own, and I find that I am very pleased with everything, but I still struggle at times with impatience.

Jesus is my best friend, and I find Him to be very human. I can talk to Him anytime or anywhere. He even told me that I can ask Him any kind of question, but I must not question Him when He asks me to do something.

Even though He is my best friend, I am very humbled in His presence. I reverentially fear and respect Him very much, because I know He is God. At the beginning, I asked to see His presence more clearly and to hear His voice more distinctly. He responded, *"My daughter, you see My spirit."*

Because He is a Spirit, I am not able to see Him clearly at all times. Whenever His presence becomes vivid to me, I am almost overwhelmed by the strong power of His anointing upon my life.

During some of the body-work sessions, I am able to make out the Lord's presence more clearly than usual. When this happens, the accompanying anointing is tremendously powerful. Since the Lord showed me heaven and the pit of hell, I have not been the same. Now, whenever I see the unsaved or I am aware of lukewarmness in a Christian's life, my heart begins to ache for them because I know what it takes to get into God's kingdom.

The urgency I feel for souls keeps me motivated at all times. Now I even want to help my enemies whenever I can. The Lord has repeated to me several times what is going to happen to people after the judgment.

He explained that only about 20 percent of Christians are actually pleasing Him. He has assured me, however, that He will give His people a final chance to purify themselves before He comes for us, and He explained that this is why He chose me to write this book.

He wants me to serve as living proof of the Bible and His prophecies, because many people do not believe what they read in the Bible, nor do they believe He is coming soon for His people. He also said that this book would be a tool for the salvation of millions of souls.

No Fear!

BECAUSE OF ALL that I've experienced, I no longer feel afraid. A new boldness has come to me—a holy boldness in the Lord. I now feel that I could stand before millions and testify to the world all that I have seen and heard.

My body and my mouth were sealed while the Lord was doing the necessary body-work and preparatory teaching in my life. The Lord told me that He wanted me to keep all this to myself until a later time that He would reveal. The timing has to be just right because I'm sure there are many people who would not believe me if I were to tell them what has happened.

After I experienced the visions and other supernatural phenomena, my writer pointed out some Scriptures that help to verify the experiences God gave to me. At the time, I did not know the Scriptures well enough to know where such information could be found.

In fact, I used to complain to the Lord that I did not know enough to be used by Him. Frequently I would ask Him, "Why did You choose me, Lord?"

He answered very clearly: *"It is because you are so teachable that I have chosen you."*

He explained that I would not do anything on my own because I understood that I needed Him in everything. That, of course, is the key to progress in the spiritual life. It is also the key to being used by the Lord—to remain open to Him and all He has in store for us.

Now, when I read the Bible, I can understand some things very clearly, whereas before I felt almost blinded to the truth. I have found that I can memorize Bible verses with great ease, and I have memorized close to 300 of my favorite Scriptures. The Lord helped because I have so much desire for His Word. This was also needed for witnessing and meditating. I realize that without knowing God's Word, it is hard to witness.

Throughout the many years of training, the Lord has disciplined me, tested me and even disappointed me to determine just how strong my faith actually is.

He removed all ungodly influences (including people) from my life. Sometimes He even permitted sickness to come back to ones He had previously healed so He could see how strong my faith in Him and my love for Him actually are. At times, He even permitted me to grow disappointed so He could see how impatient and angry I would become; but even in such circumstances I have never loved Him or trusted Him less, no matter how disappointed I became.

I cried in His presence countless times, asking Him why He was making me wait so long for the fulfillment of His promises. There were a few times when I thought He was going to fulfill His promise in a given week, only to discover that I had to go through the same training processes I had already gone through. It caused me so much disappointment that I actually wanted to die.

Sometimes I feel so run down that I want to give up everything the Lord promised. At times I have felt that I heard a wrong voice. Several times I asked Him if I was hearing other voices or my own voice. His voice would reflect disappointment, as He would remind me that I was hearing everything from my Lord Jesus Christ of Nazareth.

When He said these words, instantaneous joy would come so quickly that I would forget all of my discouragement. If it weren't for His talking with me, I don't think I would have endured.

During His training, I cried numerous times. When He was finished, however, He said: *"Choo Nam, you have passed your test by scoring more than 100 percent."* His words of praise and affirmation thrilled my soul. It was a three-year course for ministry, and I can honestly say I never disobeyed the Lord once. He knew I was always available for Him to do His work.

No matter how difficult the work became, nor how disappointed I was, I always knew deep and abiding joy and peace. After my visits to the heavenly kingdom, I feel as if I now live in the kingdom of God. All I think about is what I can do to please the Lord, and I will do whatever it takes. Things of this earth mean nothing to me now.

Often, I've asked the Lord to take me home permanently, but He has refused by saying that there is much work for me to do. Since January 1996, my daily life has been lived entirely for God. He is first, last and everything in between. He is my all. I normally pray four or five hours a day, but during the times of body-work, I spent between seven and nine hours a day with the Lord, and sometimes even more.

MY LOVING HUSBAND

HOW THANKFUL I am for the faithful love and patient understanding of my husband, Roger. I prayed for Him to come to know the Lord, and He did so a year and a half after I did. I have never pushed Roger with regard to spiritual things, but he is always there for me—a constant companion and support. I asked the Lord to help us have the same mind in serving Him, and He gave me a completely new man. The first year of his walk with God, Roger read the Bible six times.

Without His agreement, our marriage could never have survived. Roger is a true help to me in every respect, and he is a great support in my ministry.

Roger and I know that without God we are helpless. With Him, however, we both know that we can accomplish all things. There is nothing that is impossible with our perfect God. He knows everything there is to know about us. He even knows what we have need of before we express those needs to Him. Jesus said, "Your Father knoweth what things ye have need of, before ye ask him" (Matt. 6:8, KJV).

We have chosen to put God first in our lives. Jesus said, "Seek ye first the kingdom of God, and his righteousness; and all these things shall be added unto you" (Matt. 6:33, KJV). This wonderful promise has proved itself true in our lives over and over again.

I must admit that sometimes it's not easy to live a fully spiritual life, always putting God first; but I've learned that I cannot do anything without the Lord's permission. He always tells me to stay focused on Him and the work He is preparing me for. He warns me not to put anything or anyone in front of those goals.

It's been difficult, but I've learned that keeping my mind stayed on Him is the source of perfect peace, as the prophet Isaiah pointed out. If anything is bothering me, I'm not able to focus on Him, and I lose my peace. I know this is not God's will for me, because Jesus said: "Peace I leave with you, my peace I give unto you: not as the world giveth, give I unto you. Let not your heart be troubled, neither let it be afraid" (John 14:27, KJV).

The Lord is always a present help in our lives, even when we can't see or hear Him. "Jesus Christ is the same yesterday, today, and forever" (Heb. 13:8). He is living in us, and that is how He knows everything about us. I have learned that when we pray to Him or worship Him, He wants us to focus only on Him.

Chapter 20

The Heavens Opened Up

But he, being full of the Holy Spirit,
gazed into heaven and saw the glory of God,
and Jesus standing at the right hand of God,
and said, "Look! I see the heavens opened and the
Son of Man standing at the right hand of God!"

—ACTS 7:55–56

O N MAY 16, 1998, the Lord told me in the morning that I must prepare for bed early that evening. Therefore, after my bedtime prayer, a special anointing came to me, and the Lord said, *"I must show you something."* The minute He uttered these words, my eyes closed tightly and a special groaning came forth from my spirit. Heaven began to open before me.

At first everything was bright, and then I saw all of heaven. It was a place of purity and whiteness, and the roads and buildings were immaculately clean.

He took me into heaven once more, and He began to show me things one by one. A brilliance like sunlight was everywhere.

Then the Lord showed me all the oceans of the world and the whole earth. Snow was covering the earth. The Lord explained: *"I must purify My people before I bring them to My kingdom. Unless they are pure-hearted, they cannot see My kingdom."*

Then I remembered one of the Beatitudes: "Blessed are the pure in heart, for they shall see God" (Matt. 5:8).

My arms stretched out sideways, making a crosslike form out of my body. This lasted for at least ten minutes. I cried throughout that time span, but I wasn't sure if my tears were coming from gratitude, joy or pain. The Lord was repeating some of the previous lessons, and He reiterated that He wanted me to put them all down in the book.

This helps me to better understand the title He gave to this book, *Heaven Is So Real!* By repeating these lessons and experiences in my life, I grew to know exactly how real heaven is.

THE THRONE OF GOD

ON JUNE 6, 1998, the Lord told me to go to bed early once again. I knew something great was about to happen. After my bedtime prayer, a strong anointing came, and once more the heavens were opened above me. I saw God's throne, and I saw the Father sitting upon it. He was wearing a white crown and robe, and He had long, white hair. The Lord Jesus was standing at His right side. Jesus' appearance was the same as I had always remembered it.

Both the Father and the Son were wearing white. I couldn't see their faces, but I heard a voice saying: *"Choo Nam, I am releasing you to do the work I have prepared you for. You will serve Me now. I am pleased with everything about you."*

Hearing this confirmation was more thrilling than words can tell. After this vision of heaven vanished, the Lord's presence appeared once more, and He repeated what the Father had said to me. It was as if I was being launched into the service God had called me to, and it was wonderful to know this was happening.

ANGELS WATCHING OVER US

THROUGHOUT THE MONTH of December 1998, the Lord again showed me many of the things He had already shown me. He repeated some of the body-work as well. He opened heaven for me time and time again. Each time He did I would see the entire sky very clearly, including the bright stars of heaven.

Above the stars I saw clouds, and above the clouds I saw heaven. The brightness of heaven was astounding, and its vastness is indescribable. It is truly an endless expanse that goes all around the earth. Whenever the Lord shows heaven to me, I respond with constant joyful singing.

This time when the Lord showed heaven to me, he also showed me a multitude of angels flying everywhere. I noticed, also, that the angels of heaven were flying throughout the atmosphere of earth as well. The Lord told me that the angels I saw flying all around the earth were watching over His people.

Some of the visions God imparted to me came after the Lord made my fingers touch my eyes more than a thousand times in two months. He took me through each step seven different times.

Whenever this happened I would see the most beautiful sparkles, like diamonds, then I would see the beautiful stones of heaven. One stone, in particular, looked like an eyeball. At first, it appeared to be a very dark purple, then it changed to lighter and lighter colors until it looked like a sparkling, clear diamond. It is the most beautifully colored stone I've ever seen. It almost seemed to be on my hand, because I could see its sparkles so clearly.

CHRISTMAS EVE MEMORIES WITH THE LORD

ON DECEMBER 24, 1998, the Lord came to me once more in His magnificent Christmas crown and robe. His presence was the same that Christmas Eve as it had been the two previous years, but the experience was different. The minute I saw His presence this time, I knelt before Him, then sang, danced and cried with unspeakable joy. This was not something I manufactured; it all came as a result of the Holy Spirit taking control of my life.

I can honestly say that I will never forget anything the Lord showed me or said to me. He often repeated things to help me develop patience, and He reminded me that without patience, no one might truly serve Him.

He pointed out that salvation is an unmerited gift of His grace, but receiving other special gifts requires hard work. All the gifts are free, but we must practice patience to obtain them. Everything in our lives must be according to His way, not our way. We must obey Him, no matter what it takes.

He explained that during His time on this earth He lived only to obey His Father's will. He was not interested in pursuing His own will or plans, only God's. He also pointed out to me that those to whom He imparts special gifts for ministry must pay a higher price than others. He concluded by saying, *"Even if you don't want to do this work, you have to do so, because I have chosen you to be an End-Time prophetess."*

As I mentioned before, the Lord is so understanding of my needs, even when I complain. He always stands there and listens to everything I say. When I finish, He says: *"My daughter, I understand how you feel, but I must do it this way. It has to be in My way and in My time."* After His gentle rebukes I always feel humbled, and I respond by repenting of my impatience, my questioning and my lack of understanding.

A NEW YEAR DAWNS

ON JANUARY 1, 1999, the Lord showed me His beautiful robe and crown once again. It was the first time He did so on a New Year's Day. I asked Him what the significance of this change was, and He explained, *"My daughter, this is a very special year for My people."* His loving presence overwhelmed me, and I started to sing and dance and cry before Him.

On January 8, 1999, the Lord again wore His special crown and gown. The vision-voice came through me, and I began to cry. I realized that the Lord wears these special vestments only on particularly meaningful occasions, usually to celebrate a major milestone.

He told me that He was celebrating my work. We conversed for a while, then my hands stretched toward Him, and He put His hands on top of my hands. He said simply, *"Bless you."*

As He said this, the power seemed so strong that I felt my whole body was merging with Him. I sobbed under the intense anointing of that moment, and then my hands once more rested on my chest as I quieted down.

The period from January 9 through January 14, 1999, was particularly memorable for me. The Lord showed me a vision of the church I attended. In this spiritual vision I saw many people in the church who were overflowing with the Holy Spirit, and I saw handicapped people walking, empty wheelchairs and other blessings. I began to sing and dance as I also saw the church's parking lot filled with cars.

THE POWER OF PRAYER

ON JANUARY 15, 1999, after my bedtime prayer, the Lord came and we talked together. The special anointing came upon me, and the vision-voice came forth. Then I began to sing. I saw the Lord changed into His beautiful crown and gown, and I began to sing and dance. I went through several hand movements, and each was done seven different times.

After this session of body-work was finished, the Lord changed back into His normal white gown. He proceeded to tell me that He was revealing all the work He had prepared for me to do. From this time forth, He explained, I must only pray in tongues to reveal continually all the work He prepared and all His promises to me. When He begins my dancing ministry, I will have fellowship only with Him and will pray for the work. He pointed out that I would not have as much time for prayer.

For many years I've been engaged in intercessory prayer seven days a week. It takes nearly two hours for me to pray for the people God puts on my heart, and for all the nations of the world. I said, "Lord, it will be hard for me not to pray for all these people."

He responded, *"It is time for them to pray for you."*

Then He proceeded to tell me how to pray most effectively. *"Choo Nam, as you begin to pray, always praise the Father first, and then start to pray in tongues for your work and ministry."* He further encouraged me to take my stand upon His promises so the enemy would not ever be able to steal the promises from me.

As the Master taught me more about prayer, I realized how very important it is in each of our lives. He told me to pray in tongues when I rise in the morning until the flow ceases each Sunday before I go to church. Then he urged me to go to church thirty minutes early each time, and to pray in tongues without interruption until the worship begins.

Some people don't understand why I do this, but the ones who do understand are those who have a deep, personal walk with the Lord. They understand what I mean when I say that Jesus is more real to me than I am to myself.

He listens so very patiently when I talk to Him. No matter how bad a given set of circumstances may seem, all I have to do is to talk it over with Him, then the situation gets better. I talk to Him in the Spirit, but to me, He is so human and real that it's as if I've entered an entirely new dimension of life. No one understands me like Jesus does. I value Him above life itself.

My church work now consists only of praying for the church, its people, the pastors and so on. I do so daily, and I worship the Lord with all my heart during the church services. During those precious times of worship I am totally oblivious to those around me.

I usually see the Lord walking around the front of the church with a very happy face. That is why I frequently find myself laughing heartily during worship. During those times I give every ounce of my energy and attention to the Lord, and I believe that's what worship really is.

REMAIN QUIET UNTIL THE PROPER TIME

IN JANUARY 1999 I was under instructions from the Lord not to share any of what He had done in and for me with anyone. He had said He would reveal those things to the people when the proper time came. Sometimes this was difficult for me, especially as it pertained to my family and my pastor, but I had no choice but to obey the Lord because I knew I would lose the blessing if I didn't.

Sometimes this realization made me want to leave my church and go to another church where no one knew me. I almost wanted to hide from others, because I am a very sensitive person, and I hate for others to think I'm avoiding them.

It all required supernatural patience. I realized that many might not believe me about my revelation of heaven, but I was not concerned about such matters, because I knew my Lord Jesus would take care of it as He had said He would. Now I know how Jesus felt when no one believed Him when He walked this earth. Realizing what He had to go through for me always makes me feel better when I'm misunderstood or judged by others.

A POLISHED VESSEL

DURING THE FIRST part of January 1999 the Lord showed me some rough, brown-colored clay and said, *"My daughter, you were like this before I began to work on your physical and mental body. Now you are a perfectly polished vessel."* He showed this to me again, and the brown clay had become very shiny and sparkling. This revelation caused me to feel humbled once more, because I realized anew what God had done in my life.

On January 23, 1999, the Lord told me that on the next day (a Sunday) at 6 A.M. I should begin praying in tongues for all His promises and to continue until the flow stopped. He also told me to go to the church thirty minutes early, praise the Father first and to pray in tongues until the beginning of worship.

He was careful to warn me not to let anyone interrupt me. His direction was clear, *"You may go earlier, but no later than 9:30."* This, I realized, must have been the reason for the new tongue He had given to me about ten days before.

A week later, the Lord told me to do the same things. About ten minutes before the worship service began, I saw the Lord standing on the platform, and He was wearing the beautiful gown and crown He always wears on special occasions. He looked very happy, and the minute I saw His presence I experienced a heavy spiritual anointing.

I could barely stand up during worship times. After church, I prayed as usual, and I asked the Lord why He was wearing the special vestments at church that morning. He answered, *"I have opened the door for your work to begin."*

THE WORK HAS BEGUN

ON FEBRUARY 7, 1999, the Lord awakened me around 2 A.M. to let me know that my work had begun. He explained that it was a very special day for me, so I expected Him to take me to the front of the church to dance as He had promised long ago, but this did not happen.

I was very disappointed, and I cried and complained before Him when I returned home. For at least one hour the Lord listened to me, and when I finished my outpouring, I humbled myself in repentance. The Lord simply said that I must have misunderstood Him. Despite all these negative feelings, however, it was the strongest anointing I'd ever experienced during a worship time.

On March 11, 1999, after my usual morning prayer time, my hands began to touch my eyes, and the Lord showed me the beautiful stones once more. I didn't want to open my eyes. A thought came to me, and I told the Lord if I never saw anyone or anything again as long as I am on this earth that I still wanted Him to use me as He had promised He would, so the spiritually blinded people of the earth could truly see.

I have seen enough of this world, and everything it has to offer pales in comparison with the light of the heavenly vision God has graciously given me. Just seeing my Lord and serving Him for the rest of my life are enough for me, I realized, and I began to weep. I really meant every word, and the Lord knew my thoughts. He said, *"My daughter, you are doubly blessed."*

Though I wasn't exactly sure what that meant, I knew I had been telling the Lord that if I ever had to exchange my life for this book, I would be honored to do so. My life in this world holds very little meaning for me now. I only want everyone to read the book, and to discover what it takes to enter the kingdom of God.

Chapter 21

A Fool for God

But God has chosen the foolish things
of the world to put to shame the wise.

—1 CORINTHIANS 1:27

ON THE FIRST day of spring, 1999, the Lord told me many things during worship, and I almost made a fool of myself. Usually during worship times, my hands will move in every direction as I participate in the heavenly dancing and singing, but on this Sunday morning, I couldn't even lift my hands during the entire worship service, but my body was powerfully anointed throughout the time. I was confused by this turn of events.

In fact, the whole experience made me feel miserable. It was about the fourth time I had felt very unhappy since the Lord had started showing me the heavenly visions. I still had peace, but my mind was somewhat disturbed, even after the service when I was in the presence of the Lord.

After church, I complained to the Lord, and I did so again before dinnertime, but the Lord remained silent. I felt increasingly miserable. Suddenly the thought came to me that it was Satan who was doing this to me, so I cast out the devil in Jesus' name, and joy came back to me instantaneously.

I rejoiced with great smiles and happiness; then I asked the Lord for forgiveness. He responded: *"My daughter, you do not know how to protect yourself. Many Christians do not know how to cast out the enemy as you just did, and you must include this experience in your book.*

A Fool for God

"It is very important for every Christian to know how to cast the enemy out. When you are sick or you have other problems in your life, first you cast out the devil and then you pray to the Father in My name."

What an important teaching that was for me! It soon was followed by the Lord teaching me about judging others. I used to wonder why some Spirit-filled believers have so many problems with earthly things. I didn't really think badly toward them, but I must admit that I did find myself wondering about it. I would think that perhaps these Christians were living against God's will, and for this reason, bad things would happen to their loved ones. Then God used my own daughter to teach me something about this attitude.

My daughter and I had a very close relationship, and we were best friends until suddenly our relationship stopped about three years ago. She is a Spirit-filled Christian and we thought she had good marriage, but suddenly she and her husband were having problems.

Eventually my daughter divorced her husband. They had two children. It had seemed as if they had everything they needed and wanted—more than most people—but they lost everything as a result of their marital problems and subsequent divorce. Though my daughter was successful in her job, she was surrounded by unbelievers and lived a completely ungodly life. As a result, she had all kinds of problems.

Before their marriage problems began, I had noticed how my daughter was moving far from the Lord. Each time I mentioned the Lord to her, she didn't want to hear about Him or talk about Him. She went to church once a week with her children and read the Bible and prayed, but otherwise she lived a worldly life.

Before her problems began, she had taken my advice, but suddenly she quit wanting to hear anything I had to say. She was a completely changed person. Roger and I felt that we never really knew her. We felt that she had lost all of her principles.

It gave me a measure of comfort to know the Lord was watching her behavior, but I knew He would not do anything for her until she repented and gave herself totally to Him. God will never force any of us to do anything that we don't want to do.

The Lord taught us many things through our daughter. Since becoming a Christian, I have not believed in divorce or in doing ungodly things knowingly. Therefore, I was very ashamed about my daughter's divorce and her ungodly life. It broke my heart so much that she was hurting our Lord Jesus. This was the hardest thing that had happened to us since we were saved, but we never blamed the Lord once. We humbled ourselves because we knew He would take care of everything in His way perfectly.

I believe the Lord didn't like my shameful thoughts about this matter, and He gave me no choice but to include my daughter's story in this book. I had already promised Him that no matter what the situation, I would obey Him all the days of my life. Therefore, I never questioned Him about why I had to do this. I only said: "If this is what you want, Lord, I will do it."

Now her life is settled and our relationship is like it used to be, but her life is so busy that she doesn't have time for herself or others. I am most concerned that she doesn't have time for the Lord.

After the revelation of heaven I had received and experienced, the Lord mentioned to me several times that there will be many divorces, many broken families and many people dying. Among them, He explained, will be many Christians.

I learned the things that happen to our children may have nothing at all to do with a parent's life with God. The Lord explained it this way, *"Even many faithful Christians and their loved ones have bad things happen sometimes. Judging others is one of the worst sins. No one has the right to judge others, no matter what the situation is, and until you learn through your own experience, this is a hard truth to understand."*

From that moment on, no matter what ungodly things may happen in people's lives, I choose never to think anything evil toward them. Rather, I choose to have compassion on them, as Paul commanded: "Brethren, if a man be overtaken in a fault, ye which are spiritual, restore such an one in the spirit of meekness; considering thyself, lest thou also be tempted. Bear ye one another's burdens, and so fulfill the law of Christ" (Gal. 6:1–2, KJV).

WORSHIP TIMES

SINCE FEBRUARY 7, 1999, the Lord has revealed His presence to me every Sunday morning, always between 1 A.M. and 2 A.M. He uses this time to tell me what I should do during the Sunday morning service. Since March 21, I haven't been able to move my hands during the entire worship time.

Then, on March 28, I couldn't move my hands or my mouth, and I cried during the entire service with such joy and humbleness because I knew it was the Holy Spirit who was controlling my body. The Lord told me I should not ever do anything on my own when worship begins, so I always would sit there until the Holy Spirit would move upon me.

On this occasion, my body was powerfully anointed, and I stood up, but I could not lift my hands throughout the entire worship time. When the worship ended, my hands and mouth released the Lord's power.

On April 11, 1999, the Lord told me in the morning that it would be a special day, so I geared up for action in the realm of miracles. Instead, the Lord came with His gold crown and robe, and He stood by the pulpit for at least twenty minutes. That alone was miracle enough, I reasoned.

I prayed the entire time under a very heavy anointing. I could not move my hands or dance throughout the entire worship time.

On April 18, 1999, the Lord instructed me about what I should do that morning after I prayed in tongues for a half hour before worship. He told me not to move my body in my own way but to sit and wait, so that is exactly what I did.

Before the first song was over, my body stood up, but I couldn't move any part of it. Suddenly heavenly songs came forth, and the Holy Spirit moved my body to the front of the worship team, and my body turned toward the congregation and I started to dance with my heavenly song.

When worship was over, my singing and dancing stopped, and I returned to my seat with the Lord's permission. During the whole time while I was dancing my eyes were closed, fixed only on Jesus. I felt such unspeakable joy throughout the service. Ordinarily I am a very shy person, but I felt stunned with such a strong anointing this time that I didn't care what people thought or said.

The Lord directed me to tell the pastor that there will be many surprises and blessings coming for the church, and that the dance was under the prompting of the Holy Spirit. It was one of the happiest days of my life—a day I had long awaited because the Lord promised that this dance would be the beginning of my ministry.

I also saw a vision that day, after He started my body-work. I saw myself standing on a rock, looking down at the endless ocean. I was wearing a white gown, as I enjoyed the vision by dancing and singing on the rock.

RACHEL IN HEAVEN

ON MAY 6, 1999, after my nightly prayers, the Lord directed me to include in the book the name of a high school student shot during the

Columbine High School shootings in Colorado. Her name was Rachel.

"Rachel was chosen for End-Time use," He said, *"and she was chosen before she was born. Through her, I plan to touch millions of souls, both young and old."*

Before this I had been crying for Rachel, because it blessed me so much to know how she had stood up for her Lord in the face of death. I knew she was with Him in heaven, and that knowledge brought great joy to me. I have never felt sorry about how she died because I knew where she went after death. Whoever dies for our Lord Jesus experiences the greatest blessings of all.

The Lord told me many things about Rachel, but when I awoke the next morning in order to write the experience in the book, I completely forgot her name. No matter how hard I tried, her name would not come to me, so I thought maybe it wasn't that important for me to include her in the book.

After my morning prayer, while the Lord and I were talking, I told Him about how her name would not come back to me. He whispered, *"Rachel,"* and I've never forgotten her name again. The Lord said: *"Rachel is happier with Me than she ever was on earth, and I will bless her family. Too often people blame every bad thing that happens on Satan. If Rachel's death were Satan's will, My name would never have been brought up before she died. Satan has no power over My people if I don't allow him to.*

"Each life has a special purpose in this world. That is why I use some people in special ways. So, don't think that because someone is a faithful Christian that they will live long and perfect lives on earth. If I have to take one life in order to save another, I will do so.

"As I said before, I will have to take many lives before I return. Among them will be many Christians. Salvation is that important to Me. But always remember that I never want to see anyone perish."

REBUKED

ONE SUNDAY IN 1999, the Holy Spirit took me to the front of the sanctuary, in front of the worship team, and I joyfully began dancing and singing. Suddenly, when the pastor appeared before me, and he rebuked the dance.

The pastor grabbed my arm and took me back to my seat. I began to cry, because I knew he was hurting my Lord, but I was not ashamed or angry about what he did to me. Nonetheless, I felt very bad for my pastor, because it was the enemy that did it to him.

The dance I do during times of worship is not an ordinary dance. Because the Lord had worked with my body and hands for so many months, great power was built up within me, and the Lord directed each and every movement of my dancing. When I dance, I don't move my own hands, but the Holy Spirit moves them for me. I never try to stop my hands on my own; I let the Holy Spirit stop them.

Each step and movement is executed seven times, and I could never make these moves on my own. The Holy Spirit guides each part. It is for this reason that I go to church at least thirty minutes before worship begins, and I also pray two hours or more before I go to church, by the Lord's direction.

Then, every Monday the Lord takes me to the beach in my transformed body, and after we talk I kneel before Him. Following this, I dance before Him with a heavenly song; it is the same dance that He requires of me during church services.

Dancing, therefore, has become very important to the Lord, and I know it is part of the ministry He has given. There is so much power in my body, and after the dance, I have no strength and I can hardly stand.

After I was rebuked, I went home and talked with the Lord. I learned that He was very unhappy with my pastor. He said: *"He didn't believe you because the devil got to him. He quenched My Holy Spirit. You must never return to that church."*

For almost one month I had been dancing in front of the church, and the Lord had planned many blessings for that church. The devil ruined it.

"Only about 20 percent of churches are putting Me first; the rest of them are worrying about what people say and how much money they will have. Many churches are not concerned about reaching out to lost souls at all. That is the most important thing to Me.

"I must tell you, daughter, that many pastors will go into the valleys I showed you, then their congregations will follow. Any pastor who mistreats My special anointed servants and My prophets will not be blessed. But someone with a special blessing from Me can bring blessing to an entire church. You must put all this in your book, Choo Nam."

I begged the Lord not to require this of me, because I was worried about the effect it would have on the pastor, but the Lord reminded me that I needed to obey Him at all times. He pointed out that He wants other churches to know these things as well.

The pastor is a very anointed and loving person, but he doubted me because Satan came between him and me. We had been attending that church for more than four years, and had missed only one Sunday service because of a heavy snowfall.

My ministry at the church had been in the form of intercessory prayer, and my husband contributed a great deal of work to the building program. Roger was also the head usher, and we truly loved the pastor and church very much, but one day's experience changed everything.

A NEW BEGINNING

I HAD HEARD of Bethel Church before, but I never had a desire to go there or to any other church because the Lord had ordered me to stay where we were until such time as He would release us.

On May 16, 1999, I knew I could never go back to the first church again, and I believed the Lord would lead us to another church. My mind began to think about Bethel, and during the prayer before dinner, the Lord whispered, *"Bethel."*

That confirmed it, and my heart began to desire to go there for worship. That night we attended services at Bethel, and I experienced a warm and wonderful anointing. In fact, the anointing was so intense that my dress was soaked with perspiration.

On May 23, we attended the Sunday service at Bethel, but we had misunderstood the time of the service. We were thirty minutes late for worship, but the minute I sat down, the intense anointing of God's Holy Spirit was all over me once more. Indeed, it was uncontrollable, even though I had missed the opportunity to pray and dance before the service. To the Lord, that half hour of praying in tongues before worship is extremely important.

On May 30, 1999, we attended Bethel again, and this time I danced freely during the worship service. While I was dancing at our old church, I had felt quite uncomfortable.

The Lord had explained to me that there had been a great deal of bickering about my dancing in front of the worship team at the old church. I'm sure my discomfort had come from the Holy Spirit on those occasions. The Lord reminded me: *"Any church that doesn't let the*

Holy Spirit move the church body freely cannot be blessed. I plan to pour out a much stronger anointing upon the church before I return, and the churches had better be prepared for it."

The Lord told me that He would talk to me after the worship service about some very important things. He told me to talk to the writer about the book. He asked me to send out the manuscript for the body-work and to make a list of all the heavenly visions He has given to me over the past three years of training.

Though I had often mentioned the book to the Lord, He always told me that He would take care of it in His time and that I should not be concerned about it. The Lord was giving me some release about the book, and I was very excited.

He also told me to give a list of my heavenly visions and to share my spiritual experiences with our new pastor, Pastor Wolfson.

After three and a half years with the Lord, I realize that my thoughts and actions are no longer my own. My entire life belongs to God. My thinking, my feelings and my behaviors all have changed. I have so much compassion for lost and needy souls, and my heart aches for anyone who does not know the Lord.

Now I know that when I please my Lord and always put Him first, everything in my life will work out. My wonderful Lord has transformed me inside out, and He has taught me many amazing things about His ways. No one can make me angry any longer because the Lord's great love in my life enables me to forgive him or her.

"I will love thee, O LORD, my strength. The LORD is my rock, and my fortress, and my deliverer; my God, my strength, in whom I will trust; my buckler, and the horn of my salvation, and my high tower. I will call upon the LORD, who is worthy to be praised: so shall I be saved from mine enemies" (Ps. 18:1–3, KJV).

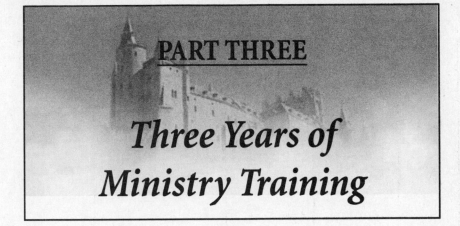

PART THREE

Three Years of Ministry Training

Chapter 22

The Time Is Short

And the Lord God of the holy prophets
sent His angel to show His servants
the things which must shortly take place.

—REVELATION 22:6 (EMPHASIS ADDED)

ON AUGUST 11, 1999, after my bedtime prayer, a very special anointing came with the Lord's presence, and it turned out to be a beautiful heavenly song with wonderful words.

Then the Lord said, *"Choo Nam, I have a surprise for you."* The minute He said this, my vision-voice came, and I beheld the Lord's presence. He was wearing the golden gown and crown as He stood before me.

My body became much stronger, and a sense of amazing power came over me. The Lord directed me to stretch my hands toward Him, and as I did so my hands moved toward Him under His power. I saw He was holding a huge gold key. Then He said, *"I am giving you this gold key for your miracle work."*

When He put the key in my hand, my body jumped and shook. I was breathless as a result of the anointing, and I started crying. Then my hand closed. Both of my hands joined together and returned to my chest for a while. Next, my hands shook uncontrollably for several minutes.

The Lord changed into His regular gown and then told me that every one of His promises was being released. He said: *"The key I gave you was the last one. You are surprised by the world, and you are my very blessed child."*

Heaven Is So Real!

Before bedtime, on December 8, 1999, after I had finished praying, the Lord began talking to me. He usually talks about my work and His plans for me, and how soon He'll start the work He has prepared me for; but tonight He was letting me know why He has to publish the book soon. He said, "Heaven Is So Real *will be the last chance for people to realize how soon I am coming for My people.*"

He also said, *"If the disobedient people don't wake up, they will not hear the trumpet sound, and they will have to go through the tribulation."* He then went on to explain that He has been warning people through events related to school children, but that we have only feared Him for a short time before going back to our old ways.

He continued: *"I have been giving them many signs to bring prayer back into the schools, but people are not really trying to do it. I will never force anyone's mind. I can only give them signs so they will know what I want them to do.*

"I have given enough warning for people to know what I want them to do for so long. I cannot wait forever for those who don't want to be ready for Me. I am coming for those who are ready for Me, and this will happen sooner than they expect."

The Lord said I must put these words in the book.

Indescribable Joy

On Christmas night of 1999, after my bedtime prayer, the Lord's presence was very real to me. After we talked for a while, suddenly a fiery anointing came over my entire body. This was followed by the vision-voice, and I saw the Lord standing before me in His Christmas gown and crown. He said, *"Sweetheart, I am happy to be celebrating My birthday with you."*

In the very instant when He said this, the heavenly songs came forth, and I began to dance before Him. This continued for at least thirty minutes. During this entire time I was dancing and singing. The anointing was so strong that all I could think about was that I wanted Him to take me home at that very moment. I was crying, but I also was smiling at my Lord, because the joy was indescribable.

The Lord Awaits Those Ready for Him

On New Year's night of 2000, I had exactly the same experience with the

Lord that we had shared on Christmas 1999. It was a more awesome experience than the previous Christmases and New Years had been. Some of the things the Lord tells me, I cannot put in this book. I can say, however, that the Lord is very ready for those who are ready for Him.

On January 6, 2000, after my bedtime prayer, the Lord showed me a vision for our church, the Church for All Nations. This is the new name of Bethel Church. I received this vision during a Sunday service while I was doing miracle-work dancing. In the vision, the Lord was standing by the pulpit, raising His right hand. In response, the entire congregation fell to the floor.

AN ANOINTING OF POWER

IT WAS JANUARY 8, 2000. On this night, before my bedtime prayer, the power of the anointing was so strong that I could hardly sit straight. My whole body became very weak, and my tongue was too weak to permit me to talk during the whole time I was praying. I simply couldn't make a sound, and my body wanted to lie down.

At the end of the prayer time, the Lord told me to get up at 5 A.M. on Sunday and to praise the Father first. He wanted me then to pray for all His promises, in tongues, and for my ministry, then to go to church before 9:30 and start to pray. He told me that I could go to church early, but not later than 9:30 A.M. He also told me not to allow myself to be interrupted by anyone.

"When you begin to pray, do not do anything on your own until you complete the dance," He directed. *"You should know all the procedures about this dance."*

The minute I walked into the sanctuary on January 9, I felt as if I were on fire, and I began to cry before I started to pray. I gave praise to the Father, and as I began to pray, I saw the Lord's presence. He was dressed in His golden gown and crown, and He was standing on the pulpit, smiling at me.

He said simply, *"I am opening the door for your miracle-work ministry."*

I began dancing before the congregation. I danced only four times at the morning services in this church during the early days when I first began attending. As time went on, however, I began to dance at the evening service every Friday while they were having a revival at Bethel. I continued to do this until they moved to the new church, Church for All Nations. There, I didn't do the miracle dance for almost two months.

NO TIME TO WAIT

ON JANUARY 13, 2000, after my morning prayer, the Lord began talking to me about my work and the book, *Heaven Is So Real!* He told me that there is no time to wait any longer. He explained that it was time for Him to begin the process of publishing it.

He also reminded me that He has given people every chance to come to know Him, and He has shown many signs to people in an effort to help them to realize He is God. He went on: *"But people do not fear Me, and many of those who know My words don't believe Me enough to live according to My commandments. But I will give them another chance through your book and many other signs."*

After He spoke these words, so strong a power came upon me that my eyes closed very tightly and a very loud voice came forth from my innermost being. It was so loud that it could be heard throughout the whole house, and this caused me to cry.

The Lord then showed me His vision for the earth very quickly. I saw many tall buildings falling throughout the whole world. After this, dark clouds, wind and lightning spread around the whole earth followed by rain, floods and tornadoes everywhere. After this, He said, *"Read Isaiah 64:3."* This prophetic passage talks about the mountains quaking at the Lord's presence.

Then the Lord said, *"I am warning my people one more time that I am coming for them sooner than they expect."* He went on to explain: *"Whoever is ready for Me will hear the trumpet sound, and those who are not ready for Me will go through the tribulation, and many of them will become Satan's. I have given enough chances for people to prepare for My coming, but they don't pay attention to My words. I will not wait for them forever. I am coming for those who are ready for Me."*

The Lord repeats many things. He wants so much for people to get ready for His coming.

Chapter 23

A Miracle-Work
Ministry

[He] was transfigured before them.
His face shone like the sun, and His clothes
became as white as the light.

—MATTHEW 17:2

O N THE MORNING of January 15, 2000, the Lord told me: *"I have a surprise for you. You must go to bed early."* After my bedtime prayer, my body suddenly began to shake very hard. I was anointed so strongly, and a very loud voice came forth from me for a while, followed by the vision-voice.

I saw the Lord appear in His golden gown and crown. The minute I beheld His presence, my voice became louder, and I began to cry while I trembled in humility before Him. At the same time I was also experiencing unspeakable joy.

I had seen Him in His golden gown before, but the anointing that accompanies this vision was much stronger than ever before. The Lord told me that all His promises were being released for the final miracle-work ministry He has prepared for me.

The Lord has often repeated things to me. I'm sure this has been His way of making sure I understand and remember the important things He has in store for me. However, you can see how many disappointments I had to go through.

Next, the Lord directed me to put out my hands toward Him. I did so immediately. Then He raised His right hand and said, *"I release your work."* After this, He instantly stood before me in His white gown, and He explained to me that the day I began to dance, my ministry was released to the church. During each dance the Lord's presence is with me. Miracles abound wherever the Lord's presence is.

Several people have told me that they feel a special anointing when I dance. These are Spirit-filled people who know how to discern the work and presence of the Lord. So many people have told me how they appreciate my dancing in the Spirit, and some have experienced the Lord's miracle-working power as I dance before Him.

MORE PREPARATION FOR MINISTRY

FROM THE FIRST part of June 2000 to December 2000, the Lord showed me many repeated visions. Simultaneously, many special anointings came, along with various hand movements. Often the movements of my hands would include touching my eyes countless times. Frequently the Lord would also show me beautiful stones, and He would give me many teachings in an easy-to-follow, step-by-step manner. Each of His teachings is very important to me.

I feel as if He gives me a wake-up call every day. Each time when I do things wrongly or say ungodly things unknowingly, the Lord lets me know right away so I won't do them again. I know I can never learn enough from Him, but I am trying my very best to learn all I can and to follow Him in all His ways.

If I cannot talk about my Lord or read His words, I am very unhappy. It seems as if many people do not want to be around me unless they are like me. Even many Spirit-filled Christians don't want to talk about Jesus all the time. For me, however, He is always first, every waking moment. Even when I go shopping I tell people about Jesus.

I never feel lonely or need anyone's company, because there is so much I enjoy about my Lord each day. His words are sweeter than honey to me. If I spend half a day with someone without God being the center of our conversation, I feel I have wasted my time. I feel a strong sense of urgency related to everything about God, because I know His coming for us is so near.

Sometimes the power of His anointing on my hands and arms is so strong that I feel as if my hands are actually breaking apart. One Sunday morning my hand touched my eyes thirty-six times, and before each of these touches, my hands made seven different strange movements.

Every Sunday morning I have to pray, spending at least two hours with the Lord, before I go to church. Then I am ready for the miracle dance. I never watch the time, but He always releases me on time so I will be ready for church. Our Lord knows everything about us, and He promises to supply all of our needs (see Phil. 4:19).

Sometimes my body becomes so weak while I am in the Lord's presence that I drop on the floor before Him. When this happens, I always praise the Father and humble myself before Him. It's only after I conclude this time of prayer with "In Jesus' name" that I am able to lift my face up.

Every Sunday morning I cry so much in the Lord's presence. This usually happens while I am praying in the sanctuary thirty minutes before worship begins. My tears enable me to humble myself before Him as I thank Him and express my love to Him.

During each of my thirty-minute prayer sessions before the miracle dance, I behold the Lord's presence either in the pulpit or at the altar. He always talks to me for approximately ten minutes before the dance. That is why I always cry, and sometimes I even laugh.

Fasting was never a part of my Christian life until I began to receive revelations of heaven. At one point during this period I wanted to fast for three days, but on the second day my body became so weak that I could hardly walk, so the Lord told me to stop.

He said, *"You don't have to fast to show Me how you appreciate My blessings in your life, for I already know your heart."* Even so, I still wanted to fast every Sunday for the Lord, just to show Him I respect and honor Him for what He has done for us. And I wanted to sacrifice something for Him, so I told my husband about it.

I wanted to fast from Saturday after dinner to Sunday dinner. This would be a full twenty-four hours of fasting for every week. Roger indicated that he wanted to participate in fasting with me, so we have been fasting this way since. During these fasts I drink only water, and Roger drinks coffee.

We are striving to make each Sunday truly the Lord's day from morning until bedtime. The Lord told me that after He starts my ministry, we must stop fasting. He said, *"You will need strength to serve Me."* He always knows what is best for us. I only know how important it is for us to spend every minute of our time with the Lord on Sundays, instead of going shopping and eating out and being surrounded with ungodly people on the Lord's day. If we have a chance to preach the gospel, however, it is a different story.

MY HEALING

BEFORE I MET my Lord Jesus, I had some emotional and physical problems. After about two months, as I attended church, every emotional problem I had previously experienced was healed and erased. For example, no matter how angry I would become, I could no longer say any bad words. This change really surprised me, because I didn't even ask for such a healing, and I didn't even know that God could do such a thing that at that time.

It was during this time that I asked the Lord to heal my physical problems, and He slowly did so. As I look back on that time now, I can see how I was sinning, with or without knowing it, so He couldn't heal me quickly. Now I fully realize that, in many cases, sin brings sickness.

I have been a Christian since March 1992. I've gone to the doctor only about two or three times since then (for physical checkups), but I have gone to the dentist many times. When I realized the Lord Jesus took thirty-nine stripes for our healing, I submitted every one of my sicknesses to Him.

I do have pains sometimes, but He always heals me. Sometimes the Lord heals me instantly; sometimes it takes time. Whatever the case, I've learned that nothing is impossible for our Lord. I am totally dependent on Him, because I know He will take care of me.

One time, about five years ago, I suffered from a severe sore throat. I had never had such a painful sore throat before. For two nights I couldn't sleep because of the pain, but I didn't have a desire to take medicine or to see the doctor. Every swallow was incredibly painful.

With each pain I thought about the stripes Jesus had to endure for me, and I cried for Him so much, fully realizing that my pain could not compare with what He had to go through for me. In comparison, my pain was nothing. I feel that I was crucified with Him. Since that wonderful revelation and healing experience, if I catch a cold, it doesn't last for more than one or two days, whereas such conditions used to last a week or a month.

A Miracle-Work Ministry

I know I have many gifts from my Lord God, but until now I haven't had an opportunity to minister to others, except through witnessing and praying. However, I know I have healing gifts, because each time I have pain somewhere in my body, I simply put my hands on that particular place for healing.

When I do this, instantly the heat comes on my body, and my physical being becomes very anointed and shakes powerfully. Sometimes I am healed instantaneously, and sometimes it takes longer.

When the Lord doesn't heal me instantaneously, I keep on beseeching Him for healing until He brings it to pass. The Lord told me, *"Persistent prayer is answered because those who believe actually expect to be healed by Me, so they continually ask until they receive."*

He also told me, *"Impatient prayer never will receive anything from Me."* Those who don't know enough of God's words cannot have faith or patience to receive all His promises. When you don't know God's words and His promises, you will not have a desire to pray.

GOD HEARS AND ANSWERS PRAYER

THE FIRST THING many Christians do when they are sick is to go to the doctor, instead of casting the devil out, praying to the Father in the name of Jesus, searching their hearts to see if they have sin within them, and repenting. However, sometimes the Lord does lead us to a doctor.

One such occasion took place when one of my wisdom teeth was bothering me for a while. The Lord didn't heal this condition for a long time, so I asked Him why. He simply directed me to have it pulled.

I obeyed, and went to the dentist immediately. The dentist took an x-ray, and he pulled it right then. There's nothing impossible for God, but sometimes God chooses not to heal us.

It's important for us to hear and know the voice of God in these situations. Sometimes, however, it is very hard to understand what the Lord wants you to do. Always pray about it first and ask Him what you should do. Then no matter what decision comes to your heart, if you have peace about it, it is of God.

Always remember that God is peace. If it is Satan's decision, your mind will be very confused. Always ask the Lord when you want something or need something. He is very happy to help those who trust Him. Our Lord God wants all His children to depend totally on Him. If you continually ask for whatever you need or want, sooner or later you will hear His voice, because you are depending on Him. That is why persistent prayer always will be answered.

Some people think that because they can't hear God's voice, He isn't hearing or will not answer their prayer. At the beginning of my Christian walk, I didn't know how to pray and I never heard His voice, but I was very persistent in prayer and I believed I would receive what I requested from Him.

During the last two years, almost all of my prayers have been answered. Now the Lord and I talk all the time, everywhere, but it seems that some prayers take a very long time to be answered. I believe God will answer the prayers of saved people first if they are obedient and their hearts are clean and close to Him.

When I first became a Christian, even though I didn't know how to pray, I prayed many times a day. I asked the same things over and over like a child. I needed so many things then. About two months later, the Lord began to answer my prayers, one by one.

As a result, I began to fear God in a reverential way and humble myself before Him. I learned to pray more often and began to read the Bible, even though I couldn't understand much of it. I began to make a habit of reading the Word and praying many times each day.

The Lord continually blessed us more and more. The more He blessed me, however, the more I feared Him. I couldn't knowingly do anything against His will. This realization and commitment led me to give up the worldly things that I had once greatly enjoyed, especially the television soap operas that had been my daily life. Once I made up my mind about this, I never wanted to see them again.

In a similar vein, I couldn't be happy with anyone if God's Word wasn't in him or her. All worldly desires began to die very quickly. I have learned that the Lord will never force us to do anything, but when we want to serve Him and give up the worldly things, then He will step in and remove our worldly desires and put godly desires into us so we can walk in full obedience in Him. Total obedience from His children is a great blessing to God.

Chapter 24

Obedience That Blesses God

You are My friends if you do whatever I command you.

—JOHN 15:14 (EMPHASIS ADDED)

THE LORD DIDN'T allow me to do any church work or anything else during my training years. He was continually telling me to focus on Him in preparation for my work and to keep on praying for His promises to be fulfilled. The presence of the Holy Spirit began to fill me, anoint me and surround me as I danced before the Lord.

He will not allow my hands to touch anybody's body to pray at such times of great anointing. Even if when I've tried to touch others, my hand would not do so. When I am anointed to dance, no one is permitted to touch my hands or body.

I actually long to put my hands on other people's bodies in order to pray for them. For now, however, when I pray for sick people, it is from a distance. During such times of intercession, the anointing comes upon my body and I shake. It is as if my own body has become a substitute for the ill body of the person I'm praying for. When this happens, I see the Lord's presence with that person. This happens especially with children.

I believe the reason for this is that the Lord wants my hands to remain pure so the Holy Spirit can dance with my hands. That is why, at the beginning of the body-work described in the second part of this book, the Lord told me, *"When you begin to dance, your hands can*

209

never touch other hands or bodies to pray."

My personality completely changed after the revelations of heaven I was privileged to experience. All my thinking has changed. Whatever I used to want means nothing to me anymore.

THE LOVE OF GOD

WHOEVER LOVES WORLDLY things and their families more than the Lord will hurt Him and not please Him. It is so important not to hurt our Lord Jesus. He told me that His feelings are being hurt so much by many of us. For Him, it's very much like what happens to us when our children hurt us.

The Lord has given me so much of His love for others that I had never really experienced before, except for the love I had for my own family. Now I have so much love for people, especially the little ones. Each time I see them I smile for them and I want to touch them. I know this is Jesus' love within me, for He loves the little children.

Now I also want to hug and touch others, even strangers. This is one thing I never wanted to do before. Similarly, my desire to preach the gospel of Jesus Christ is uncontrollable. It seems that I just cannot help myself.

Before I saw heaven, I always had a desire to preach, because I wanted to make my Lord happy and I wanted to go to heaven. My motives for wanting to preach have changed now, because I know where I am going.

I have so much compassion for lost souls. In fact, that is an all-consuming passion in my life. I used to have so much compassion for handicapped people I saw in church. Now I never feel sorry for them anymore. I realize they love Jesus more than healthy people do.

I believe the Lord has put a great burden in my heart for lost souls. That is why He showed me my parents and the other people in hell. I still cry for my mother.

Before I knew my Lord Jesus, I always thought I wanted to be with my mother after death. At that time I thought we would all go to the same place when we die. I never knew there is a heaven and a hell. Now I know how real they both are. They are as real as the planet Earth.

I am very thankful that the Lord has given special patience to my husband, Roger. Roger's patience with me for all these years, as he has walked with me in the Lord, has been a tremendous source of encouragement to me.

My husband never complained about anything I wanted to do for my

Lord. In fact, he never disagrees with me about anything related to my spiritual life. He fears the Lord and loves Him more than life itself.

The Lord keeps my husband very busy with his job. Therefore, I strive to take good care of him in the way the Lord wants a wife to care for her husband. I realize that a wife is supposed to be a crown for her husband (see Prov. 12:4).

THE IMPORTANCE OF OBEDIENCE

ON MAY 28, 2000, after my morning prayer the Lord showed me the outside of our church building, and then the vision moved inside the church. I saw the Lord's presence, in His golden gown and crown, standing in front of the pulpit. The inside of the church was filled with brightness. It was as brilliant as the sun. It was then that the Lord told me He is releasing my miracle-working dance to the world.

I want so much to see our church blessed with this dance, and I want to bring glory to my Lord. The Lord has spent countless hours with me to help me prepare for this work.

Truly, whatever I want to do while I'm on this earth is not important to me. Everything is for my Lord and for my brothers and sisters in Christ and lost souls. The Lord has blessed us with everything we need and want in our lives. What we want most now is to put God first, no matter what the situation. I want others to be blessed through me. Actually, I am a very private person, and I don't really want to be noticed by anyone at all. In spite of this shyness in my nature, the Lord has given me no choice but to be noticed by others.

A comfortable life, even for one hour a day, is not what I'm looking for. My heart feels so eager to do God's work, and this aspiration fills my every waking moment. For a long time I've been getting up before 4:00 A.M. every morning to pray. When you pray almost half a day, each day, you really don't have much time for anything else.

Since the Lord showed me heaven, I haven't slept the way I used to. There just is not much time to relax. Each day I want to learn so many things about God's words in order to prepare for my ministry, even though my ministry, at the present, simply consists of dancing. The Lord says He will do everything for me, but I still want to know so much about Him and His words. I have an unquenchable thirst and hunger for God and His Word.

There is no easy way to serve the Lord. To please the Lord, we must totally submit everything to Him, including those things we may not want to give up. We just do it because we love Him.

When difficult times come, I make myself think of our Lord's cross, and this memory enables me to endure anything. Whoever wants to be with the Lord Jesus forever must work for His salvation daily, all the days of his life. We cannot be off-and-on Christians, because we do not know when He is coming for His people.

When you get used to a lifestyle of total obedience, you won't want it any other way. When our lives are totally obedient to the Lord, we never have to worry about anything. From time to time we are required to go through certain tribulations and trials. Through these we learn that we always can depend on the Lord and that, no matter what, we have our peace and joy with and from Him.

FRIENDSHIP WITH THE WORLD IS ENMITY WITH GOD

I WANT TO tell all the disobedient Christians of this world, please don't be too comfortable with the world. Stay awake, for our Lord Jesus is coming for us. This could happen at any time. Take a moment to read Luke 17:26–36. If you are continually disobedient and enjoy the world more than our Lord Jesus, who died for you, you cannot expect to see His face.

Obedience is very important to our Lord. He has shown me many Christians who will be left behind, including some people I know personally. He is coming for those who are ready and waiting for Him, and this will happen before we know and expect it.

The heart of our Lord is hurting for disobedient people and lost souls. His love within me causes me to think about lost souls and lukewarm Christians everywhere. Because I know what will happen to them at the end, if they don't wake up, I remain very vigilant in prayer for them.

If you are a lukewarm Christian, please pay special attention to what I'm saying. You cannot love anything or anyone more than our Lord Jesus who died for you. If a preacher tells you that all Christians who go to church will go to heaven, you'd better find another church.

When we are saved, the Lord expects us to pray continually and to study the Bible. So be sure to stay awake spiritually, without depending on everybody's teaching. When you continually study and pray, then you will understand the Bible's teaching, because the anointing will teach you all things (see 1 John 2:27).

212

After we are saved, we must continually work on our salvation. This means we must obey God's Word and please Him in every area of our lives. This book has mentioned obedience many times, because this is very important to our Lord. He wants to bring everybody into His kingdom. Many Christians have many problems because of their disobedience to the Lord about tithes, offerings and giving to the needy. They still live the same way they did before they were saved.

I have studied many people who give tithes and offerings, and these included my son and daughter and my friends. Those who tithe and give offerings have lives that are continually blessed in every area. Conversely, those who don't tithe, even though they are going to church and do many things for God's work, often find that their lives are never really blessed, and they continually have problems. The Lord is very unhappy with people who are not tithing. (See Malachi 3:8–10.) The Lord showed and told me clearly that whoever doesn't tithe will not see His face because they love money more than Him.

The tithe is 10 percent of whatever your gross pay is, not net pay. God doesn't need our money, but He wants every believer to bring the tithe to His house so the church can do God's work. Offerings are love gifts for the needy and a giving of thanks to God's house and different areas of ministry. All of God's work requires money. Anyone who is able to do these things faithfully will be blessed by Almighty God the most because it is obedient and shows love. These two things are very important commands of God. If you truly want to be with Jesus forever in heaven and have a blessed life while you are on this earth, please pay close attention to what the Lord says. I have a responsibility to write the truth of God's words. I wrote this as clearly as I can so new believers and some Christians who are confused about the tithe and offering can fully understand.

WITNESSING FOR JESUS

WHEN I WITNESS to others, some agree to receive Jesus Christ as their personal Savior, but some respond by saying, "Not now." I usually tell them not to wait too long, for it could be too late. When we die, we end up going to one of two places, either to heaven or to hell. I know I will never see some of these folks again, unfortunately, because in many cases their decision to accept Christ will come too late.

When I tell others about Jesus, I often start by telling them what He did for us and how much He loves us. Whoever believes He is the Son of God will live forever with Him in heaven. After this, if they still refuse to receive the salvation package I present to them, I tell them, after God's people are taken to heaven, if you are still alive, never receive Satan's number—666.

If you receive this number, you will be with Satan, not Jesus, and you will burn in the lake of fire throughout all eternity. If you refuse to receive Satan's number, you will be killed, but you will live forever, because you died for Jesus (see Rev. 13:15–18; 14:9–13 for further information about these important matters).

I believe the Holy Spirit leads me to say these things. Therefore, I have unusual and supernatural boldness to speak this message to others. Like Jesus, I don't want a single person to perish. I began to go to church because I did not want to go to hell. I believed this message, and I was very afraid that I might die before being baptized. Therefore, I got baptized without even studying God's words.

The hell the Lord showed me was much worse than what I had heard described by other people. I hope whoever reads this book will keep on believing and staying awake to the message of salvation. Just because we're attending church doesn't mean we are going to heaven.

If we don't live by God's commandments, He becomes very displeased with us. Disobedient Christians can never enter God's kingdom. Heaven has many different levels and places. The Lord has shown me and told me this time after time.

Once we are saved by the Lord Jesus' blood, we must do our best to give up all worldly things and live for Him. We must study God's Word, because it is impossible to live a holy life without doing so. I realize that many Christians don't like to hear the truth of God's Word simply because they don't want to change.

To be reborn means that you no longer desire the ungodly things you used to desire. You want only to please God. I am saying this because I love you. I have Jesus' love in me, and that is why I am saying all these things. It doesn't matter to me what you think of me. Just believe that I care for you so much.

Chapter 25

Focusing on the Lord First

*Then David danced before
the* LORD *with all his might.*

—2 SAMUEL 6:14

A S I DANCED in the Spirit during church services on June 4, 2000,
I expected a big surprise from my Lord, but nothing out of the
ordinary happened. Nonetheless, I was very happy in church instead of
feeling discouraged like I had on other such occasions.

In fact, I had been discouraged so many times before with my dancing
because I had expected miracles for the church. When the miracles did
not take place I would complain about it to the Lord. In May 2000, however, I promised the Lord that no matter what, I would never complain
about my dancing ever again.

After I left the church services on this day in June, I began to be discouraged again. When I came home, I began to pray as I usually do after
church. This time, though, I felt worse. In spite of my feelings, however, I
prayed. While talking to the Lord, I was holding my feelings back. I knew
the Lord knew how I felt, but He seemed to be ignoring my feelings.

I believe He was waiting to see if I could keep the promise I made to
Him the last time. We proceeded to talk about the usual things and He
released me. After I was released, I felt worse than ever, so I rebuked the
enemy. Even this didn't help, however, and this meant that my feelings
weren't coming from the devil.

A few hours later, during my prayer time, I sat down and tried to pray, but I didn't want to pray for His promises this time. (Usually I pray four times a day at approximately the same times.) I told the Lord I didn't want to pray for the promises this time. It was the first time I had ever refused the Lord anything, but His response was simple and direct: *"You must obey."*

Though I understood His message, my mind was too disturbed to comply, and my resulting attempt at prayer was insincere. I said to the Lord, "I don't want any of Your gifts of work because they cause me to sin against You. I didn't ask for any of these gifts You offered to me. All I want to do for the rest of my life is worship You, please You and make You happy.

"All Your promises caused me to sin against You, because I expect too much and my desire is for all the brothers and sisters to be blessed by this dance. I cannot focus on You while I am worshiping You ever since I had to do this dance.

"During each and every dance I am concerned about miracles happening to the church. I want so much for this church body to be blessed by this dance, and most times I've even forgotten to praise You."

After all these words, new thoughts came to me. Remember, though, I was talking with my heart, not with my mouth. When I am in the Lord's presence, I cannot talk with my mouth. Suddenly I realized how many wrong things I had been doing for so long. Also, I had complained so many times about my discouragement. Upon these realizations, I began to humble myself before the Lord and ask for His forgiveness.

He softly replied, *"I have forgotten all that, sweetheart."* Then the Lord began to talk to me. He said: *"I have been saying to you that you must focus on your Lord first, then your work. You haven't been doing that. During every dance you are concerned about miracles for the people and you are forgetting your Lord's glory. This dance I created for My pleasure, not for you to be worrying about miracles.*

"When I am pleased, then the miracles will happen. They are My miracles, not yours. You must never forget how important this dance is to your Lord."

After He said these things, I felt so embarrassed. I realized then how much this dance means to my Lord. Just the hand practice alone had taken sixteen months, and all the other practice and the building up of the Holy Spirit's power in my body had taken almost three years before I even began dancing in the church.

DANCING ON THE BEACH

IN PRECEDING CHAPTERS I've mentioned some of our beach days. Every Monday morning the Lord wakes me up after 12 A.M., and He shakes my body for exactly thirty minutes. He is never one minute late or early. If I fall asleep for even five minutes, the shaking has to start over again.

After thirty minutes of shaking, the Lord's presence appears to me, and He tells me, *"Daughter, we must go to the beach."* The minute He says this, my body shakes harder and an even stronger anointing comes, then I can see my transformed body walking with the Lord Jesus on the beach, and we are holding hands. We walk on the beach on the edge of the sand for a while, then we go up the hill and sit on a long, huge rock. This beach and rock were the ones He used for the revelation of heaven.

When we get there, the minute we sit, I put my right arm under His arm, and then the Lord tells me, *"You must see the water."* When He says these words, I can see the water on the beach in front of us.

The same scenario was played out during my visit with Him after He had explained many things about my dancing and its true purpose. After we talked for a while, He said, *"You must sing."* Then I sang. After I sang, we talked for a while, and He said, *"Now you must dance."* Instantly, I knelt before the Lord and began to sing and dance.

The Lord always sits before me with His legs crossed while I do this dance. I cannot see His face, but I know when He is either happy or sad. With this dance, He always looks happy, and I can tell He is smiling. I continually smile at Him the whole time while I am dancing.

Each time I am with the Lord on the beach, I feel the same as I did when He took me to heaven. At such times I am completely focused on the Lord. I can't think of anything else. There are no words to express the joy I have when I am with Him. How I wish such times of sweet communion could last forever.

Each time I am with Him on the beach I tell the Lord I don't want it to end. This Monday morning dance lasts for more than forty minutes each time. After the dancing is finished, the Lord pays so many wonderful compliments to me that I always feel very embarrassed, because what He says seems too good to be true.

After these moments of appreciation, He says, *"You must see this!"* Then I begin to sing again, and I see the whole ocean for a while. Soon the scene changes to the whole world. After this, we talk again, and He says, *"I must take you back, so you can sleep."* With each word He says, our bodies move as if they were figures in a video.

All this takes between two and two and a half hours. At the end of our time together, the Lord always gives me a big hug, then I see Him walking on the edge of the water. I am always able to see His back clearly while He is walking.

Everything that happens on the beach involves my transformed body. My real body is lying on the bed, participating in the dance and singing. Remember, the Lord uses my spirit-body, but all thinking and feeling happens in my physical body. This means that Jesus' spiritual body and my spiritual body are together. If I had pain in my body before the visit, most of the time it is all healed after these visits with my Lord on the beach.

I want to explain everything about these experiences as clearly as I can, so when children read it, they will understand it fully. Children have a wonderful capacity to understand why this book is so very important to the Lord, because they are innocent, trusting and open to God.

It was on Monday, May 27, 1996, when the Lord took me to this beach and told me, *"I will bring you to this beach every Monday."* Until now, He has never missed once. He said this will continue to happen until the last day.

I have finally realized that my faith had been weak, and that is why I had been so discouraged and had complained to almighty God. Since the dawn of that realization, during each and every dance, I seek only the Lord's face and never concern myself about anything or anyone else when I am dancing.

I had only complained about the dance, because I had thought with every dance great healings and deliverance would happen to the church. I had thought this because He had shown me many wheelchairs in the church. Our Lord God never explains details, however; His words are very brief and to the point.

GREAT TESTS

THE LORD BEGAN to test me in every area of my life. The biggest test of all concerned my loved ones. I also believe that my complaining about the dance had caused Him to delay the fulfillment of His promises. Surely the Lord could've told me what I was doing wrong or right, but He wants me to learn my own way. His preparations in my life for the work He has called me to do have not been easy.

I've learned that He does not want us to have anything the easy way. His Word tells us that we must go through tribulation to enter His kingdom (see Acts 14:22).

DANCING ON THE PLATFORM

ON JUNE 17, 2000, after my bedtime prayer and at the end of our talk, the Lord said, *"You must hear what I say about the dance."*

I replied, "Whatever You say, Lord. I will expect and receive it."

He said, *"You must dance on the platform tomorrow morning. You must go to church early and talk to the pastor and tell him you are going on the platform to dance."*

When I heard this, my heart dropped, because this is one thing I didn't want to do until miracles began to happen with my dance. Nonetheless, I told Him, "I will obey You, Lord."

My heart was very disturbed about this, because I have been doing the same dance every Sunday, facing toward the congregation, since January 9, 2000. I had already heard from one of the pastors that church members were asking why I didn't turn toward the worshipers. I told him that I have to obey the Lord. It is not because I want to do this. My greatest concern has been that I would not disturb the worshipers, but I go against the Lord about such matters. My only response must always be that I would obey Him.

About three months ago, I thought, *What if the Lord wants me to go to the platform to dance?* So I talked to the senior pastor, Pastor Wolfson, and asked him if I could dance anywhere, even on the platform.

The pastor told me that I could dance anywhere, even on the platform. After he said this, I thought it wouldn't be a problem for me to dance on the platform if the Lord so directed me.

When I got up on the morning of the 18th, I felt happy to be doing whatever the Lord asked me to do. I went to church early that morning, but I couldn't find Pastor Wolfson. While looking for him, I ran into the other pastor, and I told him what the Lord had said to me about dancing on the platform.

This pastor said, "It's out of the question."

I then said to him, "Pastor, you are putting people before God's Word. The Lord has asked me to dance on the platform for the church's blessing."

Then the Lord said to me, *"Do not be concerned about this; I will take care of it."*

While I was praying before the dance began, my heart was saying, in spite of the pastor's refusal, I intend to go up to the platform and dance, because I must obey the Lord, and I don't care if I am thrown out of the church. If there isn't enough room in front, I will go behind the worshipers, if the Holy Spirit takes me there. Whatever the results, I didn't want to disobey the Lord.

The Lord always knows my thoughts. His pleasantly reassuring voice said: *"Daughter, you do not have to go to the platform until such time as I am ready for you. I am very pleased with your obedience. Be happy. Whenever you go there, you will stand at the very front, never standing in back of the worshipers. The whole platform is yours."*

The Lord knew how much I didn't want to stand on the platform to dance with the worship team. I believe He wanted to make sure how far I would go to obey Him, to please Him and to put Him first. I obeyed Him, and everything turned out all right.

ATTENDING CHURCH FOR THE RIGHT REASONS

AFTER THE NEW Puget Sound Christian Center (the church we had been attending previously) was built, they had to wait for an offering to cover expenses for the carpeting. It occurred to me that Roger and I could help pay for the carpets, so I asked the Lord about it.

In a somewhat unpleasant voice, He said, *"My daughter, you must not be concerned about it. I don't look for carpet in My house; I only look for the church's heart.*

"Most churches are trying to spend so much money for the church's beauty, but not many of them are trying to please Me. I want every church to train the people for preaching the gospel and sending them out to the mission field."

At the same time He also expressed His displeasure about people who come to church without focusing on Him first. On this particular morning, while I was praying for thirty minutes before the worship began, I noticed that I could hear people talking loudly and laughing; many were sharing their whole week's experiences with each other.

The Lord spoke to me: *"You see, My daughter, instead of bowing and praying before Me, they would rather talk about worldly things. You can see why some churches are never blessed."*

Chapter 26

Evangelism and Giving

For God so loved the world
that He gave His only begotten Son, that whoever believes
in Him should not perish but have everlasting life.

—JOHN 3:16

THE VISION OF heaven that I have been so blessed to receive impels me to witness to others. I buy whole Bibles and New Testaments to give to others. I mark all of the important passages within them, write notes to explain about Jesus, and include a tract concerning salvation. I give these out every time I have the opportunity to witness.

Since December 1999, I have also included our church bulletins and a tape of Mary K. Baxter's *A Divine Revelation of Hell* in the materials I hand out while witnessing. I put all of these in one package and, each time I go out, I take several with me. I have been giving them away as the Lord leads me.

I never bring any of them back. I talk to people everywhere—in grocery stores, parking lots, the mall, other stores, at the post office and in waiting lines at banks or anywhere else. What a privilege it is to witness for my Lord wherever I go.

My desire to talk about Jesus is so overwhelming that I truly cannot help myself. Sometimes this is irritating to others who go with me; therefore, I usually go out alone.

I have learned that the best way for me to begin witnessing to someone is to simply ask if they believe in Jesus. Many will respond, "I believe in God." This usually means that they don't know anything about Jesus. It is then that I begin to present the gospel message.

I do experience some rejection when I'm witnessing, but this doesn't bother me at all. I have found that younger people and African Americans are very easy to witness to.

Almost 99 percent of the unsaved young people I witness to will take the package of materials I give to them. Sometimes the Holy Spirit leads me to pray for them at that moment. I pray for their salvation and cast the devil out each time. Whenever I cast the devil out, a fiery anointing comes over me and I jump. I believe this happens because it makes the Holy Spirit happy. I never plan what to pray for people; the Lord always directs me.

Many people I've talked to know the Lord, but they don't have time for Him. So many Christians work on Sunday. A few times when I've tried to witness in the parking lot of the mall, the minute I mentioned the name of Jesus, people will say, "I don't want to hear about it," and they will run from away from me. In one case, a lady said to me, "It is because of people like you that I don't want to go to church."

I'm sure she said this because I had mentioned Jesus' name to her. To her, unfortunately, I was doing a terrible thing. She just didn't realize that all I wanted was to see her get saved. I asked the Lord to bless her and save her.

My heart really breaks for those who don't want to know about Jesus. I can never forget those who are in hell and are trying to escape from the fire, but they can't. This happened to my parents, because they never had a chance to hear about Jesus. This is one of the reasons why I must share the name of Jesus and the gospel of Jesus with people everywhere. They need to know Him. Thank God, many who don't know Jesus do like to hear about Him, and they are happy to receive the message and materials I offer them.

The Lord wanted me to include Mary K. Baxter's tape in the salvation package I hand out. It was Mary's *A Divine Revelation of Hell* tape that someone at church gave me after my revelation of heaven. At that time I had no desire to listen to it, because I had just experienced such an awesome experience of heaven and one experience of hell. At the time I felt that one vision was enough for one lifetime.

Two years later, however, the Lord reminded me about this tape and

I had a very strong desire to listen to it. When I listened to Mary's words, I immediately believed everything about her experiences of hell.

I heard that Mary's book has been translated into many languages. I know it was translated into Korean. One of my nephews in Korea read it, and it scared him to death. He believed all of it, and he is now going to church.

I believe 100 percent of Mary's *A Divine Revelation of Hell* because it is so very biblical. The Bible says liars will never see God (see Rev. 21:8). The Lord also told me that every word Mary has said about hell is true. He said, *"Some people's punishment will be worse than what Mary has said."* He went on, *"Mary's revelation book is very important for everyone to read, because this punishment could happen to anybody, even many believers."*

As a result, I have such a desire to give this tape away. I have given many hundreds of these tapes to others. I believe each tape I have given out will touch many other lives.

I have learned many things about people while doing street ministry and witnessing. I have given the witnessing packages to many Christians who don't go to church or can't go. I have also given them to some Christians who go to church so they can minister to others by sharing these materials with them.

Several Roman Catholics have received the packages. I was surprised to discover that some of them don't consider themselves to be Christians. I usually say to them, as long as you believe in Jesus, you are Christian.

Likewise, I have talked to a few Mormons and Jehovah's Witnesses. These precious folks, however, have never taken my package. To everyone to whom I give the package, I explain about Jesus, and I tell them what the tape is about. Usually they are very pleased by this. Even some unbelievers have shown a hunger to have the Bible.

We must remember to pray for Christians who find they have to work on Sundays. I believe Jesus' coming is so near, and that Satan is trying to keep Christians busy on the Lord's day. As I've witnessed, I've learned about people's workplaces. For instance, if there are five people in the workplace and two of them are saved, and three co-workers are not saved, in many cases the unsaved ones never hear about Jesus from the other two who are saved.

I know this often happens, because when I witness to the three who don't know about Jesus, then explain to them about Jesus and salvation and offered them package, most of them were very glad to receive it. Sometimes they will even say that they know their co-workers are Christians, but that they've never told them about their faith.

We need to share our faith with all those we know, for witnessing is the most important work we can ever do for our Lord Jesus. He died for sinners. The Lord told me, *"If those who are saved don't testify, how will unbelievers come to know Me?"* I believe when Christians don't talk about their salvation with unbelievers, it makes God unhappy.

THE TWO VALLEYS

WHEN WE GO to heaven, we will see that there are two different valleys outside the gates of the kingdom. I don't want to walk around in the valley forever. The Lord showed me these two valleys twice. Those who find themselves in the valleys remain outside of the kingdom of heaven.

When we go into the kingdom of heaven, and live there forever it will be 1,000 times better than this earth has been, even when we are walking here with our Lord Jesus. He has prepared all the things for our pleasure, because He knows what we like. Remember, almost all things in heaven are similar to what we have on earth. The beauty of earth can never compare to heaven. Some will say that they cannot believe these things because they are not in the Bible.

That is a matter of personal choice. However, I have discovered that almost everything the Lord has shown me has its roots in the Bible. The Lord has chosen me for End-Times prophecy so He can show me some things that are not clearly outlined in the Bible (see Joel 2:28–30). This is happening because He is ready to take His people to heaven.

THE COMPLETION OF THE STREET MINISTRY

AFTER EIGHT MONTHS of street ministry, on July 30, 2000, the Lord told me that my street ministry was over. It thrilled me to hear Him say that I had done well.

While I was doing this street ministry, I had a burning desire to give the packages out, and almost everyone accepted them. After the Lord told me my street ministry was over, I no longer experienced the same desire. However, I still tried to witness and give the packages to people, but seven people rejected me in a single day. I took great comfort in knowing that everyone I gave the packages to were God's chosen ones, and I fully believe they will not perish.

I enjoyed every moment of street ministry. I still witness every chance I get, but it is not the same as the ministry I enjoyed during those eight months. After each time I witnessed, I felt joy unspeakable. I walked around with a smile on my face and people looked at me with wonder.

Now you can understand why the angels rejoice and dance for joy every time a sinner repents. For every person I had the privilege to lead to the Lord, I continually prayed six days a week. This reminds me of a farmer who plants seed in the ground, and he knows he must water, fertilize and cultivate the seed in order to see it bring forth fruit. Intercessory prayer is one of the most powerful spiritual forces that exists.

A DESIRE TO GIVE

EVERY SATURDAY NIGHT after my bedtime prayer and every Sunday morning after my prayer time, the Lord pours upon me a very special and strong anointing. This covers my entire body, and many unusual things happen to my body during these times. It is hard to explain exactly what takes place, because both my body and my mind feel so strange to me. These powerful anointings always happen to me when I have to do the miracle dance on Sunday mornings.

Ever since I became a Christian my desire has always been to give. At first I envied those who were able to give tithes and offerings, because at that time I was not able to. We had just moved from California and my husband wasn't saved.

It was a year and a half later when Roger was saved. During the second week of his Christian life he began to pay the tithe, because that is what I asked him to do. In response, our blessings began to increase more each day. Until the present, we have never had to ask for any material thing. God continually blesses us more than we expect.

I am not bragging about this. I just want every Christian brother and sister to obey the Lord's Word about this, because I know each one who does will be blessed in the same way we have been. I can never not give to anyone who needs help.

My husband and I do have limitations when it comes to giving, but I want so much to be able to give more. My plans for giving when the Lord blesses me with His promises of financial resources are to support mission ministries and the homeless in this world. I told the Lord that when He makes me rich, like He has promised that I will be, there will be no hungry children in this world.

As I have grown in the Lord, I have learned a very important lesson about giving. Early one Saturday morning in May 2000, I passed by the children's car wash, and I stopped there to help them out and witness to them about Jesus and to give them a salvation package.

As I did so, I noticed there was a group of people on one side who had some food. They were very friendly and invited people to talk about Russia and an evangelistic crusade that would be held in June. They were collecting offerings for the Russian church.

I had only $40 with me, and I immediately gave it to them. When I went home I felt a deep desire to give more. My husband wasn't at home that day. Suddenly I thought about $500 in cash that I had saved for my own emergency use. So I asked the Lord, and He told me that I must give it.

When I returned to the site of the car wash and gave the money to them, I felt very happy. I noticed from the list that I signed that mine was the biggest offering of the day, because I signed when I gave.

After I got into the car, I began to laugh with such joy that I couldn't stop laughing all the way home. The minute I walked into the house I began laughing harder and I was jumping up and down with unspeakable joy. That whole day I experienced great happiness, and I wished to give even more.

The reason I was so happy is because I knew the Lord was happy. In fact, He told me He was very pleased with what I did that day. Ever since that month, the Lord has blessed us more than we could have imagined. For a while I didn't even tell my husband, but a few months later I told him and he seemed pleased.

Usually we discuss whatever we give, but this time I did it with my own savings. From this I have learned that whoever gives with love will be blessed a hundredfold. The ability to give makes me want to praise God more and more.

I have been saying to the Lord that I want everybody to be able to afford to read my book, especially young children. I can imagine how they will be excited when they realize what they have waiting for them in heaven, where there will be pleasures forevermore.

Our Lord has a very special love for children, and I share this very special love for them. I pray for young people and youths alike each day, asking God to save them.

My husband and I have no desire to have more than what we have already. The Lord blessed us with whatever we needed before we knew Him and we have always lived comfortably. We never have been rich, but we never really cared to be rich. Right now our desire to be rich is solely for serving the Lord and letting our lives make a difference to others.

In fact, I would feel very uncomfortable if I had an expensive house and car. This is because I realize that so many people are dying of starvation and there seems to be a lack of funds to send out for the important work of missions around the world. I believe, even if I don't want it, the Lord will bless me with a better house and car, because He already showed these things to me.

Before I became a Christian, my greatest desire and most enjoyable activity was shopping. Now all of that desire to shop is dead. However, I do want to buy nice clothes to wear to God's house for worshiping my Lord.

I know He looks only on our hearts, but I want to respect and honor Him at all times. When we are standing before almighty God, we should look our best. I used to feel very guilty when I wore nice clothes and jewels to church, because I knew some people couldn't have these things. However, the Lord told me never to feel guilty wearing what He blessed me with.

Even though I communicate with the Lord in the Spirit, I feel He is so real to me and He is watching over me both on the inside and the outside. Therefore, I fear displeasing Him so much. I tell Him, "Whatever I want to do does not matter to me anymore, Lord, because pleasing You is everything to me. My life on this earth means nothing to me if I cannot please You."

He has answered my prayer this way, *"Daughter, what you are saying is very pleasing to Me."* Usually His words are very few.

This really refers to every Christian. If you have beautiful clothes or jewelry, please don't feel guilty about wearing them. The Lord has told me that we must not hide from others what He has blessed us with. It is good that unbelievers know that Christians are blessed. I have noticed that many Christian sisters feel very guilty about wearing what they have at church. Let us not worry about other people, because showing them what God has blessed us with gives them hope of the Lord's blessing in their lives as well.

This I know: The Lord is very pleased when we look our best in His house. Many times the Lord has told me, *"You look beautiful, sweetheart, in the church."* After all, what doesn't He know about us?

WORSHIPING THE LORD

AFTER WE MOVED to Bethel Church, I only danced four times during the morning service. Then I began to dance only on Friday nights, for the revival services, from sometime in June until November of 1999.

After we moved to our new church, Church for All Nations, I didn't do the miracle dance for a while, but during each offering time, the Holy Spirit would take my body to the altar for dancing. This dance I have never trained for, but the Holy Spirit moves my hands and body according to the music. Each and every move is repeated three times.

Many people don't realize how important worship is to our Lord. While we are worshiping, we will receive the anointing, fruit of the Spirit, healing, God's desires, baptism of the Holy Spirit, and unspeakable joy, peace and deliverance. Whoever worships with a sincere heart of love and thanksgiving to our Lord, and seeks His face without distractions, will receive an awesome blessing.

A LONG PERIOD OF PREPARATION

I ASKED THE Lord why every one of His promises for my work and publishing the book are taking so long to be fulfilled.

He said: *"In this way, daughter, I am showing you that your work is a very important work for this last day. Your miracle dance ministry involves many things and many people. Therefore, I had to prepare all the people who are going to minister in your ministry and to put other things in place. Most importantly, I had to purify you completely, inside and out. Your compassion for others and all the other areas of your life are being transformed to be more like Me when I was on this earth.*

"No matter what the situation, your heart must be able to put Me first at all times, so you can obey me like I obeyed My Father when I

was on this earth. This dance I created for you to do must be completely pure at all times so the Holy Spirit can do the dance. Therefore, I had the training take place in public for so long to help you become very bold, confident and not afraid to stand before anybody.

"No matter how noisy it is around you, or how many people you're surrounded with, you must be able to focus only on Me. Any noise or any person cannot interrupt your mind. That is why your eyes are closed and I have you put earplugs in your ears while you're dancing. When I am completely satisfied with the preparation for your ministry, then I can move everything like a burning bush. Nothing will be in the way."

Chapter 27

Release
of Ministry

But imitate those who through
faith and patience inherit the promises.

—Hebrews 6:12

O N December 22, 23 and 24, 2000, the Lord woke me up at 3:30 A.M., and my body shook for thirty minutes, then His presence appeared, and He talked about twenty minutes each morning. He told me that my miracle-dance ministry would soon begin. He said that it had been a very long time of training, and He thanked me for my patience and obedience

At this same time, I knew some people were complaining about my dance in the church. I believed if people are truly Spirit-filled, they would not complain about what others do under the power of the Holy Spirit or the anointing. When the church body receives a special anointing, many members do very strange things. The Bible gives us many examples of this.

My husband and I want our church to be so blessed. We pray very faithfully, twice a day, seven days a week. My husband even prays at every mealtime. We are so thankful that our church has let the Holy Spirit dance very comfortably with my body, and the Lord continually tells me: *"I will bless this church. The senior pastor, Pastor Wolfson, is one of My very favored sons."*

He is a God-pleaser. I believe that is why I was sent to this church after I was rebuked at the old church.

A HAPPY DANCE

ON SUNDAY MORNING, December 24, 2000, while I was praying in the sanctuary before dancing, suddenly I felt a stronger-than-usual anointing upon me, then I saw the Lord in His special Christmas gown and crown. He was standing on the pulpit, smiling, and I smiled back at Him.

I said, "Lord!"

He responded, *"Sweetheart, I am celebrating My birthday with you."* The minute I saw Him I couldn't pray any longer, because my mind and eyes were with Him and I couldn't focus my mind for prayer. The Lord already knew my thoughts. Then His presence disappeared. This particular morning's dance was happier than any other time.

Upon completing this happy dance, the Lord told me that I must rest for two weeks. He instructed me that during this time I must not dance the miracle dance, but I could do the offering dance.

A CHRISTMAS CELEBRATION

IT WAS CHRISTMAS night 2000. After my bedtime prayer, the Lord and I talked together for a while, and suddenly a special anointing came upon me, and the special vision-voice came forth for a while. I saw the Lord dressed in His Christmas crown and gown standing before me with a smile, and then He said, *"Sweetheart, I am celebrating My birthday with you."* The minute He said those words, special heavenly songs came and I began to dance for approximately thirty minutes.

The joy I experienced that night truly was unspeakable. The dancing ended and the Lord's special Christmas gown presence disappeared. Then the Lord's normal presence appeared before me. He said, *"Sweetheart, you are My very special daughter in this last day."*

NEW YEAR'S DAY 2001

AFTER MY BEDTIME prayer on New Year's Day 2001, the Lord showed me His special golden gown and crown presence again as He had done four other times. Each and every one of these times for Christmas and New Year's were the same.

The only difference was that He gave me different songs and dances each time. This Christmas and New Year's, I spent a very long time dancing and singing, more than at any other time.

PRESIDENT GEORGE W. BUSH

AFTER CHURCH ON February 4, 2001, the Lord told me many things must change. He told me not to pray for His promises to be fulfilled in my ministry anymore. I had been praying the same words related to His promises for almost two years.

Ever since the Lord showed me heaven's vision, I pray four times a day, seven days a week until now. I never missed a single prayer time. Anything I start to do with the Lord, I can never quit on my own until He tells me to. This is the reason the Lord moved all people that I know out of my life. Nothing and no one was to disturb my mind while He was preparing me for my ministry.

The Lord had told me during the preceding national election year in the United States that George Bush was His chosen man for the last days president. I knew why it was so difficult to complete the election process with so many disputed votes and other problems. This was because Satan knew that George Bush would make a difference to the Christians of this world, and the enemy was so against him.

On the morning of January 27, 2001, the Lord told me that through President Bush He would lead many souls to Himself in this last day, and the enemy would try very hard to win. Therefore, the Lord told me that every church must cast the devil out and pray for the president. The people in his cabinet are praying for him daily, and I am praying for him every morning as the Lord guides me. I hope every Christian prays for him, and for your children and all the lost souls within this troubled world.

SPECIAL DANCES AND A WHITE GOWN

ON THE MORNING of February 11, 2001, when I walked into the sanctuary of our church my body was shaking uncontrollably. Again, it was a very special anointing for me. After the dance, the Lord told me to tell pastor Wolfson that the dancing I do is very important to the Lord and the church, and that He is releasing the blessing to the church. I told him to expect and receive.

After church on March 4, 2001, the Lord said to me, *"Daughter, you must get a white gown for Sunday, March 11."*

I was shocked by this, but I didn't question Him. I know the Lord doesn't like to be questioned when He tells me to do something. Also, I was very excited about it, because the Lord told me that I would be wearing a white gown at the beginning of the body-work at the outset of my miracle ministry. He showed me a vision in which I was wearing a white gown as I stood on the huge rock and danced before the ocean.

The Lord gave me very short notice to get a white gown, but I knew it was extremely important for me to obey Him in this as in all things.

Therefore, on March 5, 2001, I went to four stores in order to find a white gown, but it was very hard to find the right size unless it could be custom-made for me. I finally bought one, but it wasn't even my size.

On March 11, on the way to church I cried all the way because I felt such humility toward God. I wondered how almighty God could let someone like me wear a wedding gown to dance before Him.

While I was crying, I asked Him, if it would be possible to do so, to rapture me like Elijah while I was dancing. In this way I knew everyone in the church would know that I was with the Lord, and I knew my husband would take care of *Heaven Is So Real!* and have it published, and then everybody would believe it is true, and people everywhere would get ready for Lord's coming. But the Lord told me I must stay on this earth until the last day.

This morning, for the first time, I really felt beautiful while I was dancing before the Lord and wearing my white gown. I truly felt that I was His bride. I have noticed that when Christians gather, often only one person will be anointed for ministry at a time.

When I am dancing each and every dance, I am so anointed and the Lord's presence is fully with me, but I never notice anyone being healed, because he hasn't released me yet to serve Him in this way. The Lord has to make sure that I am ready for the world. I felt that I was ready for my ministry a long time ago, but my opinion doesn't count.

Whatever it takes, I will obey my Lord and will wait on Him until my last breath or the last day. My life on this earth holds nothing for me if I cannot please Him. There are many things that He asks me to do that I don't want to do, but I love Him so much that I can never disobey Him. I believe that whoever really loves the Lord cannot disobey Him.

After church on March 11, 2001, the Lord told me I must wear only white gowns for each and every miracle dance from then on. He said that I was never to wear any other color, but He explained that I don't have to wear fancy gowns in the beginning.

RELEASING THE PROMISE OF MINISTRY

ON MARCH 25, 2001, after I prayed in the sanctuary, the Lord's golden presence was standing on the pulpit. The minute I saw Him, I began to cry. The Lord said with a smile, *"I am releasing the promise of your ministry."* After that, He changed into His regular gown and began talking to me about the usual things.

After church on May 27, 2001, I prayed as usual. The Lord said to me, *"In your next prayer you will speak in a new tongue."*

A couple of hours later I began to pray again. A special, fiery anointing came over my entire body. It was very unusual to receive such an anointing during my afternoon prayer. Then I remembered the Lord told me that I would receive a new tongue that afternoon during prayer.

The anointing was so strong that I couldn't talk, and it turned out to be another new tongue that the Lord had given to me. I have received various tongues many times before, but this one was a very long one. It required me to pray much longer than usual. With this new tongue-talk, I couldn't understand anything that I said. The Lord told me not to be concerned about this. He assured me that He understands everything I say, and He told me that He is opening doors for every area of my miracle ministry.

The Lord told me that from that day forward I would not be praying for those I had been praying for over such a long span of time. He said that I must pray only for my family, my pastor and my church. From then on I have been praying for others in my spare time rather than in my periods of regular prayer.

NEW HEAVENLY SONGS

THE NEXT MORNING, I began to worship before the Lord at home in a very different way from which I have ever done before in the mornings. After I prayed, I started singing new heavenly songs that He gave me the day before. He gave me the words to sing as well.

Then I begin to do a heavenly dance. I always worship with dance once a day before lunch, but this morning's worship was very different, and I felt I was in heaven with the Lord. I believe He would rather have me worship Him than to pray for others. He also told me that He had heard every one of my prayers already.

I have been praying seven days a week for many years. He has always said that when He would begin my miracle ministry, I should focus on Him first, then His work, and then rest every day until the last day. This makes me realize that I will never have a social life. In fact, my ministry, once it begins, will be a very short one.

TWO KINDS OF DANCING AND SINGING

SINCE THAT MORNING I have been doing two kinds of dancing and singing. The first dance is the vision on the beach with Him and my spirit-body. In those times I sing without words. The Lord and I can talk to each other heart to heart, and I can praise Him with understanding. I meditate on what He has shown me, and I meditate on what He did with me in heaven. I also reflect on what I want to be doing in heaven when I get there, and I praise Him in such an awesome way.

Then He tells me what I mean to Him, and He shares many promises with me—promises that are related both to the time while I am on this earth and my future in heaven.

The second dance has words with it, but I can't understand these words. The second dance is exactly like the one I danced in the church for two years. The Lord calls it a miracle dance. In each of these dances, the Lord's spiritual presence always stands before me. During each dance He tells me that nothing is more joyful than that particular moment. This always makes me so joyful that I simply want to fly away. Each of these dances takes about an hour.

AN OPEN DOOR TO MINISTRY

ON THE MORNING of May 30, 2001, after prayer in the Lord's presence, He told me, *"I am putting a special anointing on you."* The minute He said this it was as if fire came to my whole body for a while, then the vision voice came forth, and then I saw the Lord's golden gown and crown presence.

It was then that the Lord said, *"Daughter, I am opening the door for every area of your ministry."* He talked about many things for a while, then He told me to put my hands towards Him. When I put my hands out before Him, He put His hands on top of my hand and said, *"I bless you."*

By this time my body was hot and breathless, and my hands were closed so tightly that they returned to my chest. After this, my hands started to clap for at least ten minutes out of sheer joy.

CLAPPING HANDS

ON SATURDAY NIGHT, June 16, 2001, after my bedtime prayer, the Lord moved my hands in many different ways. The next day, after morning prayer, He did the same thing, and He let my hand touch my eyes ten times. The Lord told me that this morning's dance would be different, and it was. This morning I was crying at church before worship, and I cried almost the whole time and the dance was the most joyful dance I had ever danced.

At the end of the dance, my hands started clapping uncontrollably. After this stopped, I began to say, "I love you, Lord." I said this over and over again, always with my hands stretched out to Him.

The Lord let me rest from miracle dancing for two weeks, from July 8 to July 15, 2001, but He permitted me to dance the offering dance those two Sundays.

Then on July 22, 2001, the Lord told me that I must dance on the first step of the platform.

AN UNDERSTANDING PASTOR

ON JULY 29, 2001, after this morning's prayer, my hands touched my eyes fourteen different times. I also saw many sparkles. My hands and arms felt like they were on fire. The minute I walked into church, I could feel Lord's presence, and while I was praying, I saw the Lord sitting on the first step on which I was supposed to dance, and we both smiled most of the time.

I had a very special anointing come over my body. It was more powerful than at any other time while dancing, and I also felt different than I did while I was dancing on the floor.

After the service I told pastor Wolfson that I had danced on the first step. He didn't know about it, because he had come in late. He said, "You have to do what God says." He also asked if anyone had said anything. I love my pastor so much. I can tell how much he loves the Lord and fears Him. I also love his preaching. Not many pastors can compare with his preaching. Some say he is a fireball. He has a special love for the young people. The Lord always says how special a son he is to Him.

I said no, no one had said anything. I told him I had been dancing from the minute worship began. It doesn't matter whether anyone is there or not, I have to go to the front when the Holy Spirit moves me. This dance is only to please the Lord, not the people. When He is satisfied, then the miracles will happen. The Lord spent countless hours in an effort to train me for this dance. When I do this dance He always smiles. This book mentions the dancing often, but this is very important to the Lord.

On the night of August 4, 2001, the Lord told me that the next morning would be my final dance on the floor of the sanctuary. All the dancing I'd been doing on the floor was training.

He told me that He is perfectly satisfied with my training. Then He went on to explain: *"I couldn't do the miracles while I was training you for your ministry. The next dance will be on the platform. The whole platform has to be yours."* How I wish He had told me this before so I wouldn't have been hoping for miracles for every dance.

SEEK THE LORD'S FACE

ON THE NIGHT of August 4, after my prayer, the fire of God went through my entire body and let my hands touch my eyes many times. The vision-voice came, and I began to see our church. While I was dancing, the Lord's presence was standing before me with a smile. He looked taller than He had at other times, and He told me: *"My presence will be before you for every miracle-work dance. That is why I trained you, so that you can focus only on your Lord while you are dancing."*

He also said: *"Each place where you will dance, someone must tell the people what the dance is for: tell them to try not to watch your dance. They must close their eyes and seek My face and praise Me with all their hearts from the beginning of the dance to the end of the dance, if they want to be blessed."*

He also told me that I must dance after worship is completed and have some worship music without words in it. He went on to explain that the whole platform would be filled with His presence and that I will be dancing before Him. Every dance I have danced, I knew the Lord's presence was before me, but it was very hard for me to see Him.

I used to pray, "Do not let me fall on the floor while I'm dancing," because each time I used go to the altar, my body wanted to fall. The Lord answered my prayers, because during each dance, even though the anointing is so strong and my body feels like it is on fire, I have never fallen yet. This is one reason why the Lord built up the power in my body for so long.

A JOYFUL DANCE

AFTER PRAYER, ON the morning of August 5, 2001, I had a very special anointing as usual. This only happens when I have to do the miracle dance on Saturday nights and Sunday mornings before the church. On these occasions, My hands touch my eyes fourteen times. After each touch, my hands make a symbolic cross.

At the church, even though I knew it was the last time I would be doing the miracle dance on the floor, I had such peace. While I was dancing, I felt very joyful, and I felt greatly relieved about not dancing on the floor anymore. I knew then, as I know now, that the Lord will take care of everything perfectly.

In fact, the Lord had worked very hard and spent thousands of hours to train me for this. After I danced, the Lord told me that I had done well and that I'd never have to dance on the floor again. He said, *"Now you could stand before millions, for you are perfectly trained."*

From January 9, 2000, to August 5, 2001, I rested only eight times between dances, for two weeks at a time.

HOLY LAUGHTER

ON AUGUST 12, 2001, during Sunday morning worship, the whole time I was at the altar a very strong power came over me, and I couldn't stand up. During the entire time of worship I just sat there and laughed. Even if I had wanted to stop laughing, which I did not want to do, I'm sure I couldn't have done so. This is because it was a supernatural gift that I call holy laughter.

Chapter 28

The Book,
My Testimony

A S NEARLY EVERYONE knows, the World Trade Center's Twin Towers were destroyed by terrorists on September 11, 2001. Ever since this tragedy happened, I have been continually crying and praying for those who lost their loved ones. My compassion went out for those who were trapped and couldn't get out or be found and for their families as well. In one sense, I am not sorry for the ones who were saved when they died, because I know they are in a far better place; but I am very sad for those who died without knowing our Lord Jesus, because I know where they are also.

On September 14, I kept on crying profusely as I thought about how much pain those people had to go through. I thought especially of the children who lost their mothers and fathers. As all these thoughts came to my mind, my heart ached over their pain and sorrow.

While I was worshiping the Lord I began to cry again. I was crying very hard and couldn't stop. A strong anointing of the Lord's presence came over me, and I noticed my Lord Jesus was crying with me. I could tell that He was very sad, and I felt that His heart was aching for these hurting people.

Remember, our thoughts are in Christ. He started talking to me, and said: "*Daughter, I can see how much compassion you have for others. My heart is aching for those who are hurting because they lost their loved ones.*"

He explained: "*I must tell you, they must concern themselves for those who are with them. No one can live for his or her dead. Those who died and didn't know Me could never have been Mine, but through their death, their family might be saved. Those who died without knowing Me, they had a chance to be saved but ignored my Gospels. It is written, do not live for tomorrow, live from day to day.*

"*My coming for My people is so near. I try to save as many souls as I can, no matter what it takes. Satan knows this and he is trying to destroy as many souls as he can before they are saved. People should realize why so many people are dying now. Every church must cast out the devil continually by prayer. My churches have been too comfortable. I am very dissatisfied with many of them.*

"*I want the whole world to know that I am a fearsome God. I love My children, and that is why I died for them. I must be first in everyone's life. Everyone needs to repent and be humble before Me. What happened to New York is a very small price to pay. There will be a great distraction in this world continually until I come for My people. That day is sooner than they expect.*"

After having received this powerful word from the Lord, I can understand a little better now why the Lord showed me many mountains and the buildings that were on fire. The fire came down from the sky and then snow came down until the whole world was covered with snow.

He wants everybody to repent daily and purify himself or herself so He can bring all His people to his kingdom. Our Lord Jesus loves us so much that He doesn't want anyone to miss the trumpet sound. He said no one can love Him more than He loves us. If I say to Him, "I love you a million, billion ways," He still says, "*I love you more.*"

THE IMPORTANCE OF HUMILITY

HUMILITY IS SO important to our Lord. He exemplified the importance of humility to us by humbling himself to become a human being when He was in this world. I'm thankful to Him for showing and teaching me humility in so many ways.

For example, he led me to a seamstress who could sew my white gowns. Others had highly recommended her to me as a woman with great talents for sewing things according to their specifications. However, when she did my gowns, they simply were not wearable.

I was taken aback by this, so I went to the Lord in prayer about it. He told me to give her another chance, and I obeyed Him. In almost three months time she made one jacket and one dress. I bought more materials to give her, but she didn't have time to sew for me. So I had her give them back to me. I didn't think she could use white material. Finally, I asked her to meet me at the material shop, and I bought something that she liked, then treated her to lunch.

As soon as she agreed to sew my white gowns, she began to have many problems. This included physical problems that both she and her husband were experiencing. It was also a very busy time for her, but she didn't want to stop our relationship. I really felt great empathy for her, and I believe she felt the same for me.

However, I could not wear the things she made for me, and I felt like I couldn't point out the faults to her. Instead I endeavored to show love to her at all times. Now I know that this was the Lord testing me.

Though I had memorized her telephone number, after she brought back the materials, I couldn't even remember her telephone number, not even a single number in it. Through this, I believe the Lord was teaching me patience and humility.

I had been praying for humility, and still do, because I want to practice humility toward every human being. I want every aspect of my being to be like Jesus. No matter what the situation may be, I never want to judge others. Instead of judging others, I want to love them and pray for them. That is what our Lord wants from each of us.

After a heavenly vision, the Lord gave me a great desire to read 1 Corinthians 13. I have been reading it six days a week and I have never missed reading it yet, but I never try to memorize it. I believe the Lord put His love into my spirit through His words. The Lord also gave me a desire to pray the Lord's Prayer each and every day after my regular prayer.

HEALING MIRACLES

ON DECEMBER 24, 2001, the Lord appeared in His Christmas gown and crown and on December 31, 2001, in a golden gown and crown.

Everything happened the same way as it had the previous Christmas and New Year's Eve. This was a more unspeakably joyful time than any other Christmas and New Year's Eve in my life.

At the end of this special time, the Lord told me, *"You are the best celebration for My birthday and New Year's Day, and I love you, sweetheart, so be happy."* With that, He disappeared.

Since I stopped doing the miracle dance, the Lord has led me to pray at the altar every Sunday morning before worship begins.

A noise developed in my right ear, and I asked the Lord to heal me. He assured me that He would take care of it. The healing came, but it took a couple of weeks.

On January 13, 2002, while I was going to church, I told the Lord that I wanted my ear to be healed that Sunday morning at the altar. Each Sunday when I go to church, the first thing I do is to kneel at the altar and praise the Father with thanksgiving. Then I pray for the pastors in the church and for revival. On this particular morning, the minute I knelt, without thinking, my face hit the steps and the fire of the Holy Spirit hit my entire body, leaving me without the ability to talk.

However, my heart was saying: "I love You, Lord. You already know what I asked You to do for me this morning." From that moment on, I continually cried until worship began. Ever since that morning, the noise has completely stopped in my ear.

Another miracle occurred on the following Sunday morning. Before I went to church, I suddenly had a terrible pain on the left side of my body and shoulder, and I could hardly move. This time the Lord didn't heal as He had on other occasions. I told the Lord, "No matter what, I am going to church and praise You, and I expect You will heal me before I leave the church."

Again, while I was kneeling on the altar, my head hit the steps, my entire body felt like it was on fire and I began to cry. After this, worship began and I praised the Lord during the whole worship service. I even forgot the pain, and then I realized it was healed.

I had experienced this kind of pain before I met my Lord Jesus. Sometimes it would take two weeks to heal. Our Lord Jesus took thirty-nine stripes in His body so we could be healed. Whoever truly believes Him, loves Him, obeys Him and puts Him first in every area of his or her life, will discover that He takes care of us just as He promised.

He could have healed me instantly as He had so many other times before, but this time He was teaching me humility before Him in public, so I could include this in the book. It is very hard for some people to humble themselves before the Lord at the altar or in public.

Yes, it is very important to the Lord that His people be humble before Him and before others. I have experienced this while praising the Lord in my seat and at the altar. The difference is that I can feel Holy Spirit fire hit me each time I kneel before the Lord on the altar.

When we belong fully to our Lord Jesus, we must not worry about what people will say or think. The most important thing is pleasing our Lord who died for us. He is the Son of Almighty God and He experienced great humiliation as He hung on the cross for us. He humbled himself unto death for us.

The Importance of Praise

ON THAT SAME morning, as I lifted my hands all the way and began seeking the Lord's face, a very strong anointing came upon my body. It's important for us to lift our hands to the Lord as we worship and praise Him. This is one of the ways the Lord taught me as a key for receiving His anointing upon my body.

Some people may think they are so blessed that they don't need to praise the Lord. This is dangerous thinking. God created us for His glory. He wants everyone who calls Him the Lord to glorify Him continually. In His eyes no one is so high or important that they don't need to worship Him. God's presence appears to His church in order to receive glory from His people during the worship services. That is one of the reasons why Jesus tells us that the Father is looking for worshipers (see John 4:23).

Marks of Salvation

THE LORD REMINDED me to write about people who claim to be saved but never go to church or participate with other Christians. Some people think that being baptized with water is what saves them. The Lord told me that the only ones who are truly saved are those who live according to His commandments and walk in His Holy Spirit.

Whoever believes in Him must love Him with their whole heart and have fellowship with other Christians. God also expects them to attend church and pay their tithes and offerings. Those who are unable to attend church must give their tithes and offerings to the local church or any other church.

Those who work on Sundays, if they desire to go to church, will be able to find a way. Jesus said, *"Anyone who is saved must share My words with others and worship Me with others as one unit. Also, those who are unable to go to church must pray for the pastors and churches, and pray for the salvation of the lost."*

JESUS AND THE CHILDREN

EVEN WHEN CHILDREN are at a very young age, the Spirit of God seeks to save them. Any parents who know God's Word and don't teach it to their children or bring them to church are guilty of grave sins.

Those women who have had abortions or mothers whose children died before the age of seven need to know that these children are all with our Lord Jesus in His kingdom. It doesn't matter whether the children's parents are believers or unbelievers; they're still with Jesus. Whoever comes to the kingdom of heaven will see any lost children they may have had. I put all of these things in this book because the Lord wants me to.

ORDAINED BY GOD

ON APRIL 4, 2002, after morning prayer in the Lord's presence, the Lord spoke these words to me: *"I ordain you."* The minute He said these beautiful words to me, a strong power come over my entire being, and a great noise came out of my mouth. It emanated from my stomach and it sounded so loud.

Both of my hands stretched in the direction toward where the Lord was standing. This lasted for a while, then both of my hands returned to my chest. In a little while the power departed from my body.

The Lord had told me that He has ordained me for the ministry. He then said, *"It is time for every one of My promises to you to begin."* The Lord ordained me many times. This same day, after the second time of prayer, another great surge of power came upon and into my body. My hands shook very rapidly for a long time, and then my hands started clapping very hard also. This shaking and clapping of my hands lasted for about forty minutes.

ABOUT THE ANGELS OF HEAVEN

I HAD EXPERIENCES with two different angels, a male and a female, about two years ago when I got to the shopping mall parking lot. The minute I parked my car I saw a young man coming directly toward me like he knew me. He stood before me. I asked him what he wanted. He said he needed help. I told him he was young and handsome and asked him why he didn't get a job. He said that he came from Canada and it was hard to find a job. I asked him if he knew the Lord Jesus, and he said he did. So I told him that I'm going to the Church for All Nations and for him to come over there and someone can help him find a job. He told me that he knew a lot about our church. I told him all about Jesus, and I hugged him and prayed for him. I gave him some money and told him to make sure that he came to our church, but I never saw him again anywhere.

He was on my mind for a long time and I still remember him. Later, the Lord told me that he was an angel. He said many people interact with individuals and even mistreat them, not realizing they are angels.

I met a female angel about six months ago during the worship service while I was sitting at the altar praising the Lord with His presence. I was under a very deep anointing when someone tapped my shoulder. I opened my eyes, and this young lady was sitting on my left side with her face tilted looking at me with such a loving smile like she knew me. So I tapped her shoulder back. Usually no one touches or talks to me during worship. After worship was over, I was looking for her but couldn't find her.

I saw a young lady in the mall after the service that kind of looked like her. I went up to her and asked her if she touched me while I was worshiping. She said no, so I asked her if she wanted the manuscript for *Heaven Is So Real*. She was so happy to receive it. From that moment on, I had a very special feeling for her.

Her name is Julie. She came to church the following weekend and sat next to me. I had never seen her until the day I gave her the manuscript. I go to the 9 A.M. service and she comes for the 11 A.M. service. She is always faithfully waiting in the mall when I go out from the sanctuary. She lives about an hour and a half away from our church, and she comes to this church because she loves the pastor's sermons. She is a single mother with three boys.

A couple of months later she told me that I was her angel. I asked why. She said that three days before she met me, she was very sad, and she was praying, crying and asking God to send her an angel. In three days she met me and I gave her the manuscript. She told me it was the happiest day for her and she also said that ever since she met me, she is very happy and has to see me every weekend to be satisfied. After she told me about the angel, I realize that the young lady that tapped my shoulder was an angel that led me to Julie. I have never seen such a loving smile on her face. The Lord told me she was an angel to direct me to Julie, because Julie needed help. The Lord also told me Julie is a very special daughter to Him. I realize Julie truly loves the Lord more than anything or anyone in this world. She is a very blessed sister. I love you Julie.

How the Lord Began to Publish This Book

THE LORD DIDN'T mention publishing the book for many years, but recently He began talking about it every day after prayer time. At the end of July 2002, He told me to send all the manuscripts back to the writer so he can go over everything and put it in order to complete it for the publisher.

I didn't know who was going to publish it; He didn't tell me. I am sure that it has to be a Spirit-filled publisher with many connections, because He has been saying that this book must be translated into many languages. He wants all the churches to read this book and prepare for His coming.

He is ready for His people, but many of them are not ready for Him, and He is not going to wait for them forever. He is coming for those who are ready and waiting for Him.

The Lord also told me to send out some parts of this manuscript to my partners, all the TV ministries and whoever else I have a desire to give it to so they can use it to share with others. I hesitated to do this but I had to obey the Lord so I sent out the manuscript to most of our partners and TV ministries that we support. I sent out over a hundred copies of the manuscript. I also gave it to many people in our church and many others I have witnessed to. I have heard that it changes lives. Many have shared this experience with others. Some have even told me that they feel unworthy to receive such a revelation of heaven.

From the TV ministries I received unexpected responses from pastors who are very famous. God bless you for encouraging me when I needed it, I will never forget you. I kept wondering when the Lord would publish the book, but I couldn't do anything about it; the Lord didn't allow me to do anything about the book.

About a month after I sent out the manuscripts, on a Saturday, the mail was brought in and I picked up one of the envelopes; suddenly my entire body was on fire. I opened the envelope and it was from Creation House Press, who was interested in publishing the book. The Lord said, I told you I would take care of it. It was a very happy day for me. We sent out the manuscript and after about a month I called Creation House to see if everything was OK. After that we didn't hear from them for five months. In the meantime the Lord continued to tell me that Creation House Press is the one He chose for this book. The way He talked, I thought I would be hearing from them in a day, but I had to wait for five months. During this time I went through many periods of testing and discouragement. Many unexpected and unhappy things happened to me also. Like He said, without patience, no one can receive a good gift. I wanted to call Creation House, but the Lord continued to tell me that before I am able to call I will hear from them.

During this time of waiting, the Lord told me that it wasn't Creation House taking the time; it is all in my hand, and I have a good reason to delay them. The book is in His hand and it has to be done by His will. At the end, the Lord told me, "Daughter, you have passed an important test. I am proud that you never thanked Me less, no matter how many times you were discouraged and kept everything to yourself instead of telling others." It is true, no matter how bad it was, I never complained to others, even to my husband. Finally on March 3, 2003, after morning prayers, I had power come over me and my voice was so loud I was almost breathless for awhile. Such an unusual heavenly song came out so loud for so long, that I was filled with unspeakable joy.

After this, the Lord told me that the window of heaven opened for His promises of publishing the book. On the morning of March 6, 2003, the Lord told me that I would hear from Creation House that day. That afternoon the secretary from Creation House called to tell me they were sending me a proposal for the book and she e-mailed it that day. I was very excited.

After seven years of waiting and training, it wasn't easy at all. Even if I wanted to give up, there was no way out. The Lord said that you are the chosen one for this End-Time work and there's nothing you can do but obey me.

During those seven years I never left the state. We never knew what worldly enjoyment is. I couldn't go anywhere without the Lord's permission except church and shopping. We visit our son in Federal Way a couple times a year as well as one of our friends.

The Lord told me that after my miracle dancing ministry begins my life will be the same as it is now. This requires so many hours of prayer, I will never have a social life until the last day. It doesn't really matter how we live here on this earth. The most important thing is how we can live an eternal life with our Lord Jesus. His word says we cannot have it both ways. I choose the eternal life, whatever it takes. I hope my seven years of endurance will help every reader who doesn't live a holy life. The Lord said many souls will be saved through this book. Please, get ready; Jesus is coming for us. I have learned that waiting is the hardest of all. My hope is that every Christian will be raptured and be able to enter the kingdom of God, instead of left behind or have to go into the valleys of heaven.

The Lord told me so often that whoever is raptured will have to stand before the judgment seat before the wedding takes place. The worst thing that can happen to any Christian is not being raptured or not seeing Jesus' face. This is the reason the Lord showed me the two valleys for disobedient and sinful Christians.

I used to think that whoever was "saved" and went to church would go to heaven and wear a beautiful wedding gown. I was wrong. The only ones who will see Jesus' face and wear the wedding gown are those whose hearts are pure as water. God is so holy that defiled things cannot enter His kingdom. That is why the Lord prepared the valleys for those who are not holy enough to enter His kingdom.

I want you to be ready for our Lord's coming! My heart's desire is that no Christian brother or sister or their loved ones will be left behind. When the Lord showed me the rapture, so many Christians were left behind. He showed me this vision in two parts. In the first vision people were going through the air like white birds. The second vision was of those left behind. The first was so exciting and joyful but the second one I cried the whole time. The noise on earth while this was happening was horrible. These visions ran more than thirty minutes. He showed me many details of both visions. I have never seen such horrified faces before. It was so bad. My heart ached for them after the vision ended. The Lord said that what I saw is nothing compared to what will happen at that time.

Our Jesus loves all of us so much that He doesn't want anyone to be left behind or go into the valleys in heaven. He wants every believer and prepare for His coming. He continually tells me this will happen sooner than expected.

Please believe and search your heart to see what kind of relationship you have with our Lord Jesus. Every believer who has a relationship with Jesus is the most important to Him. If your heart is not right with Him, do something about it before it is too late. I hope you share this message with others so they can prepare and wait for the coming of our Lord Jesus. And I pray that you will become a greater disciple for our Lord. I also pray that you will be blessed by Him while you are on this earth and see His face when you get to heaven.

FOR SALVATION

I HAVE HEARD many people say that they believe in God but don't believe in Jesus. Please believe what I am saying. Even if you believe in God, if you don't believe that Jesus is the Son of God, there is no salvation. Salvation comes only through Jesus. Jesus died for all of us because He loves us so much. He said, "I am the way, the truth, and the life. No one comes to the Father except through Me" (John 14:6).

Jesus is the only one who can save you and forgive all your sins so that you can have eternal life with Him. (See Mark 9:48.) If you have never before asked Jesus to save you, now is the time for you to do so, before it is too late. Simply say this prayer out loud, from your heart: "Lord Jesus, I believe You are the Son of God and You died for me. Please come into my heart, be my Lord and Savior and forgive me of all my sins and take control of every area of my life from this moment on. Jesus, fill me with your Holy Spirit and use me for Your glory. I want to serve You and love You all the days of my life. Thank You Father, that I am now Your child, in Jesus' holy name. Amen.

After this prayer, to work out your salvation, read the Bible, pray continually and go to church to listen to God's words and fellowship with

God's people. Your life will never be the same; you'll have a very happy life while on this earth and live forever with Jesus in heaven. God bless you.

HEAVEN IS SO REAL!

YOU MAY RECALL that at the beginning of this book I told you I had written this so that I could share with you the experiences I have had in heaven with Jesus. At this juncture—as you reach the end of *Heaven Is So Real!*—I ask only that you receive this book in the same way it was written—with total openness to the Lord and His will. I again invite you to evaluate my experiences in the light of the Word of God.

At the Lord's direction, I have done as the Old Testament prophet Habakkuk did—I have watched and waited for Him, to see what He would say to me:

> I will stand my watch and set myself on the rampart, and watch to see what He will say to me, and what I will answer when I am reproved. Then the Lord answered me and said: "Write the vision and make it plain on tablets, that he may run who reads it. For the vision is yet for an appointed time; but at the end it will speak, and it will not lie. Though it tarries, wait for it; because it will surely come, it will not tarry."
>
> —HABAKKUK 2:1–3

Like Habakkuk, I have written my vision down and made it plain, so that you who read it may "run" according to the Lord's perfect plan for you—a plan that includes a place already prepared for you in heaven if you only will believe in His Son and receive Him as your personal Lord and Savior.

My prayer for you is found in Isaiah 40:31—that you who wait on the Lord will renew your strength, that you will run and not be weary, that you will walk and not faint, and that that you will mount up with wings like eagles and soar with Jesus. For surely He is coming soon!

SCRIPTURE KEYS FOR HOLY LIVING

God loves you very much, and I hope that these verses of faith, healing, truth, and love will allow you to experience—as I have many times—the presence of our beloved Savior, Jesus Christ.

+ You are healed by the stripes of Christ. See Isaiah 53:5.

+ Those who have pure hearts will see God. See Matthew 5:8.

+ Your heavenly Father sees your humble deeds and will reward you. See Matthew 6:1–6.

+ Take the narrow road. It leads to life. See Matthew 7:13–14.

+ God knows those who do His will. See Matthew 7:21–23.

+ Separate from anything that causes you to sin. See Mark 9:43–48.

+ The greatest thing you can do is love God and love others. See Mark 12:30–31.

+ Give God first place in your life. See Luke 14:26–27.

+ Your obedience shows your love for God. See John 14:15–24.

+ You will go through trials on your way to the kingdom. See Acts 14:22.

+ Not one thing in this life will separate you from God's love. See Romans 8:35.

+ Jesus works to present you holy and pure before Him. See Ephesians 5:27.

+ Obey God with deep reverence and holy fear. See Philippians 2:12.

+ God will be seen in you as you walk in peace and holiness. See Hebrews 12:14.

+ You are healed and made righteous through Christ's sacrifice on the cross. See 1 Peter 2:24.

+ Rest in God's care, and be strengthened by faith in His Word. See 1 Peter 5:6–9.

+ Read this everyday, and watch God's heart of love overtake you day by day. See 1 Corinthians 13.

+ Build an eternal foundation that cannot be consumed by fire. See 1 Corinthians 3:12–15.

+ You are held accountable for the things you do on earth, whether good or bad. See 2 Corinthians 5:10.

To contact Choo Thomas:
E-mail: godisready@comcast.net + **Web site: www.choothomas.com**